ON ANOTHER MAN'S WOUND

ERNIE O'MALLEY

ON ANOTHER MAN'S WOUND

ANVIL BOOKS LIMITED

First published London and Dublin, spring 1936
Reprinted October 1936

US edition published Boston 1937
under the title Army without Banners

German edition Berlin 1937

First paperback edition London 1961
Reprinted 1967

This edition by Anvil Books Ltd.
90 Lower Baggot Street, Dublin 2

Hardback March 1979
Paperback August 1979

Printed in Ireland by
Cahill Printers Limited, Dublin

CONTENTS

Jacket photograph: Death of Cúchulainn by Oliver Sheppard, the 1916 memorial in the General Post Office, Dublin. Reproduced with the permission of the Commissioners of Public Works.

FOREWORD TO THE 1979 EDITION

This new edition of Ernie O'Malley's first book follows the publication in 1978 of his posthumous second volume about the civil war, *The Singing Flame*. Both books enhance and enrich each other. They are the twin classics of the period in Ireland from the Easter Rising to the aftermath of the civil war and together they make up an outstanding record of those crucial years. It was in fact the reading of *On Another Man's Wound* which induced me to discover and then to edit its sequel in order that *The Singing Flame* should continue and complement this first part of his story.

Ernest Bernard O'Malley was born in Castlebar in 1898 and died in Howth in 1957. As a child in Mayo an old woman predicted for him fighting and trouble, though he did not remember the end of her tale. His courage seems to have brought an unusual degree of immunity in the beginning and until the occasion of his first wounding, the start of many injuries to be suffered in the cause of Ireland's freedom. Nonetheless, and however incongrous in a guerilla leader, his inherent sense of chivalry remained 'the idea the other fellow should fire first.'

Apart from wartime despatches and reports, his earliest writing for *On Another Man's Wound* was the section on his interrogation ordeal in Dublin Castle, composed as early as March 1921 at the specific request of Erskine Childers who wanted his account for the purposes of Republican publicity. This passage was omitted by the British publishers of the original edition but it is here reprinted in full between pages 246 and 253. Most of the chapters, however, were written while O'Malley was journeying throughout the United States, from New Mexico to Massachusetts and New York.

One reason for the book's lasting fascination is the many-sided character and complex personality of its author. One part of him was the tactician and textbook authority who would write memos lecturing his officers for not observing commonsense security precautions. Another was the artistic impulse; hunting for some mythological dyke in the midst of hostile territory or carrying poetry books in his pockets alongside the bombs and guns.

In *On Another Man's Wound* O'Malley avoids any future hindsight as to subsequent events, yet to read it is to sense how it leads irretrievably to the next. Here he details the first five years of his military and spiritual commitment to the Irish Republic as proclaimed in Easter Week; the tragic conclusion is told in its companion volume, *The Singing Flame*.

FRANCES-MARY BLAKE
(1979)

INTRODUCTION

THIS BOOK is an attempt to show the background of the struggle from 1916 to 1921 between an Empire and an unarmed people. The Irish situation is complicated by reason of conquest beginning at the close of the twelfth century, and by successive reconquests never fully completed. The outcome of these successive attempts was the wearing down of a people who refused to surrender or submit, a withdrawal of their life apart from that of the conquerors, and the gradual destruction of their civilization. The tradition of nationality, which meant not only the urge of the people to possess the soil and its products, but the free development of spiritual, cultural and imaginative qualities of the race, had been maintained not by the intellectuals but by the people who were themselves the guardians of the remnants of culture.

To show the complicated situations and race memories I have touched on childhood and boyhood as seen twenty or more years later, then necessarily vague, ill-defined and romantic. A certain amount of our background seems necessary to explain our disturbance by certain flaring of outside events.

My attitude towards the fight is that of a sheltered individual drawn from the secure seclusion of Irish life to responsibility of action. It is essentially a narrative against the backgrounds of the lives of the people. The tempo of the struggle was intermittent, life went on as usual in the middle of tragedy, and we were intimately related to this life of our people. The people's effort can be seen only by knowing something of their lives and their relationship to our underground government and armed resistance. We who fought, effected a small part of the total energy induced and our individual effort as personalities was subordinated to the impersonality of the movement, and not inspired by it.

The relationship of events is traced as the situation developed. I have endeavoured to explain action as I then saw it and, as far as was possible to avoid all retrospective realization of the implications of events. As the survey is seen through my eyes I had to show my own progression in development. Each of the three divisions of the book deals with a certain phase of events and with my changing relation to them.

This is not a history. Dates I considered unimportant. Our people seized imaginatively on certain events, exalted them through their own folk quality of expression in song and story. Anonymous songs of the period, at the end of some chapters express what the people thought, and amplify, in so far as they are concerned, the situations described. From time to time a summarisation of events is used to relate the general development of the situation to the particular.

E. O M.

April, 1936
Dublin

FLAMBOYANT

CHAPTER ONE

★

OUR NURSE, NANNIE, told my eldest brother and me stories and legends. Her stories began: " Once upon a time and a very good time it was," and ended with, " They put on the kettle and made tay, and if they were not happy that you may." Tales of the King of Ireland's son, his strange adventures and exploits; fairy tales about the " good people"; the story of the heavy handed, mighty Fionn and his giant strength; the epic of Cuchulain, the boy hero, the Hound of Ulster; Cuchulain of the grey sword that broke every gap; of Ferdia of Connacht whose loss was our loss, for was he not from Erris in our county Mayo. That was the best of all her stories.

She sang us songs and ballads of the people and of the land :

'Tis often I sat on my true love's knee
And many a fond story he told me.
He told me things that ne'er should be,
Go dtéigh tú, a mhúirnín slán,

I'll sell my rock, I'll sell my reel,
When flax is spun I'll sell my wheel,
To buy my love a sword of steel,
Go dtéigh tú, a mhúirnín slán.

I know where I'm going
I know who's going with me,
I know who I'll love
But the dear knows who I'll marry.

Oh the French are on the say,
Says the Shan Van Vocht;
The French are on the say,
Says the Shan Van Vocht;
Oh the French are in the bay
They'll be here without delay
And the Orange will decay,
Says the Shan Van Vocht.

A Bansha Peeler went one night
On duty an' patrollin' O,
An' met a goat upon the road
An' took her for a stroller O.

With bay'net fixed he sallied forth,
An' caught her by the wizzen O,
An' then he swore a mighty oath,
" I'll send ye off to prison O. "

But this, " The Peeler and the Goat," in a quieter tone
and when we were alone.

In low and often stilly tones she told and retold ghost
stories that afterwards made us keep our heads under the
blankets. In the demesne, which belonged to Lord Lucan,
we looked for green-coated leprechauns under the trees,
listened for the ting-ting of their silver hammers and watched
the fairy dancing rings in the glades. Often on the path
close to the chestnut trees we met old Lord Lucan on his
tricycle. Although we felt inclined to laugh at his machine,
which we thought of as a child's toy, and his straight-
backed, slow crab-like approach, we answered his few remarks with serious faces. Nannie took our part against
our parents, defended us, often accepted the blame for our
small faults, which in a home atmosphere could grow to
gigantic proportions.

Life at first seemed to be a mixture of admonitions,
curly hair and velvet suits, probably due to a wave of little
Lord Fauntleroy. Governesses replaced each other rapidly ;
we had not much sympathy with that anaemic form of
spinsterhood. With the servants we spent many happy
hours talking or listening ; from them we confirmed or
changed our ideas of people. By exchanging gossip with
the girls in other houses they could view family life in
unexpected and unwished for ways. They knew our
visitors and guests well, especially if they had been a long
time in the family. Then they could advise, quarrel,
threaten to leave and often domineer ; but, except Nannie,
they were in a rank of servitude and looked upon as a third
sex. We listened to the stories of the butter woman,
watched her unroll her ridged pats and bulky ovoids from
a muslin wrap, and gathered near her when she drank her
big mugs of tea.

We were not allowed to go with other children ; few
were " good enough " for us. We could not accept the
distinctions of our elders. We divided people into those
who were courteous and those who were distinguished
according to our views. Many with whom we were not

supposed to mix passed our tests, others whom we met in the house or in the streets did not. Our chief admiration was for a boy who could use stilts, and a tomboy who could walk on her hands. The most interesting of all our illicit acquaintances was a beggar woman who was double-jointed, and the town crier who gave extra dongs of his bell when he stopped to speak. With envy we watched boys and tomboy girls at horseplay, listened to their shouts ; watched the men who cemented the outside of the house as they slithered with spades at delicious puddles.

The Royal Irish Constabulary had a barracks opposite us. They touched their caps to father. We often climbed the steps and were shown spruce weapons : carbines clipped in arms racks, blue-black revolvers, the steel of bayonets, and heavy-padded helmets. The Head Constable would talk to us in a chesty voice, a sergeant with thick gold V's brought us through the rooms. Once we saw police, no longer in bottle green, stiff-collared tunics, but like ordinary people, wearing soft caps and cloth suits. They were going to the North on special duty to keep the peace at the Twelfth of July celebrations, when the Orangemen with song, bands, banners, and fists blooded from thudding their drums, remembered the victory of William of the Boyne. Mary Anne did not like to see us talking to the police—they were Peelers, she said.

Ours was a shoneen town, as I knew it ; a shoneen, little John Bull, was anyone who aped the manners and fashions of the English as interpreted through the Anglicised Irish ; who adapted his mentality, or lack of it, to theirs ; who despised and, actively or passively, ignored the remnant of the older Gaelic civilization of the people. Father and mother never spoke of Ireland to us. If one minded one's business there was time for little else. Nationality did not exist to disturb or worry normal life. We heard long discussions at table about names—Parnell, Redmond, Tim Healy—and the words Home Rule. There was a general parliamentary election which was of interest to us ; every day we could look at the opposing parties who were presented in the newspapers as men climbing long ladders. Englishmen thought of nothing but their bellies ; that seemed generally agreed on. But when I was called Ó Máille, our name in Irish, I was insulted. That was not my name ; only the poor used it. I would have none of it.

At the concerts in the Mall, given by a band from the garrison, most of the onlookers took off their hats when "God Save the King" was played. We saw the militia stamping by on the way to a summer camp, and heard the ring of their nailed boots. Aided by the delightful remarks of shawled neighbours : Whisha look at the boyo, Kateen. Glory be to God, will ye look at Tinker Durcan; we picked out some of the town drunks noising past, clean-shaven, in khaki. The minister invited us to cinematograph shows in his house ; all Protestants were respectable and rich. Priests came to us for dinner. They were hearty men who drank their whiskeys and sodas with father or sat at the fire sipping at sweet-smelling punch ; but why did they screw up their faces after a long drink if it was not pleasant? One of them always called the " pope's nose " on a bird " the ecclesiastical part "; that meant a laugh at table. At Westport, where we had driven to Mass from the sea, a temperance preacher asked us all to stand up to take the pledge against drink for a year. We were in the gallery. Father alone kept his seat, though mother whispered : " Stand up, dear ; don't make a show of yourself " Later he lashed the cowards who, next day, would drink as usual.

The priest would read out the dues from the altar. He blew his nose like a cracked trumpet. I often tried it and I knew how it hurt. It would be fine to make a noise like that. He would pause for a long time after some names, or cough in a threatening way. He would repeat a name, as if by accident. " Patrick Joe Grimes, two shillings . . . Patrick Joe Grimes." Nannie said priests would stick you to the ground if you went against them, or put horns on you, God save the mark.

At Mass on Sundays from the centre of the chapel we could look across the partition to the right and left to the penny and tuppenny places where were low stool seats or bare ground to kneel on. We sat on high backed, varnished pews: country women knelt on bare knees. One man, at the Elevation, always hit his stomach three resounding smacks. I heard father say to a friend that he was " a regular craw-thumper." At funerals I heard women wailing and saw them beating their long, wild-strewn hair as they climbed the hill in the foot-gatherings. People lifted their hats, blinds were drawn, shops would put up a shutter. It was a good thing, when the procession passed, to turn and walk three steps after the corpse. In the town a box of clay pipes and tobacco or snuff might be left outside the chapel door whilst the corpse was lying inside.

On market days we could sense the roughness of country people. Awkward men drinking pints of frothy porter, using wiry ash plants on each other in daylight or being dragged and sometimes carried to the barracks by police. Bullocks beaten through the streets, the shrill complaining of pigs, a steady waft of speech and smells of cow dung and fresh horse droppings. Shawled barefooted women selling eggs and yellow, strong salty butter in plaited osier baskets, salty dilisk in trays, or minding bonnovs with a súgan. A ballad singer with an old song or one of a recent happening, stressing his syllables, rushing a long line into a short singing space whilst the people gathered in a circle, following the words eagerly. They bought his broadsheets and hummed the notes as they walked around. Old women with pleated frills to their white caps, the more wealthy with black bonnets shaking from a spangle of flat beads ; boys in corduroy trousers and bare feet ; rosy girls in tight-laced boots, which some had put on at the entrance to the town. Through all, talk, laughter, hot-blooded sudden blows, a sense of the bare breath of Mayo, backed by rounded mountains and sea, frayed lake-edges and the straight reach of Nephin mountain.

Nannie could tell fortunes with tea-leaves : In the space of three you'll get a letter you won't expect . . . there's a red-haired man has a great wish for you. She looked at the sky last thing at night to find out the direction of the wind and the chances of rain. The sun-wise turn was important ; we should pass the salt that way, or whatever was wanted at table. A Connachtman had leave to speak twice and to poke the fire, she said. Thunder was God's voice in anger, lightening, earthquake or tidal wave punishments ·visited on the evil. We were afraid of the dark through stories of walking death, black dogs whose eyes were yellow fistfuls of fire, and the *cóiste bodhar*, the terrible death coach. A ringing noise in the ear meant a

B

friend dead and shooting stars were souls released from Purgatory.

The gentleness and kindness of the people were all around us as children, shielding and expanding, offset by steady supervision of parents, nuns, priests and teachers. One had to be courteous to understand or feel with the people ; on the surface they were pleasant to each other, though I thought their deference, to those who were wealthier and had more social standing, to be put on. We would see their smouldering wild fierceness also. Nannie would speak of mountainy men and show them to us at a fair ; somehow they were different. Whether she came from the hills I do not know, but ever since a mountainy man, or the name itself, heightens something in me.

At school where soldiers' sons from the garrison attended, we pronounced " a " as " ah " and not as " ae," as they did. Somehow for us " ah " represented the difference between the two nationalities. We were taught a little Irish, the Our Father, the Hail Mary, and a few salutations. The few words of Irish in common use were vulgar: gob, pus; but endearing terms a ghrádh, a chuisle, a mhic, a stóir, and pulse of my heart were used naturally as well as the diminutive " een " ; Noreen, calfeen. The speech of the country people and of some of the townsfolk was rude: Tay, mate, afeard, decave, faut, twiced; Tudor words once respectable. Adjectival richness, Irish construction in English, use of Irish in an English sentence, the marked rhythm of voice, were fit only for the uneducated. We saw donkeys and jennets carrying creels of turf to sell from house to house and watched asses and carts loaded with bog-dale.

The history of our town became loosely threaded together in our minds : Dudley Costello of the early seventeenth century lingered on. As a rapparee he had fought the Planters from Mayo to Tyrone until his head rounded a spike on the gateway of Dublin Castle. . . . Outside an hotel on the Mall was the tree from which Father Conroy had been hanged in 1798. He had taken a despatch from a messenger riding hard to the redcoats, roused his parish to gather supplies for the French; but he had not fought . . . Sheriff Brown in that Year of the French had made many a boy and man dangle from the trees on the edge of the

Mall. . . . Stoball, a hill in the town said to be connected with an order "Stab all" . . . French Hill, where the Frenchmen who had landed at Killala fought and died chasing the English who had bolted to Athlone on the Shannon. . . . Fighting FitzGerald, whose house we often passed, had been hanged on a cart. The rope had broken : " The British Government can't even buy a decent rope to hang me with," he had said. We watched the judge at the Assizes clothed in scarlet and ermine. He sat erect in his carriage guarded by cavalry with drawn swords. The escort was a result of the land war ; their white spotless bridles had a metal core in memory of the slashing pikes of the '98 rebels.

We hurried home once to tell our tense rage. We had heard the story of Deirdre and the sons of Usnagh ; we were angry against Conchubar the king who had killed the three brothers and had broken his word.

On Clew Bay, where we went each summer, we learned to row punts and boats, to blister our hands sitting side by side tugging at the one long sweep with the fishermen. They carved small boats for us, models of schooners, frigates, ships, full-rigged boats in glass bottles. We learned to work a lug-sail and to manage centre keels ; we knew the names of sails and shipping terms, to the delight of our sailor-teachers. We sailed on the stout-nosed fishing smacks of the Bay, where there are few traditions. Further out, beyond the Bar, was rough sea, and the story-tellers of Achill and Clare Island. Near the steep swarthy cliffs of Achill men shot the seals that gluttoned on fish ; fishing in a chopping sea we helped to pull in leaping lines and watched gleaming blue-green mackerel and scaly silvery herrings fighting death with curved bodies. We took lobsters from floating lobster-pots and watched shells being gathered in oysterbeds. Clare Island was an adventure even on what would be called a calm day ; the open sea lashed the cliffs that faced towards Dooega Head and the rising slate blue of Croghaun of Achill. It lashed the people who lived there. To us the island meant stories of *Gráine Ní Mháille*, who had refused a title from Elizabeth— " were they not both princesses? "—a strong-minded Connacht woman who worried her husbands, flaunted Elizabeth's governors, and, as a pirate, robbed Spanish and English ships. A cable led from her bedroom in one of her castles to a galley below ; she did not leave much to chance. In the minds of the people her name, Grannia Uaile, had become a symbol for Ireland.

We lived the stories we heard of pirate ships and wrecks from the Great Armada. We stole off in a row boat on daring discoveries : there were islands near where we lived. Our sister Sweetie would be Grannia Uaile, but the orders would come from Frankie and me. She would change suddenly to be the mother of an English sea captain. "Let's play . . ." "Let me be . . ." "No, me . . ." "Me" It was hard to fight against the English because none of us wanted to be the *Sasanach*; it was an insult which could be wiped out only by having the shouting Irish, who always won in the person of Frankie, become the English later on.

One day we stole away in a small boat; the lug sail was folded around the mast, which was under the seats. When out of sight of the house we all roared orders at the same time, the boat dipped and wallowed with excitement. " There she is . . .   Bang . . . BANG.   More powder . . . SURRENDER . . . " We saw a high galley poop and the gunners with lighted cord matches whilst we bore down to leeward straight on to ram in our two-banked galley. Our wooden spears had cords attached so that we could throw them into the water and haul them in again ; they served as spears, guns, cannons and arrows. Sweetie was a nurse who bound up heads with our hankies. The curly-headed Bertie and she had to become our prisoners ; we tied them with ropes ; they were now the crew of the Spanish ship.

We learned to love the sea, to be unafraid of it ; stormy days found us out on a point watching the curve of breakers or shouting on a cliff ledge above the spray and crash. Behind the Bay was the pointed Reek, Croagh Patrick, with its yearly pilgrimage climbing the rocky slopes to hear Mass where Patrick had once fasted. Stout-bellied hookers with dun and sienna sails carried turf to the mainland ; we listened to the Achill men talking their wild, strong-sounding Gaelic, which we had heard in town at markets and in the courthouse during trials.

The islanders had nearly all been abroad as sailors ; they talked around the turf fires of their hardships and

adventures in foreign parts, but from the women we heard
the stories of the islands. After returning from a fair the
men imitated the gestures, speech and peculiarities of the
mainland people; with twisting sarcasm they mimicked
people we knew. They were quickly enraged if their lack
of energy in off seasons was criticised. At a wake I heard
the caoin, a heart-breaking cry of women in grief, caught
up by it so that it seemed to flow through them from
another source ; the wail became unified, impersonal as a
sea-moan, disembodied as grief itself. We were shown the
Dane's Hole, which had passages leading to the sea. In
one room were old swords and an Irish flag ; but we did
not go down through fear. The people had confused the
Danish Invaders with an earlier race, the Tuatha Dé
Danan.

Now we knew the country on either side of the Bay,
from grey hungry Connemara to Mulranny. The bare,
once ice-covered drumlins gave the land a gloomy look
when the sky was clouded or when rain-winds tufted black
clouds. But sun made the cold land and the dark green
glint and become lush; it shone on the crowded islands,
lifting them out of the water, making the cliffs recede. A
harsh land and lonely, hard to make a living from its
grudging soil, cruel-hard they said it was, as hard as the
hob of hell, and desolate in the winter when storms could
cut them off for three weeks from the mainland. Misty,
indefinite, the land changed its surface in the mind from
gaiety to brooding melancholy ; but it gripped hard when
one knew it or had lived there. In rain or sun we loved this
country; its haunting impersonal bareness, its austerity,
aloofness, small lakes, the disproportionate bulking of the
mountains, smells of shrivelled seaweed rotting in grey dirt-
spume, brine, storm-wood, tarred rope and riggings, sea-
wrack, and mud after an ebb tide. The glass green blue
of a rough sea, clear depths under a cloudless sky, blurred
distorted crabs and the flowing of fronds and seaweeds,
slow apricot sunsets, steel grey, white and light blue clouds
furled up by wind, splotched by rain until they mixed as on
a palette, white green undersides of waves dashed back from
pitted torn rocks, phosphorescence dripping from oars and
bow on a dark night, the bullet precision of caillech
dubh diving clean for fish. Changing swirls of moaning

wind on capey headlands, rain splashing off thatched roofs or pelting against windows, waves smashing in rough sea as the bow dipped in furrows when one lay stretched out forward, the raucous harshness of herring gulls, islanders shouting into the breeze against the clapping of sails.   Our life was ringed by the Bay ; it was a huge world to us.

An old woman told my fortune one day as I dried myself at her fire after I had fallen out of a punt.   She looked at my feet as well as my hands and kept her hand on my head as she told me of fighting and trouble ; but I do not remember the end of her tale.

CHAPTER TWO

★

AT A STATION in the midlands as the family moved to Dublin we heard loud moaning from women who were saying good-bye to their sons and daughters who were off for America. The moans became a caoin, women threw their shawls back from their heads and beat their faces as they wailed : "A Mhuire, Mhuire . . . O Katey girleen . . . O Michael boy, my son."

Our accent was mimicked, and back to back my brother and I fought a ring of tormentors ; in the end we were left alone, as we were both lithe and hardy. We told our school chums stories of Fionn and Cuchulain, but they laughed at us. They had read the latest Buff Bill, could talk of the red varmints of Indians, Colt-emptying frontier fighters, of split-up-the-back Eton suits and the rags of that other public school life of the *Magnet* and *Gem*.   Only to ourselves now did we talk about the older stories. We told lies and deceived our teachers whenever it suited us. We felt ourselves conspirators against what we considered the undue authority of school and home.

I made my First Holy Communion. It would be the happiest day of my life I was told, and I would always look back at it proudly ; but I was in the dumps. I looked at myself in the glass. I could not see the light of grace on my forehead ; perhaps I had made a bad communion.   I worried over the confession in my mind . . .

Yearly a Brother, whom we called the recruiting sergeant, came to enquire about our vocations for the Brothers or the Priesthood. We were interviewed singly and prompted about our leanings towards religious life.

I learned of comparative religion by swopping stories with a Presbyterian boy. Some of my tales began : "There was once a minister Dick . . . " His: " There was a fat old priest who . . . " My suppressed indignation lingered on, but helped me to make an adjustment in tolerance.

King Edward came to Dublin. I was sent with my younger brother and sister to see the procession pass down town from the Phoenix Park. We stood in the front rank of the waiting people. I said we would keep our hats on. Scarlet-coated Life Guards with shining helmets cantered past ; but we alone of the crowd looked at the carriage with hats on. To show my intense conviction I spelt King with a small letter. I did not like the English. Early, Nannie with a grimace of disgust told us the story of the giant who said " Fee, fah, fum, I smell the blood of an Englishman"; evidently they smelt badly. We met few English people; they seemed very grand in manner, important and serious, with loud voices.

Joe Devlin, Member of Parliament for Belfast, came to see us. Our teacher had told us about the mighty man before he visited the classroom with the Head. We stood up and cheered when he entered. He asked for a half-holiday for the school, which was granted ; truly, he was a great man. He spoke about Home Rule and Irish freedom.

We learned to mix with "gutties" in the lower schools, to sit beside patched home dignity and thrift or carelessness. We laughed at the Jesuit school, Belvedere, and invented names for the initials " B.C. " on their caps ; in examination results we beat them. We fought boys from Belvedere and Protestants from Mountjoy School ; they were Swaddlers and Proddy-dogs ; we were papishes, R.C.'s pronounced quickly and O'Connell's Sausages, from the " O.C.S." on our caps ; their " M.S. " meant Monkey Slops. At home there were still taboos as to whom we should mix with ; but our selection was based on liking. At school there was no stress on relative wealth; brains were shared equally by rich and poor, but many could not reach the higher grades because their parents needed their earnings.

Now there came a change. Here was more of a middle class concentration ; its prejudices and distinctions gripped us. The budding attractions of ties, long trousers, hair oil and girls were combined with Ruskin, who seemed as necessary for certain years as pimples. Gentility flourished easily in Ireland : very little wealth nourished it. In the towns tuppence-ha'penny looked down on tuppence, and throughout the country the grades in social difference were as numerous as the layers of an onion.

My sister was taught deportment by nuns in boarding schools, how to enter and leave a carriage, the flouncing courtesy, recitations for company, and art as applied with needles in a ladylike way to unoffending backgrounds. By the irony of Irish life she was now in St. Ita's, Padraig Pearse's first school, conducted by Miss Gavan-Duffy, a friend of mother's. Pearse, a separatist, controlled a boy's school, St. Enda's ; one of the two Catholic schools not conducted by religious. I had the accepted Catholic views of normality, in religion, morals and behaviour ; atheists were perverse, they sinned against the light. There was a pitying commiseration for them and for people of other religions.

There were strikes in Dublin, the great lock-out of the Larkin strike. Workers who refused to resign from the Irish Transport and General Workers' Union were thrown out by the Dublin Employers' Federation. Twenty thousand men starved slowly for six months whilst they fought the masters, the Irish Parliamentary Party and separatist opinion. Sheehy-Skeffington, the Countess Markievicz, George Russell, Jack White, and some intellectuals were with the workers, but the fight ended in defeat. The lock-out showed the terrible conditions under which Dublin workers had to live, and for a while the slums stank.

I heard Jim Larkin speak, a fiery orator, well loved by his men, and the calmer James Connolly who did not provoke such enthusiasm as Larkin, but whose every word told. I was in O'Connell Street one evening when Jim Larkin, to keep a promise, appeared on the balcony of the hotel, wearing a beard as a disguise. He spoke amidst cheers, and hoots for the employers. Police swept down from many quarters, hemmed in the crowd and used their heavy batons on anyone who came in their way. I saw women knocked down and kicked. I scurried up a side street; at the other end the police struck people as they lay injured on the ground, struck them again and again. I could hear the crunch as the heavy sticks struck unprotected skulls. I was in favour of the strikers. Later I saw bodies of men drilling in Croydon Park, the Irish Citizen Army. A newsboys' strike at what period I do not remember. Mounted police charging· quick-witted urchins who scattered and lured the attackers into narrow by-lanes. There the boys used stones and pieces of brick with accuracy and rapidity. My sympathies were with the newsboys.

I was at Skerries on the coast when the Howth gun-running took place ten miles from Dublin. The Irish Volunteers landed nine hundred heavy single-shot German Mausers, and the Skerries company assisted. Police and military attempted to disarm the Dublin Volunteers on their way back to the city, but did not succeed. A Scottish regiment, the King's Own Scottish Borderers, the K.O.S.B., provoked by the Dublin crowd which had heard of the attempt to disarm the volunteers, fired at close range. Three people killed and thirty-three wounded. The Zabern incident seemed small in comparison. A man came round to the hobby horses and side shows on the Strand that night : "Women and children have been shot down in the streets of Dublin," he said. "Stop your amusement and mourn for your dead." We laughed at him and walked away. Who was he, anyhow? He gathered a small group around him and kneeling they recited the Rosary. Young boys whistled a new tune :

> "We are the Volunteers, the Volunteers.
> We are the Volunteers
> And not the Scottish Borderers."

The European War came. Redmond, the Irish Party leader, pledged Ireland's support to help England; the Irish Party voted for war. Home Rule was on the Statute Book; but an amending Act was passed to suspend it until six months after the War would be over.

Asquith, the British Premier, came to Dublin, to appeal for recruits. John Redmond had already advised Irishmen to carry the war to Flanders. With a school friend I walked through the crowded streets. The approaches to the Mansion House were guarded by Royal Irish Constabulary, armed with carbines. They stood in the shadows lining the shop fronts of Grafton Street, the butts of their rifles resting between their toes. In Woolworth's we bought small siren blowers, decorated with the Union Jack. We blew them as we walked around. A procession led by Redmond's Volunteers, armed with " sewer pipes," as the large amu-munitionless Garibaldi rifles were called, had marched to the Mansion House. Posters on the tram standards announced that Jim Larkin, James Connolly and others would address an open meeting. " A counterblast to the packed meeting in the Mansion House." We walked towards Liberty Hall, the labour headquarters. A large board outside : " We serve neither King nor Kaiser—but Ireland." The Citizen Army was drawn up ; some of them carried rifles, magazine rifles, and bandoliers of ammunition. They marched across to the top of Grafton Street, a few hundred yards from Asquith's meeting, and stood with fixed bayonets as a guard to James Connolly who spoke. Outside the old House of Parliament Jim Larkin spoke to the crowd, and asked their pledge that they would never join the British Army. We had minor skir-mishes as people tried to snatch our sirens because they flaunted the Union Jack. We heard rumours that Asquith had been fired at, that the procession would be broken up as it left the Mansion House; but although there was a feeling of tenseness, nothing happened. Asquith said "Room must be found and kept for the independ-ence, existence, and free development of the smaller nationalities."

I attended recruiting meetings held in the streets. Recruiting officers were asked questions about the freedom of Ireland when they spoke of poor little Belgium. The interrupters were silenced by police, or arrested. Some-times a rival anti-recruiting meeting would begin ; police and detectives would force their way through the crowd and attempt to arrest the speakers. Men were fined for answering the police in Irish. Irish Volunteer organisers were arrested or ordered to leave the country ; attempts were made to disarm the Volunteers. Often up amongst the Dublin mountains I met their battalions on route marches or on manoeuvre. Officers in full uniform with stiff tunic collars, some of the men in uniform, others wearing equipment only, a number carrying rifles. I looked at them curiously, watched them in the evening, mud splashed after a hard day's work. At home we discussed them, laughed at them. They were play acting, trying to pull the lion's tail. Who were they going to fight? They hated England more than they loved Ireland. A crowd of pro-Germans, that's what they were. My brother joined a cadet corps, and was commissioned to the Dublin Fusiliers. My friends joined the Army. I would also join, later on.

O'Donovan Rossa died in America and his body was brought home to Ireland. He was an old Fenian and the two traditions met, the old Ireland and the new. He lay in state in the City Hall, with an armed guard of Irish Volunteers and Citizen Army men. Out of curiosity I passed by the glass coffin lid, objecting to the green-uniformed Fianna Boys who guided the long files, but I did not utter a word. I watched the funeral pass to Glasnevin Cemetery, company after company of Irish Volunteers marching by, some in uniform, some wearing uniform hats and bandoliers, others green ties only. I saw the ungainly side of the parade : irregular marching, faulty execution of commands, strange slouch hats turned up at one side, uniform caps wobbling, long single-shot Howth Mauser rifles. They provided an amusing topic of conversation at dinner.

Father asked me what I would like to do. He thought I might care for law ; but I did not like that profession. Once I had heard him say that in Ireland the law considered one guilty until innocence had been proved. I wanted to do medicine ; it seemed good to help to prevent imperfect bodies and to relieve pain. I went to the University with members of my school class. There one heard little of the Volunteers or the various other movements.

I saw the St. Patrick's Day parade of the Dublin Irish Volunteers. Staff officers with yellow tabs on their gray-green uniforms, companies marching with a swing. We laughed later when discussing them. They had no guts, they would never fight. I was still thinking of joining the British Army. Around us the people were mostly imperialists or believed in the Parliamentary Party. The old men to prove their loyalty, had joined the G.R.'s., the George Royals, a defence corps known to some as the Methusiliers, or the Gorgeous Wrecks. I was commended for my desire to join up, but I was dramatising myself. I had no interest in the war, at most it appealed to me as a physical hardening if I saw service.

The old hatred of the " Redcoats " had disappeared. Before the war, scapegoats, those in debt or in trouble over a girl had joined the ranks ; now all trades, professions and classes were found there.

There were rumours about the Irish Volunteers being disarmed ; but who would bother about them? They did not count. Police arrested and deported some, others were forbidden to enter certain stated areas in Ireland. Three men were sentenced to three months for singing " God Save the King " in an unseemly way. Fianna boys, citizen army and the Volunteers were seen more often on the streets and in the outskirts on manoeuvre. " So many fine boys dying at the front while those ragamuffins strut around," said a neighbour, " they should be conscripted." . . . The Pals Battalion of the Dublin Fusiliers suffered heavily and those who had lost sons were less kindly disposed at seeing other boys unhurt, walk the streets of the city. . . . A letter from my brother stationed at Cork. He had joined a detachment sent to the coast to prevent gun-running, and was " very much bucked." Mother cried—he was in danger, and in his own country. Father looked worried but said nothing. In the papers we read that men had landed in a collapsible boat, evidently from a German submarine, off the Kerry Coast. Two of them had been found by the Royal Irish Constabulary hiding in the sand dunes, German automatics in their haversacks. They had been removed under escort to what newspapers called an unknown destination.

MOURNFUL LINES ON THE MILITARY OUTRAGE
IN DUBLIN

You true-born sons of Erin's Isle, come listen to my song,
My tale is one of sorrow, but I won't detain you long,
Concerning the murderous outrage that took place in Dublin town,
When a cowardly regiment was let loose to shoot our people down.

On the 26th of July, the truth I'll tell to you,
The Irish Volunteers all swore their enemies to subdue,
They marched straight out to Howth and soon the people were alarmed,
When they heard the glorious news " Our Volunteers are armed."

The crowds all kept cheering on as our brave defenders passed,
But their cheers were stopped by an outrage which for some time did last.
Our gallant men, the Volunteers, were met in front and rear,
By the King's Own Scottish cowards, who are doomed for everywhere.

God save our gallant Captain Judge, the hero of the band,
Who nearly gave his precious life for the just cause of the land,
In spite of terrible injuries and weak from loss of blood ;
He fondly hugged his rifle grand, the prize of his brotherhood.

Next in the line of heroes is the scout so well renowned,
With the butt end of his rifle felled a Borderer to the ground.
He disarmed him of his weapons and soon made his escape
By climbing a wall in Fairview, for his young life was at stake.

The Dublin police were ordered the Volunteers for to subdue,
But O'Neill and Gleeson boldly replied " such a thing we decline to do,
For to fight against our countrymen would on us put a stain,
For we wish to see our native land ' A Nation Once Again.' "

On Bachelor's Walk a scene took place which I'm sure had just been planned,
For the cowardly Scottish Borderers turned and fired without command,
With bayonets fixed they charged the crowd and left them in their gore,
But their deeds will be remembered in Irish hearts for evermore.

God rest the souls of those who sleep apart from earthly sin,
Including Mrs. Duffy, James Brennan, and Patrick Quinn,
But we will avenge them and the time will surely come,
That we'll make the Scottish Borderers pay for the cowardly deeds they've
    done.

CHAPTER THREE

★

EASTER OF 1916 came.   At Verdun the French were hard
pressed.   The Allies looked to the United States for
munitions.   It was a late Easter.   Flowers bloomed early ;
the weather was warm and dry, almost like mid-summer.
I sat in Stephen's Green on Easter Saturday, basking in the
sun, watching the ducks and gulls, before I walked up
and down to do Grafton Street and meet my friends.

Easter Monday, a holiday, was warm and many people went to the races, to the Hill of Howth, Killiney, or to the mountains. I walked across the city over the Liffey to the South Side, intending to visit the older portions of Dublin. Up by Winetavern Street, through the Coombe and back around by Dublin Castle walls. I looked at the statue of Justice on the upper Castle Gate. She had her back to the city, and I remembered that it had frequently been commented on, satirically.

I passed by Trinity College; the heavy oaken doors were closed. In O'Connell Street large groups of people were gathered together. From the flagstaff on top of the General Post Office, the G.P.O., floated a new flag, a tri-coloured one of green, white and orange, the colours running out from the mast.

" What's it all about? " I asked a man who stood near me, a scowl on his face.

" Those boyhoes, the Volunteers, have seized the Post Office. They want nothing less than a Republic," he laughed, scornfully. " They've killed some Lancers; but they'll soon run away when the soldiers come."

Thin strands of barbed wire ran out in front of the Post Office. Two sentries in green uniforms and slouched hats stood on guard with fixed bayonets. They seemed cool enough. Behind them the windows had been smashed. Heavy mail bags half-filled the spaces, rifle barrels projected, officers in uniform with yellow tabs could be seen hurrying through the rooms. Outside, men were carrying in heavy bundles—" explosives, I bet, or ammunition," said a man beside me. Others unloaded provisions and vegetables and carried the food inside. On the flat roof sentries patrolled to and fro. Men on motor bicycles, uniformed and in civilian clothes, arrived frequently and the sentries made a lane for them through the crowd.

I walked up the street. Behind Nelson's Pillar lay dead horses, some with their feet in the air, others lying flat. " The Lancers' horses," an old man said, although I had not spoken. " Those fellows," pointing with his right hand towards the G.P.O., " are not going to be frightened by a troop of Lancers. They mean business." Seated on a dead horse was a woman, a shawl around her head, untidy wisps of hair straggled across her dirty face. She swayed slowly, drunk, singing :

> "Boys in Khaki, Boys in Blue,
> Here's the best of Jolly Good Luck to You."

On the base of the Pillar was a white poster. Gathered around were groups of men and women. Some looked at it with serious faces, others laughed and sniggered. I began to read it with a smile, but my smile ceased as I read.

Poblacht na hEireann

The Provisional Government

OF THE

IRISH REPUBLIC

To The People of Ireland

Irishmen and Irishwomen. In the Name of God and of the dead generations from which she received her old traditions of nationhood, Ireland, through us, summons her children to her flag and strikes for her freedom.

. . . In every generation the Irish people have asserted their right to national freedom and sovereignty, six times during the past three hundred years they have asserted it in arms . . . We declare the right of the people of Ireland to the ownership of Ireland and to the unfettered control of Irish destinies, to be sovereign and indefeasible. . . . The Republic guarantees religious and civil liberty equal rights and equal opportunities to all its citizens . . .

Signed on behalf of the Provisional Government.

Thomas J. Clarke

Sean Mac Diarmada	Thomas MacDonagh
P. H. Pearse	Eamonn Ceannt
James Connolly	Joseph Plunkett

Clarke, I had known through a friend of ours, Major MacBride, who used to come across the city to buy cigars in his little shop. Pearse I had seen for the first time a few minutes before. A man in the crowd had shouted out his name as a quiet-faced figure in uniform with a strange green, soft hat had passed slowly out through the front door of the G.P.O. He had talked with an officer underneath the portico beside a fluted pillar. His face was firm and composed. Connolly I had heard speak at meetings. I had seen MacDonagh in the University where he lectured on English, gayer than the other lectures. Plunkett was editor of *The Irish Review*, back numbers of which I had read.

They did not mean anything—only names. As I stood looking at the G.P.O. pigeons fluttered up from the roof and with flat dives flew swiftly in different directions. The Volunteers' communications were not going to be interrupted, evidently.

I was walking home when I met three boys I knew from Trinity College. Trinity had been founded by Queen Elizabeth, and had been built and maintained mainly on confiscated Irish lands. Its tone had always been anti-Irish, arrogantly pro-British, and it had always linked itself to Dublin Castle. The students all wore their college ties, black and red, carried themselves with a swagger and seemed very pleased with life in general.

" What do you think of those damn Sinn Feiners? " said one. One night not long before, when both of us were tight, I had helped him to climb the college wall and railings. He had no trace of brogue, but a polished " garrison accent."

" I don't know," I said, " but they will soon be chased out by the military."

" We are collecting our people, as we want to defend Trinity. It may be attacked. Will you come along? We'll give you a rifle. There are plenty there belonging to the O.T.C."

" I'm going home now, but I will be back to see you later," I said.

" You better hurry on or you may not be able to get through. Cheerio! " and they walked away.

As I continued on my way I met another boy whom I knew. He was jubilant. " There will be fighting," he said. " We have expected it for a long time past. There's going to be dirty work at the cross roads."

So he was in favour of the rebels. He was a student at the School of Art. We had never discussed politics ; I had not any to discuss, save to laugh at other people's opinions.

" Well, I am going back to Trinity in the evening. I was offered a rifle," and I chuckled. Was it not pleasant to have a rifle and to feel that there was going to be excitement? This was a lark. He stopped suddenly and looked at me hard.

" Why? What is Trinity to you? "

" I said I would go back there to defend it."

" But it's not your University. Remember you'll have to shoot down Irishmen, your own countrymen. You bear them no hatred. If you go in there you cannot leave; and, mark my words, you'll be sorry ever afterward. Think it over."

I parted from him and went home thinking of what he had said.

Near my house people stood at their gates, discussing the situation. The Loyalists talked with an air of contempt. " The troops will soon settle the matter in an hour or two, these pro-Germans will soon run away." They were sure of themselves. The trouble would soon be over. The Redmondites were more bitter: " I hope they'll all be hanged," said one. " Shooting is too good for them. Trying to stir up trouble for us all." People who, although they were next door neighbours, had never previously spoken, now chatted eagerly, like old friends.

Rumours circulated and recirculated, changing as they passed on. The Four Courts had been seized and Stephen's Green; Dublin Castle had been captured. The country had risen, men from outlying districts were marching on Dublin. Other positions in the city had been occupied. The rebels were shooting everybody they met. It was not safe to be out. All through the evening rumour piled on rumour. I had thought over what the art student had said; somehow I did not go to Trinity. At home the seizure of the buildings was taken as some kind of mild joke. Dublin had been used to strikes. They had provided excitement but were never very serious.

In the night time I went down towards O'Connell Street. I heard the noise of firing; random shots in the distance. People from the slums, the crowded, dilapidated tenements of the eighteenth-century grandees, had looted some of the shops. Boys walked around with a bright yellow shoe on one foot, the other bare; women carried apronsful of footwear, stopping at intervals to sit on the curb and try on a pair of satin shoes; then, dissatisfied, fling them away and fit on another and different variety. Boys wore silk hats perched on their noses or backwards at a drunken angle. Three of them had cut slits in their hats and placed them over their faces. Water pistols in hands they were Kelly the Bush Ranger and his gang, with their bullet-proof, bucket helmets. Pickets from the G.P.O. fired at the looters, but they fired in the air. Clery's store, a large one, was like an ant heap. Men, women and children swarmed about, carrying off furniture, silks, satins ; pushing baby carriages filled with sheets, stockings, garters, curtains. Trails, winding and twisting, showed what they had discarded. Pickets were strengthened, looters were fired on, the shots were lower. The looters dropped their armsful and scampered away, cursing the armed men. " You dirty bowsies, wait till the Tommies bate yer bloody heads off." They came back when the pickets had moved further up the street.

I spoke to a sentry standing in front of a pathetic looking strand of barbed wire. He had a Lee-Enfield magazine rifle, wore a slouch hat, a bandolier and a pair of green puttees neatly wound. He was about sixteen, and blue-eyed ; he looked at the looters as if they had staged the performance for him. He spoke eagerly, glad to give good news. " The country is rising. Kerry, Cork and Limerick and men from the North are marching. We can hold Dublin until they come," and he smiled. " Our wireless is sending out word to other countries."

I walked round in a detached manner. I had no feeling for or against, save irritation at those fellows doing the unexpected, seizing the Post Office and the other buildings. I wondered why the troops had not attempted to clear the Post Office, the rebel headquarters. The Dublin Garrison numbered nearly two thousand five hundred and we had been told that other troops were on their way from the Curragh of Kildare. The rebels were not numerous—the reports of their numbers varied from twelve hundred to three thousand—and their positions were not in a proper state of defence. Groups of people stood and talked. Everyone had something to say and something to add. "Only for Eoin MacNeill's countermanding order there would be more of those men in there. It's a shame to rush young boys into trouble," said a neatly dressed woman. On Sunday I had read an order in the morning papers from Eoin MacNeill, President of the Irish Volunteers, and their Chief of Staff, countermanding the manoeuvres which were to be held all over the country on Easter Sunday.

Opposite the Pillar a tramcar had been overturned,

blocking the approaches from Amiens Street Station; but there had been no attempt to barricade the wide stretch of O'Connell Street. Two women stood in front of a sentry— the same boy I had spoken to. "If only my Johnny was back from the front you'd be running with your bloody- well tail between your legs." The boy shifted his rifle a little but did not reply. That night the military proclaimed martial law in Dublin.

During the night stray shooting, then spells of silence. Next day troops from the Curragh shelled positions near the Phoenix Park from the Abbatoir, and drove the defenders towards the city. The G.R.'s, who had been out for a route march the day before, had not returned to their homes. The anxious loyalists heard that some of them had been killed. "The cowards, to fire on old men!" Perhaps the trouble, the Rebellion, was going to last. People thought of food and tried to buy extra supplies. Prices had risen; only small amounts were sold. The anger was loosed on the rebels. "Why don't the military act?" An element of doubt now. The mobile column from the Curragh, with another unit, had reinforced the Dublin garrison. Close on five thousand troops in the city. Perhaps the rebels had received help.

I found little change in O'Connell Street next day. The G.P.O. had been more thoroughly barricaded. Other shops had been looted: Lawrence's toy bazaar and some jewellers. Diamond rings and pocketsful of gold watches were selling for sixpence and a shilling, and one was cursed if one did not buy. Women and girls, some clad in Russian leather boots, smart tweed skirts and a shawl, wore rings on every finger, throbbing rows of them, only the joints showing. Ragged boys wearing old boots, brown and black, tramped up and down with air rifles on their shoulders or played cowboys and Indians, armed with black pistols supplied with long rows of paper caps. Little girls hugged teddy bears and dolls as if they could hardly believe their good fortune. Kiddies carried golf bags and acted as caddies to young gentlemen in bright football jerseys and tall hats, who hit golf balls with their clubs, or indeed anything that came in their way. This was a holiday. Some of the women with wispy greasy hair and blousy figures, walked around in evening dress. Young girls wore long silk dresses. A saucy girl flipped a fan with a hand wristleted by a thick gold chain ; she wore a sable fur coat, the pockets overhung with stockings and pale pink drawers ; on her head was a wide black hat to which she had pinned streamers of blue silk ribbon. She strutted in larkish delight calling to others less splendid : " How do yez like me now? Any chanst of yer washing, ma'am? " In the back streets men and women sprawled about, drunk, piles of empty and smashed bottles lying around. The troops were slowly surrounding the city, hemming in the rebels and trying to isolate their posts.

All Ireland was under martial law, we learned, so there must have been trouble in the country. Rumours and more rumours. The Germans had landed in the South and were marching inland. German submarines had come up the Liffey. The rebels in the country had surrendered. The rebels were nearing Dublin.

Rifle fire began slowly, increasing in scale, then the deliberateness of volley firing and the sharp, quick continuous sound of machine guns. The fighting had begun in earnest. The troops had advanced beyond the canals which almost ring the city ; the bridges were held by different regiments.

I crossed towards the North Wall and found Lancers firing at snipers in a very unmeaningly impressive way. The neat puttied legs of the kneeling Lancers were sheltered by a bridge parapet or they stood up straight to fire somewhere at nothing ; behind them grouped a garrilous crowd to stop return bullets. After each shot a small ragged boy dashed forward, seized the empty cartridge case and waited for the next shot. He was making a bandolier out of empty cases. People moved around behind the line of fire, indifferent to the shooting. They were curious, interested, seemingly unconscious of danger. A frightened looking elderly man was dragged forward by two soldiers. A woman walked beside them. " He's a dirty bloody sniper, blast him," she shouted, excitedly. " Take him away." There was flour on the man's clothes ; he protested. The crowd watched in silence. A man beside me muttered, " She's a dirty spy," and spat. I made my way to O'Connell Street, the headquarters of the rebels. There were few people there now and the sentries had withdrawn. Bullets whizzed in the distance. The boys offered to allow me the use of a pair of prismatic glasses to see the snipers firing from Trinity College. " Only tuppence a look," but I refused.

I kept a diary of events, entering everything I had heard. When I tried to sum up the day the account was conflicting —rumour, counter-rumour. I had no feeling about it. I might have been a foreign news correspondent who had just landed, knowing nothing about the country, the people or the cause of the present Rising.

At night the din increased ; artillery was being used. I slipped out of bed, got quietly over the back wall and went downtown. There were few people out. " It's dangerous to go near O'Connell Street," a man said, " three people have been badly wounded near the Parnell Monument." I reached the monument and turned in to Moore Street. From the G.P.O. came the sound of cheering, then a voice singing :

> " Then here's their memory—may it be
> For us a guiding light,
> To cheer our strife for liberty,
> And teach us to unite !
> Through good and ill, be Ireland's still,
> Though sad as those your fate ;
> And true men, like you, men,
> Like those of Ninety-Eight."

Men took up the chorus ; their voices echoed through the bullet noise. The unlit streets gave a strange quality to the words, the chorus zoomed in a loud shadow between rifle crashes. I felt I would like to join in that song.

I stood near the Pillar. I heard a voice say, " Run for it, quick," and I ran. The houses on either side of Mary Street swayed.

" We were trying to blow up the Pillar," said a uniformed officer of the Citizen Army in Moore Street. " It's too good a guide to warships in the bay or to the artillery over there," pointing across towards the Liffey. But the Pillar remained.

" How's the fight going? " I asked.

" We hold Boland's Mill, the College of Surgeons and posts on the South Side. The English have landed and are trying to fight their way through, but they have been held up."

" And when they get through? "

" Oh, well, when they do it will be hot here." He said good-bye in Irish and walked towards the G.P.O.

I went back home in the early morning and got into bed, unnoticed, save by my brothers. I felt faint stirrings of sympathy as I wrote in my diary. I did not feel indifferent now to the men holding Dublin.

The shelling and noise increased. The people seemed a little cowed as if they did not understand what it was all about. Civilians fell wounded here and there ; the presence of death was close. Military posts pushed on slowly down the city. Spent bullets fell around and the whirring noise of live ones could be heard. I tried to get down to the centre of the city, but I could not get through the cordons. In the evening I was in a whirl ; my mind jumped from a snatch of song to a remembered page of economic history. I walked up and down the garden at the back of our house. Distant sounds of firing had new sounds that echoed in my head. They meant something personal ; they made me angry. The men down there were right, that I felt sure of. They had a purpose which I did not share. But no one had a right to Ireland except the Irish. In the city Irishmen were fighting British troops against long odds. I was going to help them in some way.

The note of resentment softened a little among the people. I heard expressions of sympathy " for those poor devils in their rat traps." " Damn it, anyhow," said a man, as if discovering it for the first time, " they're Irish—they're our own." I felt the same, but I did not know how to help.

I met a boy who had been to school with me—a tall boy, in home-spun suit, with grey eyes and laughing mouth. We found that we were of the same mind about trying to aid the men in Dublin. He had, I remembered, been a member of the Gaelic League, but had never joined the Volunteers. " I know where there's a rifle," he told me, "my father was given one, a German Mauser, as a present by a soldier who brought it back from the Front. There's ammunition also in clips." I arranged to meet him that night not far from my house.

In the meantime we would separate and get as close as we could to the soldiers' posts and find out any information. If possible we would attempt to get down town in the night time. I examined the positions occupied by the troops and wondered from what place we had best open fire. Towards the centre of the city there was a gleam in the sky; after twilight buildings were burning. The soldiers advanced with fixed bayonets, telling the lingering people: " Get home, get to your homes at once."

That night we met near the railway line, a hundred yards from my house. He carried the rifle wrapped up in canvas. We undid the covering. He pressed in a clip of cartridges down the opening and the grooved cartridges clattered noisily into the magazine. We walked along the railway embankment for half a mile. " This will do," he said, as we halted near a bridge. He settled himself down flat on his stomach. He fired in the direction of the canal bridge, where I had seen a military picket in the evening. The Mauser made a sharp, curt report. There was no reply. He handed me the rifle. It kicked up towards my face when I pulled the trigger. The suddenness of the noise gave me a shock. It was the first shot I had ever fired. " Shove it in tighter to your shoulder the next time," he said. We saw rosy dots in the darkness; we heard buzzes which changed in sound as they passed over and went on. We went back to a metal bridge and climbed up together. We gripped the steel trestles with our feet and knees.

" I can't see the foresight," he said.

" I wish I had thought of some phosphorus."

" I'll wrap my hanky around it."

Leaning on the narrow steel parapet one looked into the darkness, observing, whilst the other fired. The sound of the rifle shot rang along the metal. We changed positions and lay quiet, listened to the sounds in the distance, and watched the flames far away. We could make out different rifle shots : the heavier thuds of what we thought must be Volunteer snipers, the sharper lash of the English rifles, and the cold relentless precision of volley firing; then the startling hammer-hammer of machine guns. Darkness added to the noise; bullets made the most of the night. The sounds made my heart thud with excitement. Yellow and red flames climbed high out of a hole of blackness; they seemed to float in the sky, jumping above each other. The undersides of clouds glared; bright ghosts of buildings came and passed.

Volleys were sent at us; bullets clanged off the bridge. We looked up towards the canal after each shot, not thinking of the answering spurts. Feathery red lights spread out further on the sides. " They're trying to surround us," I said. We moved further away. We were very cold. In our excitement we had forgotten to bring coats or scarfs. Before dawn we hid the rifle, shook hands, gripped for a long time, and went to our homes, arranging to meet the following night.

In the morning smoke could be seen, and flames. It was terrible to watch. Why had I not known about the fight earlier? I thought of all the chances I had had of joining the Irish Volunteers, instead I had laughed and scoffed. Now when I wanted to help I could not. A Dublin Fusilier, a friend, came to visit us during the day. He drank his large glasses of whiskey and was eagerly listened to. He was an authority. His officers had told him: " Every man you see in green uniform, regard him as a German soldier, as an invader, and shoot him down." " We examine all suspects," he said, " and a bruise on anyone's shoulder means that he has been using a long-barrelled Mauser. I'd like to stick them up against a wall instead of taking them prisoners." He was hailed by many, who were anxious to shake hands, as he walked away.

Rumour said the headquarters in the G.P.O. had been burnt out, that the men had surrendered, that they had escaped by boring their way through the walls of houses down to the side streets.

I examined other posts in the evening. Near midnight, I left my house by a back window, without noise, and met my companion. We crept nearer to the soldiers and sheltered behind a low stonewall. A machine gun answered his first shot. We lay low and trembled. Then we gained courage; we did not even duck our heads. I found myself singing :

> " At the risin' of the moon
> At the risin' of the moon
> For the pikes must be together
> At the risin' of the moon."

I was hit by a fist in the ribs. " Shut up, do you want them to find out where we are? " he said. We changed from one position to another until all our ammunition had been fired.

We looked toward O'Connell Street and tried to imagine
what the men there were thinking. The fire had spread;
it seemed as if the whole centre of the city was in flames.
Sparks shot up and the fire jumped high as the wind
increased. The noise of machine guns and rifles was
continuous; there did not seem to be any pause. We
reached our beds before dawn.

Later in the day came news of the surrender of the men
in the Post Office. For another day the firing continued,
then it died away, save for the bullets of isolated snipers.
The Volunteers and Citizen Army men marched to surrender with the rifles they had kept in safety for years.
People taunted, jeered and spat at them as they swung by
singing. Some few waved handkerchiefs or shouted a
greeting. The grand adventure was over.

People moved about more freely now. British officers
at temporary headquarters, in shops and houses, issued
passes to those who wished to go inside the cordons. I
obtained three at different posts and brought them down
town thinking they might be useful. The G.P.O. was a
shell, from which the tri-colour still floated. The stout
walls were blackened, but they held. On top the statues
had pieces missing. The lower portion of O'Connell
Street was in ruins. What houses still stood were being
hauled down by wire ropes attached to traction engines.
Houses were smouldering on Moore Street, Earl Street,
Abbey Street, the Quays. Kelley's, at the corner of
O'Connell Bridge, had been battered in by machine gun
and shell fire—Kelley's fort it was called. Liberty Hall,
though it had not been occupied, had been shelled by a
gun-boat which had come up the Liffey. Everywhere glass
had been shattered or neatly drilled by bullets. I was
frequently questioned by pickets and had to show my pass
many times before I reached the South Circular Road.
In a house there, in " digs," was a medical student who had
been out fighting. " They're going to make a house to
house search in this area and I want to get out," he said.
I told him about the passes. He went to give them to
others and they passed through the lines. Then the three
passes were returned by somebody who was not suspected
and other men used them.

The prisoners were transferred to the different Dublin

barracks ; raids and arrests took place and prisoners came
to Dublin from all parts of Ireland. The bitterness of the
people against the Volunteers was tinged with a little
admiration. They had fought well against the regular
troops. Many hoped they would all be hanged or shot,
and said so to everyone they met. Stories of the fighting
circulated and of the murders of civilians in the North
King Street area, where the troops had been unable to
break through. The number of men holding Dublin was
found to be less than eleven hundred, whilst the British
had from twelve to fifteen thousand.

Four days after the surrender a brief announcement :
three men had been shot at dawn, Padraig Pearse, Tom
Clarke, Thomas MacDonagh. Next day four were executed
and the following day, one, Major John MacBride. I had
felt resentment at the death of the others ; now a strange
rage replaced it. I had known MacBride. He had been
to our house a week before the Rising and had laughed
when I told him I would soon join the British Army. He
had patted my shoulder and said : " No you won't." I
wandered around all day wondering what I could do to
help, cursing under my breath, meeting few I could feel
any sympathy with, for my friends were all hostile to the
spirit of the Rising.

The executions continued. Men of the detective division
of the Dublin metropolitan police picked out prisoners who
were leaders. The Dublin papers reappeared and said their
say. The *Irish Times*, a Unionist paper, wrote : " In the
verdict of history, weakness to-day would be even more
criminal than the indifference of the past few months.
Sedition must be rooted out of Ireland, once for all. The
rapine and bloodshed of the past week must be finished
with a severity which will make any repetition of them
impossible for many generations to come." The *Irish
Independent* pointed out that " certain of the leaders remain
undealt with and the part they played was worse than those
who had paid the extreme penalty," meaning, the limping
Sean MacDiarmada and the wounded Connolly. James
Connolly, set up on a stretcher, was the last to face the
firing squad.

Before the last two men to be executed faced the dawn,
Bernard Shaw's letter in an English paper proved that their

spirit had awakened chords : " My own view is that the men who were shot in cold blood, after their capture or surrender, were prisoners of war, and that it was therefore entirely incorrect to slaughter them. The relation of Ireland to Dublin Castle is in this respect precisely that of the Balkan States to Turkey, of Belgium or the city of Lille to the Kaiser, and of the United States to Great Britain. . . . An Irishman resorting to arms to achieve the independence of his country is only doing what Englishmen will do if it be their misfortune to be invaded and conquered by the Germans in the course of the present war."

Some of the people resented the executions. The men had fought well, their prisoners had been well cared for, they had held the capital for six days. Something strange stirred in the people, some feeling long since buried, a sense of communion with the fighting dead generations, for the dead walked around again. Even the soldiers who wished to make further examples felt the anger of the people. Tri-colour badges were worn on coats, caps and hats ; songs were whistled and sung. " The Soldier's Song " began to be known ; soon one could hear it in the streets. "Who Fears to Speak of Easter Week?" replaced "Who Fears to Speak of '98?"

> " I'll sing you a song, a soldier's song,
> With a cheering rousing chorus
> As round the blazing camp-fires we throng,
> The starry heavens o'er us.
> Impatient for the coming fight
> And as we watch the dawning light
> Here in the silence of the night
> We'll chant the soldier's song."

* * * *

> " Who fears to speak of Easter Week
> Who dares its fate deplore?
> The red-gold flame of Erin's name
> Confronts the world once more.
> So Irishmen, remember then,
> And raise your head with pride.
> For great men and straight men
> Have fought for you and died."

Songs were copied by hand, or typewritten, and handed around. Poems were learned by heart. The surge of a rebirth of feeling, of a national spring in the air. The fierce exultance of song expressing a buried national feeling.

General Maxwell, the British Commander-in-chief, was known as " Bloody Maxwell." Photographs of the executed leaders were in every small shop. Names of men who had been practically unknown two weeks before were now on the lips and in the hearts of many. P. H. Pearse, Thomas MacDonagh and Joseph Mary Plunkett were poets. Volumes of their poems and plays were republished. Dr. Browne of Maynooth, Ella Young, Francis Ledwidge (then at the front), Seamus O'Sullivan, James Stephens, wrote poems about them. I reconstructed their work and their ideals. I bought and read everything that breathed their spirit : Connolly's *Labour in Irish History*, a vigorous work, overthrowing national idols; the works of Ethna Carberry, Alice Milligan and other poets and writers. I covered them with brown paper or with the covers of novels, and kept them in my shelves in the study, unnoticed.

There was much distress amongst the people. Over three thousand had been killed or wounded. The arrests, numbering over three thousand, meant a further drain on resources, for the dependents of the imprisoned men had in the majority of cases no support. The secret reports of the Royal Irish Constabulary had been given due credence at Dublin Castle, and a very miscellaneous assortment of prisoners passed through the country jails on their way to Dublin. Irish Volunteers, members of the Gaelic League, people interested in Irish athletics, school teachers, writers, journalists, those suspected of being in favour of the Rising, all mingled pell-mell in overcrowded jails. Rebellion, disaffection as it was called, was going to be stamped out. The spirit of the people was to be dealt with as Staff Officers work out a strategical distribution on the map at headquarters before an attack. Pins change places, are moved here and there, the enemy is crushed.

A National Aid Society was organized, and, despite the odium attached to such work, people came forward to help. Australia forwarded the first large sums, but voluntary contributions came in from all over Ireland. In Dublin, people who three weeks ago would have sneered at the Volunteers as toy soldiers now stinted themselves, happy to be able to help. I helped at the National Aid Office where Fred Allen, a city engineer, was in control. A young man, Michael Collins, came there later to help. I tried to organize area collections and had students in the University to assist. Masses were said, The Month's Mind, in honour of the dead, on the days they had been executed. I organized collections at the church doors with some newly-made friends. We pieced together a large tri-colour flag which I carried around after the Masses; standing above the people we sang songs—" Ireland, Ireland, 'fore the Wide World." Into our hats and caps the people who gathered about outside the churches poured money, copper and silver. They cheered us as if we were doing something daring. The money helped to keep some of the dependents' women folk from starvation.

A gift sale was organized and the Mansion House, the residence of the Lord Mayor, was used. Women brought their brooches and rings, family heirlooms were handed in proudly, though beneath the pride were tears ; book lovers carried their most beloved books. One man, a poet, and a lifelong collector, gave his entire library ; artists, including Lavery and Orpen, supplied blank canvases, setting six hundred pounds as the purchase price for the portrait of the buyer. Throughout the day a procession, the poor, the very poor, the needy, the rich. Their contributions all handed in joyfully, proudly, some pathetically, some with a gesture that made one's heart beat wildly.

The executions had caused bitter feeling, and the arrests and the strict enforcement of martial law helped to intensify it. The people as a whole had not changed ; but the new spirit was working slowly, half-afraid, yet determined. The leaders had been shot, the fighting men arrested and the allied organizations had been disrupted. Without guidance or direction, moving as if to clarify itself, nebulous, forming, reforming, the strange rebirth took shape. It was manifest in flags, badges, songs, speech, all seemingly superficial signs. It was as if the inarticulate attempted to express themselves in any way or by any method ; later would come organization and cool-headed reason. Now was the lyrical stage, blood sang and pulsed, a strange love was born that for some was never to die till they lay stiff on the hillside or in quicklime near a barrack wall.

In an English court an Irishman from the North, Roger Casement, who had helped the Irish Volunteer movement, was on trial for high treason. He was one of the men who had been captured by Royal Irish Constabulary a few days before the Rising on the sand dunes of the coast of Kerry, after landing from a German submarine in a collapsible rubber boat. He had been in Germany; there he had succeeded in getting arms for Ireland, but the German captain blew up his ship off the coast of Cork after capture by the British.

During Casement's trial people in Ireland waited and prayed and hoped. Many again went through the fierce anger they had felt at the first executions. Petitions for reprieve were signed by large numbers in England. But the result was to be expected. Casement was hanged.

The University was changed now for me—new associations, new affiliations. Some of the boys had been " out," and had escaped arrest; others who had been in the country had not received orders. I reconstructed my world slowly. We were being hammered red hot in the furnace of the spirit and a spark was bound to fly and disclose us to each other, with a word, a look, a chance remark. Lectures became the unconscious part of the day's work. Conversations in Stephen's Green, seated among the trees, leaning over the bridge, staring into the water; tramps up amongst the Dublin Mountains, beyond the Pine Forest climbing Two Rock; walks in the night time—that was what counted. Always Ireland, Ireland, Ireland: story, legend, song, poem, planning. Perhaps we, too, would get a chance to fight or die. That seemed to be the end of all, the beckoning fate. The European War faded into an indefinite misty distance.

The effort at repression continued. Boys were arrested for marching in groups, for singing the Soldier's Song, for carrying the tri-colour; concerts were prohibited, newspapers heavily censored. Baton charges broke up meetings, freedom of speech was denied, bayonets began to glitter and threaten. The people met the new measures passively; but militarism, without excessive physical repression, evoked the same memories and produced the same results as it had once done when it could shoot and hang, burn and confiscate, transport to the West Indies or employ the boiling pitch-cap.

Christmas came and the Volunteers met in scattered groups. I was asked to join the fourth battalion on the south side of the river ; but the meeting places were too far from my home. My absence might be noted and too many awkward questions would be asked. A medical of my year asked me to join his company. " It's on the north side, in the first battalion area, and it will begin to meet in a few days' time. I'll bring you along with me." In the days that passed we smiled knowingly at each other, for we kept a secret that nobody else was aware of.

I met him near Parnell Square and he brought me to the Gaelic League rooms. The front door was half open. Inside seated on a table was a man idly swinging his legs, with an evening paper in his hand. He eyed us sharply, recognized my companion and grasped his hand warmly, then he nodded his head towards a room at the end of the hall. We entered ; the room was a large one, the blinds were drawn and gas mantles without globes lighted up the space. Over the mantelpiece was a blackboard ; seated on chairs were eight or ten men, some well dressed, others in shabby clothes. At a table between the windows two men were writing on a wooden, unpainted table. We walked towards them, my companion saluted and shook hands with one of the men. He had a ruddy face and huge shoulders.

" Your name has been submitted and approved of," he said, turning towards me. " You know the objects of the Irish Volunteers? "

" Yes, I do."

" Well, read this first, and then sign your name." He shoved forward a printed leaflet stating the objects of the organization:

1. To secure and maintain the rights and liberties common to all the people of Ireland.

2. To train, discipline and equip for this purpose an Irish Volunteer Force.

3. To unite in the service of Ireland, Irishmen of every creed and of every party and class.

I, the undersigned, desire to be enrolled for service in Ireland as a member of the Irish Volunteer Force. I subscribe to the Constitution of the Irish Volunteers, and pledge my willing obedience to my superior officers. I declare that in joining the Irish Volunteer Force I set before myself the stated objects of the Irish Volunteers and no others.

I read down the sheet and signed my name. The Captain, for it was he who had spoken to me, shook hands. I saluted and sat among the others, all of whom had been out in the fighting. I was a member of " F " Company of the First Battalion. The Captain ordered us to " Fall in." He asked the addresses of former members of the company, and men volunteered to look them up and try to have them on parade next week. A section commander took us for drill. After a time we were dismissed. I walked home, happy, an official of a Volunteer company.

THE DUBLIN BRIGADE

It was on Easter Monday the boys got the call
To join their battalions in park, glen and hall,
In less than an hour they were out on parade
There were true men though few in the Dublin Brigade.

When they got their orders they took up their posts
Though few were their numbers 'gainst England's proud hosts
There was joy in their hearts, not a man was afraid
There were straight men and great in the Dublin Brigade.

There was much work to do in getting things right
But the old and the young were all anxious to fight.
Every man worked hard at his own barricade
And rifles rang forth from the Dublin Brigade.

For a week without rest not a man showed a frown
Till the cowardly Saxon set fire to the town.
To save it our leader had to be obeyed
For he was the pride of the Dublin Brigade.

CHAPTER FOUR

★

WE THOUGHT " F " Company the best in the battalion. At first the company was sufficient in itself, " battalion " was a name, then I sensed its organization. At the University, later, we talked of our companies staunchly, and of other companies in mild depreciation. We discussed volunteer life after classes. We recruited slowly and carefully ; we had to know our men thoroughly before we asked them to join the Irish Volunteers. The Dublin Brigade was formed of the first and second battalions on the North side of the Liffey, the third and fourth on the South side.

Stories like Lieut. Malone's defence of Mount Street Bridge and of the other exploits in Easter Week made us feel that the fighting spirit, frittered away by irresolute leaders in risings since 1798, was there still. The Volunteers meant business. For the moment we would share their greatness, then the talk would drift on to the chances of getting recruits or ammunition. Some day I hoped I would see de Valera and Cathal Brugha and others I had heard of.

I had known one man, Major John MacBride. He had been kind to us as children; he would leave the other visitors to talk to us. With him we dropped our best company manners and felt at ease. Story-tellers, sailors and soldiers were very important—and he had been a soldier. He told us about the Boer war. He showed us an unminted gold coin, which had once been in the Boer mint. He had a commission from President Kruger and the flag of the Irish Transvaal Brigade: he would show us them one day. He spoke in jerks. We knew the stories of Boer Commanders and the names of officers, long rides searching for food in the burnt ruin of farmhouses and the bitter hate of men who had fought whilst their women and children huddled in death in British internment camps. MacBride had little in common with the Gaelic cultural associations of the dead leaders or with the revolutionary economic programme of James Connolly and Padraig Pearse.

I got many a scowl from my volunteer acquaintances when they met me walking with my brother or a friend in khaki. I tried to tell them that some of these soldiers honestly believed in the Party leader, Redmond; some thought they were fighting for Ireland when they fought abroad. In the Wicklow I had met a group of officers from the P.B.Ls., Poor Bloody Leinsters. Two of them had been influenced by the Rising. They had followed Redmond; now they thought that by promising Irish help without getting a working measure of freedom in exchange, he had failed. No longer they believed in what they were fighting for; but, in honour felt bound to return to their battalion in France. " When I come back next time," one began,

D

but did not finish, as we shook hands. Both were dead within three weeks. When I spoke of these two I did not find sympathy or understanding. Men in the company had relatives and friends at the Front; their creed was simple. They believed either in an uncompromising Ireland—or not at all.

Officers in Irish regiments were indignant at what they had misnamed the Sinn Féin Rebellion; but there was a half understanding; risings and attempted risings were part of the country. I heard an English officer say with dawning surprise: " Why, those people look upon us as the Belgians do the Germans." He had been used to Ireland as a good hunting country in the same way as he had looked upon Northern Scotland as a fine place for grouse, deer, fish, and the wearing of kilts. As long as the country provided a Somerville and Martin Ross atmosphere of hounds giving cry, strong brogues, roughish wit, discreet familiarity of servants, and a sure eye for picking out " the quality," and letting them know it; then Ireland could be understood.

Our Company had ten or twelve men when it was re-organized after '16, but others slowly returned. A big percentage of the " old crowd " as they were called, had answered the muster roll on Easter Monday morning. Some who rejoined had not been seen by their comrades since the fight, or they had met in prison or internment camp. Many were out of work; their employers dismissed them when they found they had fought. Some had again obtained employment; their new situations were not as good as the old ones. There were no vain regrets, a shrug of the shoulder, a smile; " It was all in the day's work," and here they were back again in the ranks.

We, like all city companies, were mixed : professions, unskilled labour, students, Government clerks, skilled labour, business men, and out-of-works; mostly young men, some boys. University students were scattered among the city companies where they learned to meet and know that fine type, the Dublin working man. Through him and others they were brought into touch with the slums and with living conditions; they found the Cause had united men of different classes, outlooks, creeds. On my right in the ranks was a newsboy, a "guttee," on my left an out-of-work; covering me in the rear rank was a Master of Arts, since professor of Romance Languages, next to him a final medical. There were no class distinctions. One judged a man by his previous training, courage, efficiency, and ability; results by zeal and willingness to learn. Names of proposed recruits were read to us on parade by our captain. The list would pass to all the companies in the Battalion. " Does anyone know this man? " he would ask. " What do you know about him? Do you think he's safe? "

Our drill hall was in the Gaelic League rooms at 25 Parnell Square, and we met once a week. Once we were hastily converted into an Irish class; we dragged forms into rows. A blackboard appeared, my section commander became the teacher, but the report of our scouts was not followed by a rush of Dublin Metropolitan Police, or of " G " men, as the detectives were called. Our scouts watched the approaches to the square; any undue movement of police or " G " men would be quickly reported. For a time, to avoid suspicion, we met in the hall of the American Rifles in North Frederick Street; when there was a special detective mouching in the neighbourhood we left in groups by different doors. Dancing and Irish classes were held in the hall, men and girls passed in and out, and suspicion was not easily centred on our gradual arrival. Companies that had no halls met outside the city, or as half companies or in sections, to avoid numbers of men being seen on the roads.

Some of us worried over our drill, arms drill and bayonet fighting; we practised with broom handles. The handles rattled with precision at arms drill; they cut and skinned our knuckles and scarred our hands in bayonet fighting. Each section was expected to have a number of men trained in Musketry, Engineering, Signalling, and First Aid. Classes were held for these special services. We were asked to volunteer for them. I joined a signalling class and was selected for a non-commissioned officers' class. I had to refuse the N.C.O. class. I found it difficult to attend parades punctually. My people did not know I was in the Irish Volunteers; they would never allow me to belong. I had no latch key. I had to account for all my movements save on one night a week. I had arranged to study physiology two nights a week with a boy whose parents

were stout Gaelic Leaguers. He was not a volunteer ; but
he could say that I had been to his house if any questions
had been asked. I called to him before going to class or
parade. I dressed for drills as if I was going to a party
or to meet a girl.

We expected to fight in the city, when, we did not know.
The real call might come through a sudden hasty mobilisation, and perhaps at night time. We walked around the
lanes and back alleys of the North side. We selected
observation and sniping positions, or checked up on the
food supplies in shops in given areas. We climbed to the
tops of buildings to get panoramic views of the city, or to
study roof tops, and we learned to know by sight the big-
footed men of the " G " division.

Some few of us read the Official British Army Military
Books, and text books of different services. I had a friend in
a bookshop opposite Trinity, who at first thought I was in
a training camp, but when, by accident, he found I was on
the other side, he continued to order the books as a joke.
Official books were difficult ; they were used to supplement
military lectures and practical demonstration. Read by
oneself, they were tedious, dull, and badly written. They
were as hard as the origin and insertion of muscles and
relations in anatomical text books, which had almost to be
sung to be known. And there were no involved neumonics
or rhymed couplets with strong twist of word to help. When
we had a working knowledge of standard books, we branched
on to more advanced works on tactics and strategy. These
we supplemented by military journals. I took paper covers
from novels and pasted them on to military books ; I put
them below my medical text books on the shelves so that
they would not attract the attention of my mother or of a
raiding party.

Frank, home on wound leave, often sat on the edge of
the table as I read in the study. " What are you up to now?
Oh, military stuff again. Why don't you swot your
Phys? " We would argue over a problem, or the use of
ground on a contoured map ; at times he pulled himself
up abruptly and looked at me. Then I knew what he was
thinking of ; he, an officer in His Majesty's forces, was
hotly debating with a rebel. Then we returned to the map.
" It's no use," he'd say, " you might as well give it up ;

you can't beat the regulars. None of you know how to handle men; you must fling them about all the time; I wish you were with me, though, out there." Frank and I were bound by affection. We had always stood by each other. My beliefs did not make any difference to him nor did they to his fellow-officers. It was easier to talk to men who had fought; they were usually more dispassionate. Frank had changed; the army caste system had gripped him: contempt for politicians and civilians, elimination of the human factor in the military world of decision, narrowing of the world to a tested comradeship, meticulous attention to social convention. He was now a regular and spoke of Kitchener's mob, the new army, with regimental contempt.

I had no unit to experiment on. My three younger brothers helped me to cover up my doings; they believed as I did. They were too young to join the Irish Volunteers, but there was Fianna Éireann, a boys' organisation, which trained as we did. I took charge of their company on manoeuvres, worked out all kinds of protective formations, trained them as scouts and experimented with tactics. The experience from the European War I got from small booklets issued privately by the British. It was comforting to know that " the information therein was strictly private and confidential, and was not to be communicated either directly or indirectly to the Press, or to any person not holding an offical position in His Majesty's Service." The home situation was complicated by the hidden uniforms and equipment of my brothers and by their attempts to attend their parades. I was commended for the long walks which I now took with them in the country.

Frank MacCabe was our company captain. He had very broad burly shoulders; he carried himself squarely and wore dark green riding breeches on parade. He seemed slightly conscious of his dignity as commander of the company; sometimes as if he knew of this feeling his face blossomed; it became a spreading pink when he gave an order. Although he made gross mistakes when explaining musketry theory, I did not lose respect. He had been out in Easter Week, and that covered the here and the hereafter. I was in awe of any rank. Diarmuid O Hegarty, battalion vice-com., who visited us at long intervals was a kind of minor god.

Paddy Hoolihan was our physical drill instructor. His chest had banded muscles; it kept the pronounced curve of the pridefully conscious Guardsman. His own strength made him abuse ours in setting up exercises; smiling, he kept us in tortuous positions. One evening in underclothes and trousers we were doing floor exercises for abdominal muscles—the newsboy always said abominal muscles—somewhat flushed we were brought to attention by our Captain. "A lady, sister of The O Rahilly, killed in the Easter scrap, is going to inspect you. She will probably give some of you religious medals. If there is any laughing you will bloody well hear from me afterwards." We tightened our lips as he walked expanding down our ranks past many a torn shirt with a grey-haired gentle faced woman, Mrs. Humphreys. She asked our names, talked longer to those who had fought, gave them a medal of Our Lady of Perpetual Succour.

Liam Archer, thin-faced, brim of hat turned determinedly down, who worked in the General Post Office, later took charge of us. He was a better officer. He would have been dismissed if it had been known that he was a member of the Volunteers. There was little loose talk among men in the Brigade, yet weekly fifteen hundred paraded, attended special classes and manoeuvres. When I passed Archer in the street he gave me a wink. Civil servants had now to take an oath of allegiance. Many left the service but some remained; a few had been told to take the oath.

The Battalion was commanded by a semi-mythical being called Byrne. Byrne the Boer, he was called. It was rumoured that he had served in the Irish Brigade under Major MacBride. We spoke of him with awesome respect. He had been out and had escaped imprisonment. As a sniper he was said to have potted away for four days after the surrender. As he came in to the drillroom there was a low whisper : "It's Byrne." A tall man in a waterproof spoke in a heavy voice, holding his chin stiff.

Diarmuid O Hegarty, the vice-com., inspected us. Once he said that we were marking time only, we wouldn't long keep that up. A volunteer must always hold himself ready. He had a rapid utterance, his hair flopped on his forehead with the intensity of his words. His hair gave him an untidy look, he was careless in his dress. What did he mean we asked afterwards; it looked as if there would soon be something doing. During the Easter scrap I was told he had wandered about with a puttee trailing loose; when one looked at him one remembered the puttee. A Civil Servant, he had been arrested, released and reinstated.

Weekly we paid threepence or sixpence, our Quartermaster marked the amounts in on the little linen-backed green cards which we brought on parade. They were a badge of membership, but a danger if we were arrested. We paid for the privilege of belonging, the carrying out of orders might mean, if arrested, imprisonment and the loss of occupation. "If all armies were like ours," said a van driver in my section, "soldiers having to pay for kit, rifles, and amm. there wouldn't be so much bloody talk about war." Walking home at night with some of the men I listened to their talk and learned. Some had read steadily and well, others had a personal opinion on much that was generally accepted without thought or inquiry. They had learned to be independent in mind. Arts students in the University, with their constipated knowledge, Chesterbloc complex and embryonic pedantry would probably look down on the simple independence and bright alertness of these men. I was taught their songs:

Step together—be each rank
Dressed in line, from flank to flank
Marching so that you may halt
'Mid the onset's fierce assault
Firm as the rampart's bank.
Raised the iron hail to weather
Proud sight
Left, right
Steady, boys, and step together.

*   *   *   *

When Wexford and New Ross could tell
And Tubberneering and Carnew,
Where many a Saxon foeman fell,
And many an Irish soldier, too.
Hurrah, brave boys we vow to stand
Together for our fatherland
As did that bold devoted band
The gallant men of Ninety-Eight.

The newsboy I often saw a bit of the way home; but that meant we both saw each other home as he would then walk back in my direction. He lived in a tenement behind Marlborough Street. One night he said : " Come on up." Smells of bacon fat spiralling up insistently, the lingering decay of cabbage and a steady strength of sewage. I caught my breath in short, greasy coughs. Dirty paint hiccupped off the wall, banisters were splintered or broken away; " for fuel," he said. Gaps in the wooden stairs, broken windows patched with cardboard or open to the rain ; doors swung dully on lopsided hinges. He lived on the third floor with two brothers, a sister, father and mother. The boys were asleep in one corner covered by grey army blankets, there was a mattress in another corner. His mother was bent, sewing over an oil lamp, the father was slumped in a chair, his overhanging moustache dewed and a breathy stale smell of porter coming from him. Afterward the boy came down to the door. Two shawlies on the steps were holding a loud banter across to a woman who leant out from the third-story window. " My God, the people shot landlords all over Ireland to get a piece of land and a home ; but nobody has shot a Dublin landlord for an extra room." "Oh, we're used to it now," he said. I walked up to what had been sententiously called the widest street in Europe; a woman grasped my arm : " Dearie, do you want a short time? Come on. I haven't been heard for days."

By degrees I paid for my rifle. It cost £4. My rifle was a long .303 Lee-Enfield. Our quartermaster unscrewed the stock for me. It was a proud night for me when I brought it home. I wrapped the two parts in brown paper and carried the parcel past police on their night beats. If they only knew what I had, I thought. I left the parcel outside the side gate in the shadow of a laurel. I waited until all had gone to bed. I made a dump for it in my room by sawing a piece out of the floor boards, adding two uprights for supports so that it fitted back in stool shape. I had bought Rangoon oil, and a tin of 3-in-1. I brought my treasure upstairs. It was very heavy. I looked at it carefully ; it needed cleaning. I thoroughly scoured it with boiling water, cleansed it out with rags in the pull-through, and oiled it. I stripped and cleaned the bolt action. I put a plug of vaseline in muzzle and breech, smeared the steel with it, screwed on the stock and wrapped an oiled rag around the rifle.

I removed the piece of board, tied a piece of string to the leather sling and muzzle, and shoved the rifle in as far as my arm would go. I tied the cord to a nail which I had previously hammered in at half-arm's length from the opening. I put a bundle of the *Irish Volunteer* and *Sinn Féin* beneath the opening. In case of discovery by mother, it would seem to be a hide for papers only. I pulled my brothers out of bed early next morning. I showed them how to work the rifle, told them how to clean it; in case I should chance to be arrested, I got them to promise that they would look after it.

I had placed my two revolvers in another hide. At times one of them was kept by a retired member of the Dublin police. He kept a shop not far away. He received my mobilisation orders as they could not be left at my home; I passed his shop each day on my way to the Medical School. Each section had a despatch rider who left word with us during the week of changes in the time and place of parade. In case of a special day or night mob. he knew our home and working addresses. The company could be quickly brought together when needed.

We had not more than seven or eight rifles and a fair number of small arms, though our strength had increased to sixty. Often our captain announced that weapons offered to him had to pass to other companies in the battalion, because there was not enough money in our Arms' Fund to buy them. The Tommies sold us rifles and kit, but one had to be cautious when approaching them. Some had been used as decoys by their officers. We looked longingly at gunsmiths' shops in Dame Street and on the Quays; but we could not buy arms or ammunition, even shot-gun cartridges without a special permit from the police. Once, when a man from another company, who could not hold himself in any longer, broke a shop window, he was told off and the automatic was handed back.

This was a new world and a strange one. The men had little use for anyone who was not of the physical force belief. Gaelic Leaguers and members of Sinn Féin Clubs who did not belong to the Volunteers were sneered at. Most of the men had joined Sinn Féin and the Gaelic League.

Like the thoroughgoing pragmatists we were all our associations and contacts in life and literature were diverted to the one purpose. Gaelic Leaguers stressed the incentive of the language towards propagandist nationality; few had disinterested literary values. Some of the men I met had become knarled and bitter by the corroding thought of injustice which they grafted from the general to themselves. This indriving had warped them, their expression of feeling was from personal to general, and their emotions became rhetoric.

The men in the company thought the English were contemptible. They were cowardly, their word, as far as Ireland or Imperial possessions were concerned, could never be trusted. When I argued the question of cowardice giving instances of English at the front throwing themselves on top of grenades to save their comrades, I was told that the story was all " me eye."

Only by fighting had Ireland ever gained its own self-respect or any practical advantage. The only way to speak to the English was down the barrel of a rifle. When I spoke of the army, meaning the British, I was understood to mean the Volunteers, or I was asked pointedly what the hell did I mean: We were the army! There was with some, a grudging respect for the Unionists, blueguts; they were a planter race who held the land grants they had won cheaply, or by the sword, but they gave their blood to the Empire. The shoneens——those who through snobbery, acquired wealth, inclination or steady boot-licking had reached an intermediate position, neither food, flesh or good red herring——were held in supreme contempt.

I had to prevent my people knowing of my activity; but my new friends were remote from their lives. The personal isolation of people in a Dublin suburb, where one scarcely knows the names of one's second next door neighbour, was an additional protection. My sympathy with unrest was known, however.

Amongst the books at home was a copy of Wolfe Tone's *Autobiography*, published by his son in America in 1826. The leaves had not been cut. I read Tone slowly. He had been the first to unite Catholic and Presbyterians in the national effort. In his time the North was the most strongly revolutionary part of the country; clearer thinking than romantic Munster which smuggled men abroad to fight for foreign kings. Other leaders, with the exception of

Hugh O'Neill, had been abstractions; at school we had read of them in relation to events; they had nothing to do with living. Tone was the first human note, "drunk again," in his diary meant much: it brought him down to mortal level. Too many people had a leader's image in their minds that was a cross between a Calvinist's ideals and a nun's; he must possess the virtues they lacked:

> And righteous men shall make our land
> A Nation once again.

Few of the boys I met had studied Tone, Fintan Lalor or James Connolly. I had often listened to their quotation of Fintan Lalor: "Somewhere, somehow, and by someone a beginning must be made." But not: "Political rights are but parchment. It is the social constitution that determines the condition of the people." Irish history had not been written; it was the history of the underdog.

We dismissed the agony, blood, and misery of the trenches as we dismiss another's sorrow. There is an Irish proverb: "It's easy to sleep on another man's wound." When I read the casualty lists for news of my brother I found friends and acquaintances amongst the killed and wounded. I could see mother's face when she read the morning paper and a hand involuntarily going to her throat if there came a sharp knocking at the door. It might be a telegram: "We regret . . ." from the War Office.

The first Russian Revolution came. The provisional government and the coalition under Kerensky. We were pleased; we had read of Siberia, secret police and of underground movements, but none of my volunteer friends spoke of Lenin or the 1905 Revolution. Since the execution of Connolly there had been no revolutionary leader, no one made a contact between extreme labour and the separatists. Our company strength was mainly working men: but I was too intense on the new spirit of volunteering to feel their other allegiance. The Volunteer spirit in essentials was hostile to Labour, afraid that any attention to its needs or direction would weaken the one-sided thrust of force.

CHAPTER FIVE

★

CÉILIDHES, IRISH DANCES, were always crowded. There, one met only people who were all right, meaning separatists. Volunteer dances to collect money for arms were supposedly for some imaginary club or literary society, as they should have otherwise been suppressed. In between each dance were ballads, jigs, old songs, and fierce recitations:

> In Dublin's town they murdered them
> Like dogs they shot them down.
>
>   .   .   .   .   .   .
>
>   .   .   .   .   .   .
>
> May peace and plenty be her share
> Who kept us from want and care
> O God bless England is our prayer
> Whack fol the diddle ol the di-do-day.
>
> When we were savage, fierce and wild
> She came as a mother to her child
> Gently raised us from the slime,
> Kept our hands from hellish crime,
> And sent us to heaven in our own good time.
> Whack for the diddle ol the di-do-day."

Or the anti-recruiting:

> God save the King and God save Ireland !
> Get a sack and start the work to-day ;
> Pick up all the socks you meet,
> For the English Tommies' feet,
> When they're running from the Germans far away.
>
>   *   *   *   *
>
> In Dublin's fair city where the girls are so pretty
> I first set my eyes on sweet Molly Malone.
> As she wheeled her wheelbarrow through the streets
>   broad and narrow,
> Singing Sinn Féiners, pro-Germans alive, alive O !
>   Alive, Alive O—O,
>   Alive, Alive O—O,
>   Sinn Féiners, pro-Germans
>   Alive, Alive, O.

I got to dances by climbing out of the back window by a
ladder or the drain pipe when all were in bed. Often I
took a chance. I went over the back wall before father had
gone upstairs. At dawn I was in my bed.

I brought over much from my other life. I made excuses
in my mind for bad manners, sloppy clothes, sweaty hands,
bombastic ignorance, but the clash lessened. I lived on a
mountain top where there was no need for speech, even.
I felt an understanding, a sharing of something bigger than
ourselves, and a heightening of life. People could be more
expressive, natural and affectionate. They were direct, and
immediate contact was not difficult. Older people had no
conscious outthrust of age or experience; we all shared
the adventure. The important ones did not surround
themselves with barriers of authority or of organised
dignity. I could not see myself now. I could not see my
friends through the movement; the critical faculty came
up every now and then, but I hit it on the head.

I joined the Five Provinces Branch of the Gaelic League
Night classes were well attended, people seemed eager to
learn the language, and to use whatever words they knew
in the middle of an English sentence. The League had
been founded by Douglas Hyde, a Trinity man. It
had helped to preserve and teach the language, gather to
some extent its folk lore and foster literature. Out of this
movement had come respect for the wealth of a mere
peasant's tongue and a fresh source for those writing in
English. Many, because of it, had taken on a new interest
in the country, to some it had given a background through
cultural association. All contemporary Irish movements
might be said to spring from it. Most of the officers and
men in the recent rising had had some knowledge of, or
had been students of, Irish.

Through ceilidhes and general association I got to know
Cumann na mBan and Fianna. Cumann na mBan, the
League of Women, had been organised as an auxiliary to
the Volunteers. The girls were formed in companies and
organised by districts. They were expected to be trained in
First Aid, to prepare field hospital supplies and general
equipment. They organized concerts and dances and helped
the Arms' Fund. They were not controlled by the Volunteer
Executive. Fianna Eireann had been started by the

Countess Markievicz. They were scouts trained to the use of arms, modelled somewhat on the ancient Fianna of the legends. But that part of training depended very much on who commanded the company; usually they were prouder of the arms-bearing part. When eighteen years they passed to the Volunteers. Fianna and Cumann na mBan had helped in the Easter fighting.

In the University Volunteers from different faculties knew each other and kept together. We subscribed to Irish papers, learned the latest songs, wrote very bad verse, and read books on Anglo-Irish poetry. We used the Sinn Féin post when writing to each other in Dublin. Special stamps were sold by trusted news agents and letters could be left with them for quick delivery. The British opened mail and it was no use to leave anything to chance. Walking across town during the day, I met men from other companies and was always sure of a hearty greeting in Irish or a half military salute. We discussed such important matters as whether or not we should salute our officers in public. They must have liked the honour, despite the danger, for none of them forbade it.

In the college we disliked those who spoke in favour of the European War, yet saw the fight from a safe distance. They looked down on everything to do with an Irish-Ireland movement as if it would contaminate their social atmosphere. They sneered at the Volunteers, hinted at supplies of German gold, walked proudly with a background of the climbing urbanity of Jesuit schools. With some, one found that rebellion has its vintage ages. They could talk with savoury pride of a real or imaginary ancestor who had carried a pike or sword in '98, or had helped Emmet in 1803. That period was accepted, it had gone into song and everyday speech, Moore had sung of it in London drawingrooms. 1848 was respectable; there had been much romantic and propagandist poetry written and one futile gentlemanly fight. 1867 was doubtful; little poetry, much organized purpose, which was not apparent in the capture of a few barracks; there had been few gentlemen. Nineteen hundred and sixteen, only a year ago, was a dirty stab in the back. There were others who belonged to the Gaelic League or who played Gaelic football and hurling. Boisterous, very contemptuous of Rugby and golf, and soccer, tennis to them was the last straw. They spoke of the English with inherited contempt, attended public meetings in the streets, approved of physical force in talk, but made no attempt to join the Volunteers.

D.O.R.A., Dora, as the Defence of the Realm Act was affectionately called, added new Irish clauses. Anyone whose " behaviour is of such a nature as to give reasonable grounds for suspecting that he has acted, or is acting, or about to act in a manner prejudicial to the public safety or to the Defence of the Realm," could be arrested. Men were sentenced for " making use of language calculated to cause disaffection," for "whistling derisively" "The Peeler and the Goat," when passing police; the air had once been the marching song of the Royal Irish Constabulary.

> Oh, mercy sir, the goat replied
> Pray let me tell my story O,
> I am no Rogue, no Ribbonman.
> No Croppy, Whig or Tory O;
> I'm guilty not of any crime
> Of petty or high treason O,
> I'm sadly wanted at this time
> For this is the ranting season O.
>
> It is in vain for to complain
> Or give your tongue such bridle O,
> You're absent from your dwellin' place
> Disorderly and idle O.
> Your hoary locks will not prevail,
> Nor your sublime oration O
> And Peeler's Act will you transport
> On your own information O.

At the Abbey, Lady Gregory's play *The Rising of the Moon* was banned by the Castle. Formerly it had been considered by the separatists to deal with the police too kindly. The Royal Irish attended all meetings, concerts and Gaelic sports ; if unable to take a report in writing their " mental notes " were accepted as evidence. In Dublin a meeting was broken up by police, the crowd resisted, an Inspector of police was hit on the head with a hurley——later he died. The carrying of hurleys was prohibited. A new song to the air of The Wearing of the Green:

> Then shoulder high your hurleys, boys,
> And keep your rifles bright ;
> The mangy bulldog can but bark
> He's got no teeth to bite.

I was hemmed in during a baton charge in Westmore-
land Street, a heavy baton walloped off my shoulder. I
jumped for the large target of a policeman's feet and with
the help of a grocer's curate from my company toppled him
over. A squad of police charged to rescue him; we ran
with his baton.

The power of the Irish Parliamentary Party seemed to be
on the decline; three men had been returned in bye-
elections on the understanding that they would not attend
the English House of Commons. Tri-colours were tied
or nailed to old castles, telegraph poles, wires and trees.
The police tore them down. The branches of trees were
lopped and the trunk greased or tarred, then the flag
floated. Authority now rested with the individual policeman or British Officer. The official mind thinking in
schedules was not able to hold its own against quick wit
and gay carelessness.

Prisoners, in Mountjoy Jail, treated as criminals, demanded political rights. They were refused. Thomas
Ashe and others went on hunger strike. A school teacher,
he had fought, in South County. He was of powerful build.
He had been convicted on the " mental notes " of an R.I.C.
man. He was popular with his comrades. More men
attended the parades of our company. We felt that
something would happen. Forcible feeding began; bed-
clothes were taken away from his cell which he had tried to
wreck before the strike. The wind was cold and damp, his
cell windows were broken. My examinations began in the
University; but I could not think of anatomical relations
or of hydrogen-ion concentration and basal metabolism.
Something was bound to happen. Liam Archer had told
our company, tightening his mouth : " this sort of thing
won't continue long; we won't stand by and see a Volunteer Officer fight by himself." My food did not taste the
same. I was disgusted when I found myself as hungry as
ever at meals.

Thomas Ashe died. Examinations were now of no importance. There was a special mobilisation of the company.
Men in the Volunteer reserve, who could not attend parades,
were in the ranks. The company was practically at full
strength, that in itself was exciting. Diarmuid O Hegarty
inspected us. He spoke slowly now; the Irish Volunteers

were going to give Commandant Ashe a military funeral. The Brigade would be mobilised. Officers and men would carry small arms and twenty rounds of ammunition. Our pockets were to be emptied of papers before we paraded on Sunday. We would be told by dispatch of the mobilisation ground. We read into his words what he didn't say.

Next day in the University we discussed Sunday. The British would interfere, they would never allow companies to march in military formation, wear uniform or the firing squad to carry rifles. On the streets more tricolour buttons, Fianna Fáil cap badges of the Dublin Brigade, and crowds after dark. An inquest was held, the jury found that " the hunger strike was adopted against the inhuman treatment and as a protest against their being treated as criminals."

I cleaned and overhauled my rifle and revolvers and polished the brass clasps on my accoutrements. I might be recognized by my people or by some of my loyalist friends ; that could not be helped now. On Sunday morning I took father's leggings and borrowed a slouch hat which I pulled down hard on my forehead. Inside my coat I carried my thirty-eight in a thin, kid holster. I had one hundred rounds of ammunition with me in different pockets and a first field dressing and bandages. We had been told to bring twenty rounds but I wanted to be sure. I expected that the British would try to prevent or break up the funeral.

Our company fell in at the top of Whitworth Road. Across the canal was the grey bulk of Mountjoy Prison. Other companies fell in. We shouted to them when we were allowed to stand easy. We, " F " Company, were sixth in order down the road; behind us stretched the rest of the battalion. That gave us a feeling of strength. Byrne the Boer again came out of myth. A tall figure in uniform with linked chain epaulettes on his shoulders ; he inspected each company, then from the top of the road ordered us to move off. His voice carried well. We halted outside Glasnevin cemetery whilst a curious crowd watched us. I made a mistake in taking a turn. My section glared at me. One said " What the bloody hell do you think you're doing? " I felt miserable as we stood to attention. I had let down my company before the public. We were detailed off in sections. Mine was marched down the road towards

Finglas village; we halted and formed across the road. Cars and people on foot were not allowed to pass our cordon. During the day we wondered what was happening in other parts of the city. Late in the evening after the crowds had gone we rejoined our company and marched past the grave. We reformed again and swung down town, singing. We were dismissed at Parnell Square. The Volunteers had held the streets of the capitol, had kept order, had marched in the forbidden formations, had worn uniforms. A firing squad had carried rifles and had fired volleys.

*   *   *   *

The Irish Constabulary, on military lines, had been organized by Sir Robert Peel in 1822, hence " peelers " and " bobbies." Recruits had to have their own and their father's records looked up in the local barracks; if there was no taint of rebel blood they went to Dublin Castle for examination and, if approved of, to the depot in the Phoenix Park for six months' intensive training. They were, unlike the police of England and Scotland, independent of the local authorities, and could not be dismissed even by their Inspector-General without the sanction of Dublin Castle. Officers were nominated by the Chief Secretary, and after training became District and County Inspectors—D.I.s and C.I.s. They were a costly force.

Throughout the winter of 1917 all organisations increased in number. Arthur Griffith, President of Sinn Féin, had been its founder. It was organised in clubs, and councils whose area corresponded with that of Parliamentary divisions. An elected executive dealt with policy. Sinn Féin intended to fight elections on the abstention plan until there would be enough elected representatives to form a government. The various movements were lumped by the British as Sinn Féin; sine fine, they pronounced it. At a general convention of Sinn Féin the constitution was changed. Eamonn de Valera was elected President.

. . . Sinn Féin aims at securing the recognition of an Independent Irish Republic . . .

. . . a Constituent Assembly shall be convoked, comprising persons chosen by the Irish constituencies, as the supreme national authority to speak and act in the name of the Irish people, and to devise and formulate measures for the welfare of the whole people of Ireland."

Directors were appointed to organise what would be later departments of government. Cathal Brugha was responsible for Ministry and Commerce. Diarmuid Lynch, a former Lieutenant of our company, dealt with food control.

At a secret convention of the Irish Volunteers Eamonn de Valera was elected President; Cathal Brugha became Chief of Staff and I.R.B. controlled the resident executive of the Volunteers in Dublin and neighbourhood. The Irish Republican Brotherhood, the I.R.B., had been founded in 1858 by James Stephens as a secret oath-bound society to bring about Irish freedom by armed force. It had been called the Fenian Brotherhood and its members Fenians. Now it was spoken of as the Brotherhood.

The organization unit was the Circle of ten men camouflaged under stranger names for meeting; each Circle elected a County Centre. In Ireland the thirty-two counties were divided into eight Electoral Divisions. There were three between England and Scotland. These eleven each elected a Centre to the Supreme Council which then co-opted four more. The Supreme Council declared itself to be the government of the Irish Republic, and its President was the President of the Republic. It had power to levy taxes, raise loans and make war. Through its Military Council it had planned the Rising of 1916. Again reorganized in internment camps and gaols it was getting a hold on all separatist organizations by placing men in key positions. As well it had men who did not take an active part in Irish Ireland life; they worked quietly as professional men, in Government offices and in civic life.

Cattle, oats, dairy produce, and food stuffs had been shipped in excess to England, which relied largely on Ireland for the feeding of her people. The Irish Food Control Committee protested, but the power was with the London Food Controller. Sinn Féin tried to organize a food census and attempted to warn the people of danger. The famine years were yet living memories—over a million had died.

I got a mobilisation order. I cut my work in the dissecting room. I met two men from " F " Company at the

corner of the North Circular Road ; soon a group collected
from our battalion. Boys came on bicycles and tram cars.
A milkman drove up, he handed over his horse to a friend
to finish his round. We loitered about in threes. Down
the wide road from the cattle market cattle and pigs were
driven to ships at the North Wall. Drove after drove of
bullocks went past, drivers whistled and shouted, and
twacked mud-splashed rumps of their beasts with ash
plants. A herd of pigs came poking their noses from side
to side, halting to sniff after jerky runs. They climbed
footpaths, went into open garden gates, reluctant, as if
they sensed their fate. A sharp order, the pigs were surrounded ; protests from the startled drivers were ignored ;
with wild whoops and in protective formation we rounded
our spoil towards the corporation yards beside Binn's
bridge on the canal.

We stood amongst carts, dust buckets, shovels and
brushes until butchers arrived. The air quivered with the
desolation of dying pigs. We took off brush handles and
pointed them with penknives as we guarded the yard.
A force of Dublin Metropolitan Police in charge of a resolute
inspector arrived ; tall burly men marching in stolid heavy
footed ranks. There was a talk with Dairmuid Lynch, the
Director of Food Control, whilst we laughed at the police.
We looked at their long black baton cases and heavy
helmets, and wondered what they would do. " Stick your
pole in their guts ; bayonet work," said the milkman, " if
they look for trouble." The police surrounded us. More
volunteers arrived, another batch of police strengthened the
cordon. At dusk the procession started off, the police made
way, then fell in behind. Drays had been requisitioned,
the still bodies lay uncovered as we moved across the city,
our advanced flank and rear guards with brush handles
and butchers' knives. Through O'Connell Street, past
Trinity and a turn into Dame Street. Where were we going
we wondered. This went past the Castle. Past Dublin
Castle ; surely the soldiers would be turned out ; we readied
our spears. Up the hill by Christ's Church cathedral and
down the old streets of the Coombe. Where the hell were
we going ? At Donnelly's bacon factory we delivered our
dead. The seizure of the pigs caught the imagination of
the people. As a result Sinn Féin markets were held in

some towns.   It was arranged that the surplus food of one county be exchanged for the needs of another.   The resurgent Nationhood was planning.

*   *   *   *

THE CONSTITUTIONAL MOVEMENT GOES ON AND ON

We're leaders of this mighty Irish Nation
Though some folk say our leading days are done.
But don't forget what ere may be our station
The Constitutional movement must go on.

Chorus :
And on and on and on for ever more.

Gather the Party round Sinn Féin a scorning
And let your speeches roll across the floor
For the Constitutional Movement now take warning
Must go on and on for ever more. . . . Amen.

We've Home Rule now the Statute Book adorning
It's there to be seen by every mother's son
We brush the cobwebs off it every morning
For the Constitutional Movement must go on.

Four hundred pounds a year is very handy
It helps the Party now to carry on
In London boys, we all can act the dandy
For the jobbery and corruption must go on.

Now Ireland can no longer be excluded
Lloyd George he flung his speech across the floor.
No matter what you think about conscription
But the Constitutional movement must go on.

When Lloyd George will threaten Ireland with conscription
We'll stop him with our gas, lead on by John
And the *Freeman* will write a grand description
For the Constitutional movement must go on.

GOTHIC

CHAPTER SIX

[MARCH—AUGUST, 1918.]

★

IT HAD BEEN increasingly difficult to avoid suspicion at home. I had to listen to my comrades being laughed at and their motives questioned. Our set did not believe in giving their services voluntarily; they were satisfied and the existing order was good; was it not " the Government "? An idea would be viewed from the point of gain; what good would it do one personally? If instead of gaining one would lose friends, position, status, liberty, then madness lay that way. There was no sense in it; sense being the standard by which they interpreted other ideas in terms of their own. Often I flared up and said what I thought about the situation, then again I would sit quiet, listening whilst I boiled inside. I had to invent too many excuses. Already it was like a guerrilla war. In my own territory which I knew I could cover my tracks carefully, appear somewhat disinterested to friends of the family, meet my ordinary acquaintances who were pro-British, and yet keep in touch with my friends.

My point of view would never be listened to, much less tolerated. My brother could join the British Army, that was respectable, acknowledged as such by clergy and laity. I would associate with people who were looked down upon; once they had been called the " mere Irish," now people of Irish birth had got into the eddies of the British caste system. Once the English held the country solely by means of garrisons; in the last century by garrisons and society; now by patronage, caste and its outlying webs in the smallest towns. The further from the centre the more illogical and perverse it became. The Irish, always hateful of change, now held to the new mentality; patronage threw them some chaff, but they could not contribute to the constructive building of their own country, and political impotence clove to their own meaningless interests.

Some day or other an explanation would be demanded; I would be given a choice of paths, or police interference

might decide. I would disappoint their hopes of a profession and be a black sheep. I carefully oiled and greased
my rifle, wrapped it in oily rags and made my brothers
promise take care of it. Then I left home in March of 1918.

My body was hardy enough. I had an Erewonian
contempt for disease. At home we each went our own way,
there was not much sentiment. The younger members
laughed at families who sang the praises of their own, at
sisters who adored their brothers. The bond was one of
good fellowship and reliability; we supported each other
by an understanding which could meet outside blame or
praise dispassionately. Mother was methodical; we had
been well cared for. Father had given me a respect for
law, a conventional approach to accepted authority, deeply
felt kinship with the dispossessed people, and a belief that
the British Navy would end the war. The elder members
of the family said sir when they spoke to him. I contributed my own haphazard thought on the ultimate
outcome of our actions and their meanings, and a temper
which I could obligingly blame on my O Malley name.

The Dublin Brigade Adjutant told me to report to Dick
Mulcahy in Dungannon; he gave me my train fare. I
travelled with some Dublin officers. Before we reached
Drogheda our carriage was filled up by men of the Royal
Irish Constabulary, who on first entering, spoke with
Southern accents; but for the rest of the way hardly
opened their mouths although no order had been given.
They were fine-looking well-built men. Their movements,
even their lack of movement, conformed to an outward
induced sense of authority as if they wore an extra skin.
They had a ceremonious dignity about them that made
ritual out of what would seem to us unimportant details.
They had a black swarthy complexion, the only colour
there was came from a patch of claret cloth backing their
cap badge, the crown above the harp, and the salted-butter
yellow on the sergeants' V's. Their uniforms were blue
black with a touch of green, the colour of the cheap ink
we used at school. The colour darkened their appearance.
They carried batons in heavy leathern cases, carbines and
bayonets. They wore padded cupola helmets. Their
great coats were rolled neatly and slanted across their
chests.

We, on the opposite side of the compartment, looked at them curiously, talked of the East Tyrone election and laughed; we wondered if we should soon have broken heads. But in between the laughter and the chat I had an empty feeling pressing cold on my stomach, as I had always when I returned to school after the summer holidays. Life had been sheltered and remote enough from actuality up to this.

In Dungannon I reported to Dick Mulcahy, Assistant Chief of Staff. He had been in my class at the medical school; but I had been too much in awe of his rank to speak to him. He was seated at a table in a small, bare room, writing. I saluted: " I have been instructed to report to you, sir."

" By whom? "

" By the Dublin Brigade Adjutant."

" Your name? "

" O Malley, ' F ' Company, First Battalion."

" Can you handle men? "

" I have helped to train a Fianna Company on the North side."

He was in grey green uniform. It fitted well. He wore a soft, slouch hat, one side was pinned up by the Fianna Fáil badge of the Dublin Brigade. He looked neat and trim, quiet. He had a shrewd cold look. There was little expression on the muscles of his mouth or cheeks when he spoke. He spoke slowly, stressing words nasally. His face was of the thin type, clean-shaven with bushy eyebrows.

" You can remain with a family in the Main Street. I'll instruct Captain Donnelly to let you parade a half company to-night."

I wondered if my word of command would be good and if I would make mistakes. I went over drill movements and commands as I walked to the square in the evening. I marched the men as far away as I could from onlookers. I was able to handle the half company; my assurance gained as I changed to extended order.

Mulcahy spread an Ordnance Map on the table. " You'll take charge of the Coal Island district with the rank of second lieutenant. I'll send some officers to help you, later." He pointed out company areas and gave me a

list of officers. Most of them were O'Neills. The many-
times disinherited clansmen had crept back slowly to their
old lands and the names of the planter stock that had held
the lands were now a dim memory. The men told me of
the O'Neill legends.

I drilled and skirmished up and down the streets with
the men who came with hurleys or straight long sticks. We
stood misdirected volleys of stones and eggs as we protected meetings. I met Dublin officers: Peadar Clancy
on the shores of Loch Neagh, and Simon Donnelly who in
Dungannon showed me how to give calm orders when men
were excited. They accepted me. No one commented by
look or word on my inexperience. That began a friend-
ship with these Dublin men whom I had not known before.

Mulcahy told me to report to the Director of Organization. I found Michael Collins in his office on Bachelor's
Walk, Dublin. He was pacing up and down. We shook
hands. He jerked his head to a chair to indicate that I
should sit; he took a chair which he tilted back against
the wall. On shelves were green membership cards, heaps
of *The Irish Volunteer Handbook*, and stacks of white copies
of the organization scheme. Behind his desk was a large
map of Ireland marked with broad red streaks radiating
from Dublin. He was tall, his shoulders were broad;
his energy showed through rapid movement. A curving
bunch of hair fell on his forehead; he tossed it back with
a vigorous head twist.

" I'm sending you to Offaly, there's an election coming off.
I want you to organize a Brigade in that county. There
are a few good chaps in Tullamore and they're ' on the
run.' " He had a strong singing Cork accent; his brown
eyes studied me fixedly. He pointed out companies on a
map and mentioned officers' names.

" It looks like conscription," he said. " That'll make
some slackers wake up."

He pointed out communication routes on the wall map.
I was to improve and keep them tested by despatch riders.
He gave me a bundle of organization schemes, instructions
for the preparation of emergency rations, lists of equipment
that could be made locally. "Read that and see what you
think of it." He handed me notes on the destruction of
railways, bridges and engines with and without explosives.

It was signed by Rory O'Connor, Director of Engineering. He crossed to the window whilst I read. " My bail is up," he said. "They're looking for me now." "They," meant the " G " men, who carried out political arrests in Dublin. Collins had been arrested for a Volunteer recruiting speech; he had been released on bail. That was unusual. Volunteers were not allowed to accept bail. " Two nights ago ' G ' men brought off a raid; they found empty packing cases and a pile of cartridge wrappers in a store. Bruton said: This looks as if there were brains behind it; I bet it's that fellow from Mountjoy Street." Collins laughed; it meant himself. " Good luck now, Earnán," he said, as he shook hands. As I walked across O'Connell Bridge I wondered at the risks he ran, coming and going to and from his office, whilst detectives watched for him.

Austin Stack of Kerry who had recently fought a jail war in Belfast was in Tullamore with Darrel Figgis. Stack had a quizzical turn in his deep brown eyes which he half shut when he told a long story. He was grave and quiet; he spoke slowly. Figgis was not popular; it was thought that he was too vain. Stories were told about his Christlike beard. His manner, his insistent focus of attention for his words, was of the porcupine quill effect of an artist amongst those who thought of nationality alone. He was egotistical; it could be seen in his face and mannerisms; his image was reflected in the half suppressed smiles of his listeners. He had come from another life; he would find it hard now, I felt. I had read his novels : *Children of Earth* was the best book I had read about the West of Ireland. He was pleasant when he talked to me of his books; but he had an unfortunate habit of making enemies.

Eamonn de Valera was due to arrive. There was intense excitement; work speeded up. Volunteers, Cumann na mBan, and Sinn Féin Clubs arranged a parade. I heard a new song : " Convict 95," his number when on penal servitude.

> 'Twas in Kilmainham prison yard our fifteen martyrs died
> And cold and still in Arbour Hill they are lying side by side,
> But we will yet pay back the debt for the spirit is still alive
> In men who stood thro' fire and Blood with Convict 95.

Eoin Plunkett was with me in English's Hotel when de Valera walked in. We made a machine spring to attention and remained tense, glued with admiration till he spoke to us and asked us to sit down. He was tall and lean; his hair rifted on to his forehead. His face was long and sallow. He wore rimless glasses. He had a very deep voice that welled up, a fairly immobile face save when he spoke, and then the muscles, to one who had watched them in repose, played tricks. On the platform there was a hard unemotional feel to his voice and he twisted his body in emphasis.

His gravity we noticed most; he was patient and kindly to the many demands for his signature. " Have you seen Dev? " I would be asked in the country. It was easy to take on heroic build if one had seen or talked to any of those whom the people admired.

An Irish Convention called by Lloyd George had been in session for nine months; Sinn Féin refused to send representatives. It met and talked. The Irish vote in Australia had helped to defeat conscription there; a second referendum would succeed, Premier Hughes said, if the English could in any way settle the Irish Question. Irish Americans fighting for small nationalities and to make the world safe for democracy made their government anxious to have some patch-up in Ireland. The first draft of a Conscription Bill was passed in England the same day that Lloyd George announced the failure of the convention; an emasculated Home Rule Bill was to be given as a gift.

In England conscription had been imposed by degrees; in Ireland all males between eighteen and fifty-one could be taken. As a nation Ireland was not deeply concerned with the world war. Propaganda about territorial violation and outrages could be paralleled at home. The people had long watched politicians play their thimble trick at the Imperial circus: " Walk up gentlemen. See freedom is here. You cannot lose. You give your youth and you take your chance." The wild Irish who always looked for fight, who were never happy unless smashing heads with ponderous shillelaghs now wanted to fight to prevent themselves from fighting. What an Irish bull; the dear, delightful Irish, so picturesque and such charming brogues; they were broths of people; they were entirely.

A meeting of political enemies was held in Dublin.

They issued a statement : " The passing of the Conscription Bill must be regarded as a declaration of war on the Irish people." The Irish Parliamentary Party left the House of Commons as a protest. Labour carried out a day of general strike. A parish fund was organized to raise money.

In Offaly committees and subcommittees worked on Transport and Food supply; statistics were compiled; offers of help came from strange places. I paraded battalions in Tullamore; we skirmished and manoeuvred through towns and the country side followed by police. Officers were arrested and at once replaced. To save the officers I commanded the companies of a parade in turn. I was not interfered with. In small towns I drew my gun when police asked me my name.

In daytime I could now enter a town to practise quick mobilization. Shop boys, carpenters, shop owners, clerks, fell into line quickly. They practised bayonet fighting with brush handles up and down streets; they sat on pathways or in halls to listen to my talks from the destruction of railway plant to street fighting.

Men relieved each other during the day to mould lead to buck shot; gun cartridges were collected and refilled. Jewellers and locksmiths made revolver springs; they repaired weapons. Telegraphic clerks held classes with buzzers and tappers or taught Morse to signallers; harness and boot makers worked at belts and equipment, smiths and carpenters made pikes and pike handles. Cumann na mBan sewed signalling flags and haversacks. They gathered medical supplies, made splints and packed first field dressings.

Shops were raided for cartridges and detonators, quarries for explosives. Volunteers came to houses whose owners were hostile or had permits from the police; the police searched Volunteer and friendly houses for arms. One raiding party often followed close on the other.

Railways would be destroyed when conscription came; through communication routes by road were worked out. There were many branch lines in Offaly and Westmeath. Some companies were always on duty. Day and night, despatch riders on bicycles tried to improve time speeds. All despatches had time sheets; the time was checked by each company through which they passed. The time sheet from Dublin to Castlebar or to Tralee would be lengthy. Despatches were hidden in the collar or tie; sewn up in the coat, put in a part of the bicycle or in socks. The despatch might be a smelly remnant when it reached its last station.

I was told that warrants had been issued for my arrest. I changed my sleeping quarters frequently. In Clara I slept in the house of a publican. The owner came into my bedroom one night. He found two improvised hand grenades on the floor and a revolver beside my bed. He hurriedly made piles of empty porter barrels at points inside the back wall to help my escape.

Three Royal Irish halted me in Philipstown. They carried revolvers in black holsters. "What's your name?" the sergeant asked in a deep voice; the thumb of his right hand was stuck behind his broad flat belt.

"My name is O Malley, do you want more information?" I half drew my gun from inside my coat. The police were irresolute. They had evidently intended to arrest me. I waited. The sergeant took out a note book; he wrote quickly with a pencil. They watched as I cycled away.

People remarked that officers had been afterwards arrested for drilling when I had been in charge or for carrying out my orders. Some said I was a spy and that the police did not want to arrest me. A few women said I was leading the boys astray. I met mutterings in many forms.

In an island of the Bog of Allen which covers a large part of eastern Offaly I had a farmer friend. "We'll give them what's what in the bogs," he said, "if it wasn't for them bloody peelers less than a snipe 'id never get in here." He had a white horse for me. "When the fighting begins up you get and lead us all against the English." I liked the white horse. He was a fine mettlesome beast and he could "lep a house," but he savoured of the range mark. I could see myself stuck up to my middle in bog water or crawling close to gorse and heather instead of leading a procession against the nearest post.

* * * *

I was in Athlone. I had met an Irish battalion sergeant-major from the Castle barracks. He had been fifteen years in the British army and had seen much fighting. A tall man, sturdy with independence; he was resilient in well trained muscle. He had a well-handled, pointed moustache. He was willing with some soldiers to help us capture the magazine; they would fight, if necessary, during the raid, and they would join us when conscription came. I received a despatch from Collins; I was to go to South Roscommon at once.

*   *   *   *

Arrests increased. Courts martial sentences ran from a few months to five years; a boy was given a month for carrying a Sinn Féin flag; a man five months for " being in the company of boys carrying a Sinn Féin flag," a man one month for " whistling derisively at the police "; two years for singing " The Felons of our Land," a song written fifty years previously. A sentence of from six months to two years for having a copy of the Irish Volunteer paper, An t-Óglach, which was printed and distributed in secret. Our men had been captured when armed. G.H.Q. issued an order to all armed volunteers to resist arrest.

I read the order to four companies on parade in a demesne beyond Ballintubber. Two police, one a sergeant, had followed a company from County Galway. They heard me read the order; they took notes. I gave a lecture to the men; then manoeuvred them across the estate. We were able without permission to select our manoeuvre grounds. The police kept close to me that day. In the evening returning home with Brennan, the Brigadier, three of them came into a shop in Ballintubber. I drew my revolver; they left the shop.

I had a half battalion parade to inspect in County Galway one night. My bicycle chain broke; I walked pushing the bicycle along a muddy road. I crossed the bridge on the Suck, which was the county boundary, at Ballymoe. Beyond the whitewashed police barracks a sergeant and a constable stepped from the footpath and fronted me. " Halt," the sergeant shouted. He took a blue paper from a tunic pocket. He began to read it aloud. It was a warrant for my arrest.

I drew my revolver; as we looked at each other the sergeant said, " Draw," the constable drew his Webley. The sergeant had a fair moustache, red hair showed at the sides of his soft service cap; we had met in the demesne.

" Fire," shouted the sergeant. I had a mixture of respect for law and the idea the other fellow should fire first. I felt a sharp thrust in my wrist as I half turned to fire twice at the constable who had run to a doorway. I pointed my gun at the sergeant; he did not move nor did he put up his hands. He shouted orders; police rushed out from the barracks. I threw my useless bicycle to the ground. I rushed up the street. Shots followed me. I sprawled and nearly fell as I felt a burn in my right ankle. I took the first corner at racing speed and dashed at an impossibly thick hedge of thorns and brambles. I got through. I ran through the fields till I was tired. I came back to the road, crossed it and lay down. My wounds began to pain now.

Thorns and sharp brambles had cut my face and hands as I had crashed the hedge. Blood ran down my neck and on to my coat. An artery in my left wrist had been cut by a bullet and my hand was slippery with blood. I tore a piece of gauze which I always carried, then made a tourniquet by twisting a pencil through my handkerchief. My ankle was numb with pain; the sock was tightly stuck to the flesh. I could bandage the ankle afterwards, the important thing now was to find exactly were I was. I was in County Galway; I did not know that county save through map study, and though I had inspected companies there I did not know any houses where I might stay.

Darkness came quickly. I spread out my map on the ground whilst I searched for matches. Rain fell. I heard the noise of bicycle chains; men halted to talk outside the hedge; they were police. Rain drops pattered off my map; the drops sounded like revolver shots; the linen map would make more noise if I tried to fold it. The voices stopped. I gripped hard on my .38 handle. Two birds flying low wheeled suddenly when they saw me; they quacked harshly, wild duck. The police did not notice them.

By match light I cut away my sock and pulled off clinging shreds. I had a bone wound, but not a deep one, the bullet had passed through. I used the remainder of the iodoform gauze and bandaged the wound tightly. I limped when I tried to walk. I found my exact position by using compass and map. I decided to wait until dawn;

I would then wade the Suck and get to the Roscommon side. I had no coat; I was wet from the rain, and cold. I put my wrist inside my shirt. I could hear curlews whistle to each other and there were rustles in the bushes. Later I heard an otter's low bark and a splash as he slipped into water.

In the grey of dawn I stepped into the Suck. It was deeper than I had thought and very cold. I came back to the bank and tied a tin box of cartridges to my wounded wrist, then holding my gun out of the water, I swam. I saw two bog larks go up high to sing in the morning. I was in a marshy land amongst rushes; further on I found quaggy bog which squelched beyond my knees. I heard the bleat of a young lamb; then it sounded like a kid. There was someone lost beside myself. I circled around looking for the lost lamb. I imitated the noise. The sound came again and then I laughed as I saw what it was. Above me a jacksnipe was rising in spirals then curving down with a rush; the beat of his wing made a noise like that of a young goat. I must have been close to the nest and I might have saved myself trouble if I had remembered the Irish name for jacksnipe, *mionnán aerach*, the airy kid. Perpendicular shafts of silver rain fell to the west, then grey clouds went away and the sun came out.

I stumbled across drains which I could not now leap and crashed through hedges on my right side. In the distance Ballintubber barracks on a hill crest dogged me. I twisted trying to avoid it, but it still looked down on me. I went ahead then. Miles beyond the barracks a man ran towards me. "Thanks be to God, it's you," he said, "the peelers are searching the Galway side and the soldiers. They have an aerio-plane." He was a volunteer. I again washed and dressed the wounds in Brennan's of Castleplunket. I borrowed a bicycle; with scouts in front and behind, I cycled beyond Roscommon to the Shannon shore on Loch Reagh. I was very stiff; I had to be lifted off the bicycle.

"I guessed it was you," said Collins when I saw him in his office on the Liffey bank, "your shooting is certainly not your strong point." I had been moving from house to house at night as a general round-up was expected. It came. Three weeks previously Dora had been altered so that Irishmen could be deported to England without trial.

Now, newly elected T.D.'s and the Sinn Féin Executive were arrested and brought by destroyers to England. The new Chief Secretary Shortt said: " the number of Irishmen and Irishwomen who are in co-operation with the German enemy is very small, but many of them might unknowingly become involved."

The leaders out of the way, Conscription would be easier to enforce. The round-up had been expected; deputies had been appointed to direct Sinn Féin; the leaders waited for arrest. But the army thought otherwise; the Staff kept out of the way. Collins going home to Mountjoy Street early in the morning saw troops raiding McGarry's in the same street. " I waited till they had gone, then I slept in his bed; I knew it would be the safest bed in Dublin," he told me.

* * * *

I lived under the bare sandstone ridge of Slievebawn. I was glad to be close to a mountain again; for the past three months the Hill of Allen, a mound, fort, or moat, or the line of Eskers running across the midlands had been the only uplifts since I had left the Slieve Bloom mountains. To the west from Slievebawn's top I could see a mesh of lakes and small streams. To the east were bends of the Shannon as it ran to Loch Reagh; in the North was country rising to Arigna and mountainy rugged Leitrim.

The Black Pig of legend had shown himself. His huge bulk, bristling spine ridges and wicked glaring eyes had been seen on dark nights beyond Elphin. People were afraid to walk the road after dark. The Black Pig had always meant trouble, sorrow and war. Around the fires I heard versions of St. Columcille's prophesies. The dark shadow of the Pig loomed through them. The Spaniard would help . . . the last great battle of the Gael would be fought in the valley of the Black Pig . . . women would walk a day's journey without seeing a man.

Across the Shannon a man with two thumbs on his right hand had been straying the roads of Leitrim, things had been heard at night near the caves of Rath Croghan; there had been blood in the sky. Legends were remembered by older people; great happenings were looked forward to.

A man near Strokestown told me of the Pig. Words went away from him as he stumbled in description . . .

as big as a house. Man, dear, and a back . . . God help us . . . I wouldn't be seen near the place for all the gold in the Bank of Ireland . . . take my advice, now, like a good gossoon and don't meddle with it." He had talked to someone who had seen the Pig at the back of the school-house. If I went there at midnight and called three times the Pig would appear.

I knew of the Black Pig's Dyke through successive lines of ramparts and entrenchments that guarded the changing prehistoric boundaries of Ulster. I had seen lengths of the ramparts in different counties. The Pig had wound its way in and out of pagan and Christian belief. It meant something now, whatever it was, and, though a series of debates with myself did not give any logic to my action, I was going to call it out.

One dark night I walked down towards the schoolhouse, my hob nailed boots for company in the stillness. I was nervous enough, even though I put my hand a few times to the handle of my .38, yet I felt inclined to laugh at myself for being a bigger fool than I thought I was. I was at the school, before midnight. At twelve o'clock I shouted : " Come forth." Silence. " Come forth," then a pause. I heard my own voice when it had gone away. " Come forth," but no ridge of spines or yellow eyes came out to frighten me.

I cycled past many a broken demesne wall, once the sign of entrenched ascendancy, now the symbol of a passing order. The walls were built when the day's labour of a tenant was tuppence ; bullock's blood had been added, it was said, to bind the mortar, and people's blood, too. The Big House might be spruce, or gaunt in decay; weeds on the avenue and families without issue. Virtue and strength was going from the leeches who had sucked life from the people. The arid brittleness or the harsh brilliance of the ascendancy mind remained. I made the men manoeuvre in demesne land to rid them of their inherent respect for the owners. Even yet their fathers touched their hats to the gentry and to the sergeant of the police.

I cycled towards *Reilig na Rí* the royal burying place of Connacht. Seated on Rath Cruchan I thought of Nannie and her stories of the Táin. I could not imagine where she had learned the story, for the Red Branch tales were not known to the people. I had read many versions of the Táin, but I remembered her stories well. I had searched for place names and fords mentioned and had followed the route of the invading army that had left Cruchan as far as the Leitrim border where police raids often made me sleep across the Shannon for the night. From the top of Cruchan Queen Maeve had reviewed her warriors and allies before they left to invade Ulster. I could see low hills, stretches of lake-plain towards the Shannon, rings of earthen forts and an odd grove of trees with the smoke of turf floating about.

The police did not bother the hill country; towards Arigna, the land was rugged with small stretches of wood. Plantations were scarce enough; the war had made the unfortunate country barer than ever: soon it would rival Iceland. Near Loch Meelagh there were ferns and dense growth, green sedge blades flowering brown and purple and a damp leafy smell of humus. Below the Curlew Pass, Loch Key with its wooded islands and legends. I rowed to the islands; from the Rock of Courage, I used my field glasses on Rockingham House. Lord French, the Commander-in-Chief, was there and we were interested in his entertaining and the state of his health. Over the swarthy, cold looking shores of Loch Allen rose *Sliabh an Iarainn*, the Iron Mountain; one could pick up stones weighted with iron in the Shannon. The R.I.C. had few friends here; I walked where I pleased, but further south it was more difficult. Police and troops from Carrick tried to scent out the classes which I held for officers.

A long barn smelling of oats and horse harness might be our classroom or a school house. Seated at the desks the boys and men noted my diagrams and chalk headings from the blackboard. On the roads our scouts were placed; they held bicycle lamps with red and green glass. A red flash meant something strange or uncertain; a succession of red, enemy drawing near. Outside, boys waited for the flashes or patrolled the outskirts in case of a surprise approach. The mobilization ground was always carefully scouted; a despatch might have been captured and enemy might be lying in ambush for us. Once an excited scout rushed into the schoolhouse and shouted breathlessly: " They're coming . . . They're coming . . . Police," then he fled. I ordered the officers to parade behind the school. They gathered their note books, rushed out in panic and began to scatter. I followed and threatened to shoot if they did not at once fall into line. The police had heard my shouting. Another scout to report that they were retiring. Military and police tried to capture us when on night manoeuvres, but this was good practice. Our attacking and defending parties used to carry out a rear-guard action; and our scouting improved. We never lost a man.

Late at night I left a class. I went across fields to come to the house I slept in. I halted in a path on the edge of ripening meadow. I crouched down. I saw three forms standing beyond the next hedge. Clouds hid a thin moon. I worked back to a small lane running up to the house. I moved up it slowly. I could hear whispers, feet moved. Perhaps they were not peelers. The moon was in hiding also, but it peeped out and came into the open. I saw the glossy shine on a peaked cap and a dull glow on carbines strapped on their backs.

I walked away. I did not know who were my friends in the neighbouring houses. I had been used to getting around quietly; the people at my house would not tell the neighbours I had been with them. Always I had a local man with me, who was known, when I came to a new house. If I knocked at a hostile door the police would hear about it; they would concentrate on the area and search it thoroughly.

I had walked for an hour. I was cold. I was going to pull down hay from the next rick I met and sleep on it till morning. I passed a small thatched cottage. I heard the sound of voices rising and falling. The family was saying the Rosary. I listened. An old man began the "Hail Mary," voices joined in the response. At the end of the decade another voice began in Irish: " *Sé do bheatha, a Mhuire, atá lán de ghrásta,*" a girl's voice came through the answers: " *A naomh-Mhuire, a Mháthair Dé . . .* "

The Litany ended. I was ready to knock when a woman's voice began the prayers for the dead of the family and their relatives. An " Our Father " and three " Hail Marys " for each. The trimmings, as they are called, kept on. Many the time I had felt my knees getting sore on the rough flags of such a. kitchen. Would they never end? At last—a prayer for Ireland.

I knocked. I heard whispers inside. Light shone out as the door opened slowly. I could see an old man's shape. " Who's there? " then " *Céad míle fáilte*, why it's himself," said a boy. I walked into the kitchen. " We were just talking of you before we began the Rosary," said the boy. He had been a scout for three nights at the schoolhouse. The family had waited up till he had come back from a fair. The father and mother shook me by the hand, telling me I was welcome. " You're cold, *a mhic*," the woman said. " Push in and take a hate of the fire. Bridge, hurry and ready the table." She hung the kettle from a black crane above the crimson turf. She added sods from a skiv and twisted knots of bog deal. The fire blazed up. Soon I was warm. I watched the rinsing of the tea pot; the pot was put to draw on pieces of broken burning turf to one side. I ate thick cuts of white cake roofed with strong, salted butter as I drank. We sat around the fire and talked until the woman of the house said, " Whisht, maybe he's tired, God help him." The boy made down a wooden settle that served as a seat in the daytime. I slept on the flags near grey white ashes that covered fresh turf.

CHAPTER SEVEN

AUGUST 1918—FEBRUARY 1919

★

COLLINS WAS NOW in St. Ita's, the first school founded by Padraig Pearse. The room was called the dug-out. It had been a cellar of some kind or a storeroom; the door was not easy to find. I had a moustache, a bushy unkept growth; it changed my appearance, and gave me, I hoped, the weight of age. Somehow a moustache made one more serious-minded. The door was half-open; I walked in. Collins was working at a big wooden table, his back to a bare white-washed wall; a pile of addressed envelopes in front of him. He stood up quickly when he saw me. He looked as if he had been taken off his guard. " What the bloody hell," . . . he began. I laughed; he recognized me. I had forgotten about the moustache. He continued to write; the pile of envelopes increased. I watched him;

there was envy in my look for I found it hard to make enough work to keep me busy. After a time he looked up: Would you like to do work in London?"

"Yes."

"It's I.R.B. work and important." I had taken the I.R.B. oath the previous year. "It may lead to something; you'll have to impersonate a British officer. You've done that before, haven't you?" I nodded in astonishment. I wondered how he could have heard of it.

It had been this way:

In 1917 my brother wounded in the advance against Bulgaria was home on leave. He was a Lieutenant in the Dublin Fusiliers; around town he wore mufti. I thought that if I could take his uniform when he was out I would be able to buy a gun. I needed a good revolver; every weapon counted, and civilians would not be given arms without a permit. I made a parcel of the uniform and brought it across town to the digs of a medical of my year, Dan Crowley. My brother was six feet one and alterations were needed. With pins, safety pins and thread Dan made the tunic fit; the slacks were well up to my chest. We took a taxi to Callaghan's of Dame Street, military tailor and gunsmith, where I looked at small arms and ammunition. I had £6 with me: that would buy a shiny thirty-eight Harrison and Richardson revolver with two hundred rounds. "Where's your permit?," asked the attendant.

"I did not think an officer needed one; I'm just home from the Front."

"It's a regulation, but you can easily get a permit in the Provost Marshal's office. It's in the Castle, down to your left towards the City Hall."

I thanked him, went out to the taxi and saw Dan.

"I'll have to go to the Castle; nothing doing here without a permit."

"My God, don't do that, it's pure madness. You'll be had like a rat in a trap. It's never worth it."

But I was going to see the thing through now. I looked at my bull-dog forty-five, an ancient six-chambered weapon with five cylinders loaded. I put it in my front trousers' pocket intending to fight it out if I was caught. I adjusted the Sam Brown belt to cover the second button of my tunic. "You remain here," I said, "if I'm coming back at all I'll be here in fifteen minutes." He shook my hand firmly.

" *Beannacht Dé leat, anois*—it's no use talking to you."

I walked down Dame Street towards the Castle, turning to the left when I saw the heavy gates of the lower Castle Yard. I was nervous; this was Dublin Castle, the symbol of all that was hateful in the British domination of Ireland. The sentry at the gate saluted by touching his hand to the butt of his rifle. I returned the salute. A little further on were two tall Dublin Metropolitan Police. They saluted as I came near. "Where's the Provost's office?" I asked.

"It's up there, sir;" one pointed, "beyond the detective office; go through the big door." The detective office; well, I was not known, but my eyes strayed towards it as I walked stiffly across the yard past the Chapel Royal.

I walked upstairs to a landing where was seated a sergeant and his guard. They came to attention; he saluted.

"Where's the Provost's office?"

"Up the corridor to the left, sir."

I wondered if I should change the name I had intended to give—Sheehan. I had selected it because I knew him, and I had his card with me. What if the Provost knew him? I knocked, a voice said, "Come in." There were two officers, one studied a chart on the wall; the other was seated at a desk writing. I crossed over to him and saluted.

"I want a permit for a revolver and ammunition, sir."

"What calibre and how much ammunition?" he asked, reaching for a form.

"Thirty-eight and two hundred rounds."

"Your name?"

"Jack Sheehan."

"Regiment?"

"Royal Dublin Fusiliers, 3rd Battalion."

I filled in the form. "I'll give you a permit to remove that sword-frog of yours," said a voice behind me. I turned round. The officer who had been looking at the chart was facing me.

"I'm sorry, sir, I've just returned from Salonika."

"All right," he murmured.

The form was countersigned. I saluted; thanked the officer at the desk and left the room. I saluted the sergeant, the police and the sentry more nonchalantly ; I felt more sure of myself, but I took a good deep breath when I turned into Dame Street. Dan was sitting despondently in the taxi. " Did you get it? " he asked.

I handed the form to the assistant in Callaghan's with the money. " You have only signed for a revolver," he said. In my excitement I must have forgotten the ammunition. " Will you go back to the Castle? "

" No, I'm going South this evening. Can you get the permit for the ammunition and send the parcel around to the Wicklow? here's my card."

" Yes, I can manage that, sir."

I bought a copy of *King's Regulations* and *Small Wars: Their Principle and Practice* in Ponsonbys on my way to Dan's digs. Three days later the parcel was at the Wicklow Hotel.

After a parade in " F " Company I told Captain Archer who was curious to know how I had so much ammunition. He laughed. I expect he must have passed it on to Collins.

" Do you see any difficulties? " asked Collins.

" I want a Cox's cheque book—they are the army bankers."

" Right, you shall have one. In London you can get in touch with Sean McGrath and Art O Brien. I'll send word to them beforehand and I'll give you introductions as well. Anything else? "

" Can I carry a gun? "

" No, you mustn't resist arrest and you'll have to recognize the Court and take your medicine ; maybe you'll find yourself in the Tower," and he grinned. " If you succeed, I'll send over other men and you can direct them. It may have big results." I saluted. He stood up and grasped my hand firmly. " *Beir buaidh agus beannacht Dé leat anois, Earnán.*"

I met the London Irish, handed over my despatches and stayed with men who were well known to Scotland Yard. A friendly tailor took my measurements, and soon I was a Captain in the Durham Light Infantry, with a wound stripe and a detailed knowledge of the regimental history and contemporary actions of my battalion. With zeal I saluted every " brass hat " I met. There was a certain element of humour in the undercurrents of the situation which distorted casual contact with brother officers and civilians.

I bought a small amount of ammunition and a number of revolvers, but I needed a permit. I was told by the gunsmiths I could fill a form at the War Office. Art O'Brien said it was foolish to visit the War Office. He sent word back to Dublin, whilst I visited gun shop after gun shop and pleaded hurry; but it was of no use. The second-hand stores gave me a little but it was a slow process. At the Front officers could use small arms of calibre other than the army revolver, but they had to supply their own feed. I could get a permit for a fairly large supply of small arms and ammunition for other officers of my regiment, I felt, if I went to the War Office. I reported regularly at the Gaelic League hall in uniform, under protest, and at Mooney's pub, where across the creamy pints of my companions, I told of my ill success and listened to their conspiratorial whisperings; a very different atmosphere from the Irish one. I changed my addresses a few times, and always received a hearty welcome from exiled Irish, some of whom risked their Government positions by having me in their homes.

One felt the war in London : food ration cards, women in khaki, wounded soldiers, the great number of " brass hats " out of all proportion to other ranks, darkened streets and mourning. I had a good supply of food cards; my friends and I could eat as we wished. The English did not talk about the war; nor did they grumble. Munition workers were rich; their women wore fur coats and jewellery; hate from civilians cleft the air. On the surface the nerves of the Empire in crisis seemed sound enough.

Walking around watching the wealth and power of the West End and the squalor and filth of the East End I could feel our own unimportance. We were puny, the lion would only have to yawn to crush us. I feared only the provosts and their assistants. The identity of officers was often asked to discover masqueraders who were having a good time with false checks and uniforms. If I dressed in ordinary clothes there was the danger of being questioned also. At the time anybody staying in England, Art O Brien told me, even for a few days, was liable for military service.

I had been told by Collins not to tell my mission to anyone save to those whose names he had given me. In Liverpool I met Cathal Brugha; when he asked me what I was doing, I said I was over on special work. He did not question me further. He wore a double reefer jacket; he looked at times like a seaman ; of medium height with broad shoulders, steady grey blue eyes and a determined chin. He wore a green tie. That to me typified the man. It seemed the symbol of his nationality in a hostile country. He might change his appearance, but the tie meant the cause to him. He was the most uncompromising of all the army officers. He was over on special work himself ; if conscription was attempted in Ireland the first blow would be struck by shooting the British Cabinet. Men had come over from Ireland for the purpose and were waiting.

I went aboard with a ship's crew at Liverpool and was taken care of by the gunner of the anti-submarine gun. He was drunk. As I lay in a sailor's bunk he talked : " If I can't give the gun to the lads before conscription comes, then I'll have a slap at the first torpedo chaser I meet.''

Collins was in the Mansion House attending a Sinn Féin Convention. I waited outside for him. When the delegates came out I saw him with a scarf wrapped around his neck and chin. Members of the detective division were in wait for him, scattered through the crowd, but he attended his meetings regularly. In the dug-out we studied a map of Donegal. " You'll freeze to death up there," he said, cheerfully.

The county had a mountainous core extending in every direction. The mountains made communications difficult, railways ran in the extreme north and south with the main roads. The nature of the country meant two brigades. One, West Donegal, ran along the coast from Bundoran to Burtonport ; on the north coast there were no companies. In the east there was some depth where the country was less rugged; the land flattened out through the Lagan planted by the Scotch, and through Strabane, Letterkenny and Barnesmore Gap.

My name was Gallagher now ; I tried to clip my words. In the valley of the Finn, the people called me Kelly, thinking Gallagher was my real name. In some places I had three names and once four. A strange name would easily be noticed and, if warrants had been issued, the R.I.C. would be inclined to pay more attention to it.

We had no means of buying arms except from our Quartermaster-General; but a few revolvers, some ammunition and maybe a rifle or two each year did not make much difference in the arming of a county. The further away the area the less chance of getting arms from him. In Killygordon, in the valley of the Finn, we decided to hold up the guard on the R.I.C. barracks, whilst the morning patrol was out, and seize rifles, revolvers and ammunition. The barrack routine was carefully observed. On the morning we had decided for the raid I heard that the sergeant's wife had been confined overnight in the barracks. If there were any shooting it might have a serious result on her. Reluctantly, for I was leaving for West Donegal, I postponed the attempt.

Fear of conscription passed away with the European War. The numbers in the Volunteer companies decreased and we had more opposition. In houses I could feel an atmosphere of the thing half said, an awkward silence or a sudden rush of speech. I would read their thoughts in what they did not say or through plays of words and indirectness. I would grope for words in return and an out of proportion sentence would become strain, and I would feel myself inarticulate. I would be drawn into the feeling of that house and be glad to get away, but there was no discourtesy. The sons of the house might get a lash of the tongue, but it would only reach me indirectly. Donegal was not good; the material was there, but they had no leaders; the Finn valley was the best in the east.

Cycling was hard in amongst the mountains; the roads were boggy and rutty, running through waste heather. A wind from the north-east cut across the country, often I had to lie down and put my back to the wind; its full force in my teeth stifled me. The coast was bare, with hardly a tree. Trees did not grow well in the sodden salt air; inland they were bent by the wind. Mountain valleys running north-west broke up the chains, in them were long, narrow, deep lakes. To cross Donegal from east to west one had to switch in angular zig-zags from north-west to south-west. The mountains were fine; Errigal towering high like a pyramid, a flame when it caught the evening sun on its slanting crags and Muckish, Pig's Back, always sheer. The grained red granite of the long Barnesmore Pass opened its thin bright gullet in the distance.

At Bloody Foreland, the sunset ruddied and drew blood from the cliffs, the white dome of Slieve Sneacht became rose. I met a man on horseback: he talked.

"Do you know why the bishops are against Sinn Féin?" he asked. "Because themselves and the priests have all their money in the war bonds." The people seemed open and friendly. I had known the Brigadier, Joe Sweeney, in the University; a student at Pearse's school he had fought with the St. Enda's Company in Easter Week. The brigade was poor, there had been little supervision. I followed the companies along the ins and outs of the coast to the cliffs of Glen Columcille and Slieve League, along the pleasant bays between Killybegs Harbour and Donegal town. The brigade ran through Ballyshannon with its precipitous streets to the long sea rollers of Bundoran. Drivers on the Donegal Light Railway were friendly. They often stopped to pick me up on the line or to let me down before the train drew into a station.

I spent some evenings with Arthur Darley. He played folk songs on his violin, his own composition: "The Lament for Michael Dwyer" and others, and a fine version of the "Lark in the Clear Air." Tall, gaunt and courteous he eagerly gave me the airs I asked for. His playing was a direct extension of himself, simple, sincere, with a clear restrain.

The general election came, and it was easier to avoid attracting attention. The Sinn Féin election system had been thoroughly organised; the ground work had been covered months before. There was no dearth of workers; canvassers, bill posters, motor drivers, boys with whitewash to decorate bridge parapets and dead walls. Rival posters flaunted each other or were imposed and superimposed until by their weight they peeled off. Republican flags hung from old castles, until the peelers, in despair, tired of trying to take them down. Successive directors of elections were arrested, but others took their places.

Through all their work was eagerness, talk, and gaiety. This was an important election, the result would show if

the people wanted the sovereign independence of Ireland.
Irish Labour withdrew from the contest. Redmondites,
Unionists and Sinn Féin could fight it out.

Sean O Muirthile seemed to be in charge of the election
campaign in the West. A big burly man with a thick
moustache and a prosperous air, pudding rolls at the back
of his neck; he gave the organization a strength of bullock
fed ease and was, I'm sure, considered a man of weight in
contrast to the young organisers and passionate orators.
I did not like him from the first. He tried to control the
Volunteer forces for election purposes; but he had to change
his mind. I was told later that he was important in the
Irish Republican Brotherhood.

He spoke Irish fluently, interlarding his remarks with
stories about his work in the Easter Week Rising, in which
he had not taken part, and with short humorous stories
which appealed strongly to his listeners.

One wild stormy night I went with two speakers to a
village on the coast near Dungloe. We were greeted by
men and women along the roadside holding flaming torches
at the doors; the blackness of the winding road was dotted
by the leaping flames of light as the car moved on. An old
man spoke in Irish, a rush of words, soft, sibilant, vibrant;
all I could catch was an occasional " is." I listened in a glow
to the inflections of his voice, interrupted by cries of
" *maith thú!* " from the crowd,

Again I visited the companies from Ardara where home-
spun is made to enrich retailers far away, to the Rosses,
the Irish-speaking district. Bare, boulder strewn land
backed by purplish heather and misty mountains. The
people lived close to the soil pushing back the soft bog
and making it give food; a barren troubled existence.
Yet this country grips their body and soul; it haunts the
imagination in its cruelty, strength and beauty and the
bleak coast with its wild angry sea, changing skies, crashed
rocks, as if old gods had sported with pieces of granite
mountain, can be recalled when sleek fat land is forgotten.
There is a hunger for the soil, an elemental feeling that
even the stranger or foreigner can sense. There was little
tillage, very little grass save under the lee of the rocks
where it was sweet. There was no wood for firing; in
places no turf. The coarse top scraws were dried in the

sun. The sea had smashed the Rosses into islands, slashed out bays from the land and spattered it with lakes.

Sea gulls with despairing cries flew in before storms, wind roared inland, seas crashed in awful desolation and the air was misty with spendrift. Steel grey mornings came with daffodil skies, days of brilliant hard sunshine and sunsets of pale rose and mauve. White fronted geese in wedges flew overhead, their sharp penetrating cries came down the wind or their foolish laugh, and gannets with ruddy throats cruised slowly or dropped suddenly for fish. There were nights as if I was on a fishing boat at sea; house lights dipping through the washing of rain and wind blowing salty in the throat.

"An stranger" I was spoken of in their houses. It would be easy for information to be brought to the police, but though the people talked much amongst themselves, as if making up for lost time when they met, yet there were walls between them and the outside world. Tales of the Spanish Armada, ships that had been wrecked off Aranmore, stories of the O'Donnells and Fionn . . . Ghost stories with the by-ways of elaboration so that with a wrench "to make a long story short" they came back to the subject. . . . Spirits, good and bad left at cockcrow. . . . . The dead walked around, there was an acceptance of their presence, no horror and little dread, the wall was thin between their living and their dead. The fairies; accounts of their shape and the clothes worn; their fear of iron, and the prayer when they see a sudden unexpected swirl of dust for "They're surely in it."

They were hardy. The boggy land and faulty drainage predisposed them to tuberculosis. Never the poor mouth, always an attempt to have an egg for my breakfast, which with many a sleight of hand I induced the children to help me eat. I preferred the Rosses and the North where I founded companies and felt at home. It was a pleasure to see a clump of trees; but, if they were in any quantity it meant good land which had been planted by English or Scotch settlers.

The election results were a surprise: seventy-three Sinn Féin, twenty-six Unionist, six Irish Parliamentary Party. Thirty-seven of the elected Sinn Féin T.D.'s were in prison.

On the road near Glenties I was halted by a police patrol, all of them huge men, but perhaps the darkness and my imagination heightened their stature. I had no light on my bicycle. They questioned me in deep-sounding weighty voices. What was my name? Where did I reside? what was my occupation? "Gallagher," I said, "from Killybegs."

"How long are you in Killybegs?"

"Not long—some months, I came from Letterkenny."

"But you don't belong to Letterkenny. What part of the South do you come from?" This in a Southern accent.

My clipping of words did not amount to much. "I'm from Castlereagh," I said. I held my bicycle with my left hand and drew my revolver. I held it by my side wondering if the thirty-eight bullet would go through a heavy police great coat. There was a pause. "I think there's too much water in the lamp, because the acetylene does not seem to work," I said. "I'd be the last to go without a light on this switchback road if I could avoid it."

"All right, Mr. Gallagher; but don't let us find you with an unlighted lamp again. Good night."

I was cycling towards Lettermackaward in the Dungloe direction. I was close to the long bridge on the Gweebarra River. The road ran above the sea. I heard a noise of wailing. I wondered what it could be. I could not see any lights of houses, nor, though I had passed there a few times in day, could I remember houses. The wailing increased, then it fell, and seemed to moan itself out. I lifted my bicycle over the ditch, drew my revolver and made in the direction of the noise. All was silent now. Suddenly the sound began again. I gripped the butt tightly as I tried to make my way in the darkness. The sound increased. My knees trembled, and I was afraid to advance. I turned and ran for my bicycle, scrambled across banks until I reached the road ; then pedalled with my head well down until I became tired.

Another night, in the rain, I took a wrong turning. My bicycle pushed up a narrow stony hill path. I used so much force on the pedals that I had to stand from off the saddle hoping anxiously that the chain would not break with the pressure. When I reached the hill top the bicycle ran wildly down the far side swerving as it bumped. I jumped off as the brakes were bad. I heard a clang far below. I searched but could not find the bicycle. I continued on foot. Next day the remnants were found on the rocks beneath a high cliff.

The officers were slack. They talked but none were willing to come with me when they had to. I could feel the rugged wild nature of the land, the craggy, cliff-bound or shelving coast with its jutting headlands and small bays; but for the most part it was a blur, undetached from the bleakness of my mind and the bumpings of my body on the penance of a bicycle. "What the hell was I doing this for?," I often asked myself on a stormy night trying to follow a by-road. I would argue the question, cursing myself for having to drive the men, but finding no solution; I was driven myself, more than they were, if they only knew it. I had to keep my ammunition and gun well hidden. The danger of what might happen in a raid would be given a definitely objective fear if my thirty-eight was seen; often as a result I was asked to leave the house.

My thoughts and moods came between me and the landscape. Often at the end of a day's cycling or walking I would have a hazy idea of my journey. I had made the mountains scowl, and the landscape become bitter when I failed to improve an area. But that would not last long. Stretches of wild sea, or bogs and lakes amongst the rugged soggy mountains would bring some peace. There the elements were raw and pure, nature was uncaring, savage, real; one saw its core. Spring would come, then I could at least sit down without being sodden or cycle without being drenched.

I was beginning to realize that I knew nothing of organization. It was a conservation of energy, a directing of control into proper channels; but here I was doing the work of brigade, battalion and even company staffs, fraying my nerves with irritation, bulling around as they might say. The officers were happy-go-lucky; organization, like their former views in politics, was something to delegate to another person. There was a Headquarters, that was their work. Short of kidnapping officers I could not see how I would make them inspect their commands. Inspection parades were no index of the ordinary. I knew that every effort would be made to have a good muster, men from

neighbouring companies would be lent surreptitiously; a
G.H.Q. officer was an event; at councils, where I listened
to and noted their reports, figures were often cooked.

After parade an escort would come with me at night ;
they filled their pockets with stones in case we should
meet police. Often their presence nearly brought me to
trouble. Near the sea, at Meenacross, I formed a company.
I was told police would raid at night the house I was
staying in. The acting company captain had been twenty-
five years in the British Army. I went over the approaches
with him and the lieutenant. We selected a small sand
cutting near low dunes. I worked out the men's positions
with them on the sand. I had already told the men to
parade with any arms they had.

At midnight everyone of the twenty-five was on parade,
ten had weapons; they varied from two single-shot
Martini-Enfields to muzzle-loaders. The captain then
realized we would attack the police cars. He protested;
it would be hopeless. As I grasped his shoulder he quieted.
He again became the sergeant-major, the muscles on his
chest expanded as he clicked his heels. "Very well, sir."

Unarmed men went out as scouts or filled their pockets
with stones to help our first volley. We heard the wind
moving inland and sea breaking on the sloping shore. At
dawn I dismissed the men.

I climbed the gleaming Errigal; it had two peaks, but
they merged from below. The Poisoned Glen was shut in
by the barren reach of Dooish and the white cliffs of Slieve
Sneacht, Snow Mountain; Dooish, Black Back, was too
boggy to climb. On a warm day I sat out on Horn Head;
the light was clear and the breeze was as mild as in Spring.
The cliffs had a white back to their blaze of colour. I
looked through my glasses at the birds ; I had never seen
so many and their notes were harsh as if they had colds.
Red beaked puffins with a hoarse grumble, dark shags in
strident croak, sheldrakes with green heads and white
collars edged with orange mixed a growl with a quack and
clumsy green backed cormorants had a sharp cough. Their
colours matched the cliffs.

I had the address of a man in Fanad Peninsula. I might
be able to start companies there, although they would be
isolated. In the distance were the red sands of Rosapenna ;

on the estuaries, orange-legged oyster catchers waded.
Fanad was remote, wild, out of the world. Near a small
lake at the foot of a hill was the shop of the man I was
told was friendly. He bade me welcome. I could stay as
long as I wished. He would help me all he could with the
young men, but there were no Volunteers in the peninsula.

I remained a week in Fanad, organized two companies,
then left by road for Letterkenny. A dispatch from the
Adjutant-General had been sent by road from that town
to Donegal; it had followed me along the coast through
the Rosses. I was ordered to report to Dublin at once.

CHAPTER EIGHT

MARCH—MAY 1919

★

DÁIL EIREANN, the new Parliament, had met in the
Mansion House, Dublin, in February, in defiance of the
British proclamation that forbade all public meetings
without a permit from the military or police. The meetings
had been open to the public. A provisional ministry had
been appointed.

The Declaration of Independence had been read in the
Dáil. . . .

" Now, therefore, we the elected representatives of the
ancient Irish people in National Parliament, do, in the name
of the Irish Nation, ratify the re-establishment of the Irish
Republic, and pledge ourselves and our people to make this
declaration effective by every means at our command.

" We ordain that the elected representatives of the Irish
people alone have power to make laws binding the people
of Ireland and that the Irish Parliament is the only Parliament to which that people will give its allegiance."

Later the Democratic programme was read : " The
Nation's sovereignty extends not only to all men and
women of the Nation, but to all its material possessions, the
Nation's soil and all its resources, all the wealth and all the
wealth-producing processes within the Nation."

At the dug-out in St. Ita's I met Cathal Brugha, Dick Mulcahy and Mick Collins. Brugha was Chief of Staff, Mulcahy, Assistant Chief; Collins, Director of Organization, Adjutant-General and the unofficial Quarter-Master-General. Collins in riding breeches and brown leggings was striding up and down the narrow room cursing; his strong Cork accent more emphasized. Mulcahy looked at Cathal Brugha who thin-lipped, wide-mouthed, sat at one end of the bare wooden table. Brugha had never talked much to me; always he seemed to be holding himself in check. He showed little of his many wounds save round his mouth and eyes; his face was often grey. When he had to talk he spoke with directness and finality as if the matter had been thought out and was now finished. Mulcahy never said anything stronger than bloody; he did not smoke or drink. Cathal Brugha neither cursed, smoked nor drank. Collins was an adept at all three.

The situation in Clare had provoked the outburst and the long silence. Collins' thick shock of black hair bounced up and down his forehead as he walked the room. The Chief of Staff explained the situation in Clare; all three had been there recently. There had been a brigade in Clare; headquarters had been at Meelick, a few miles from Limerick City, although Carrigaholt on the Shannon was nearly sixty miles away. Control was, as a result, uneven. The county had gained strength in recruiting, and the Staff had divided it into three: East, Mid and West Clare Brigades. The Brennan brothers Padraig, Michael and Austin had helped to build the Irish Volunteers in their county. Padraig and Michael resented the formation of three independent brigades; they wanted to form a division to control the brigades. The Brennans had minds of their own, but they were not sufficiently impersonal. Padraig Brennan had been dismissed. Michael was now in charge of East Clare.

Collins during a pause said, " the bloody bowseys." Mulcahy did not speak. He was always calmer than Cathal Brugha, less taut and more impersonal. His lean jaws seemed to prevent emotion; his eyes seemed to avoid it. One always felt a quiet insistence, a tinge of something that has no human warmth, but there was always confidence. "You will have difficulty and opposition," Cathal Brugha said, "but you know how to manage situations by this.'

The brigade Vice-Commandant, Maurteen Devitt, and the Quartermaster, Peadar O'Loughlin, were on the run in their part of Mid Clare. They had more time for Volunteer work and knew the by-roads and the general direction of police patrols. Maurteen was thin in body, pale faced and energetic with a sharp turn of tongue in speech and wit; satiric.

Maurteen Devitt's father was an old man, an Irish speaker, his favourite curse being, " the curse of the crows upon you", but he sympathised with us and did not regard us as half wits, as many others did. Once I arrived early in the morning, tired out, as I had walked a long distance, I knew the sons were out at a dance and that the father was alone. He came to the window and when I told him I wanted to get in, he said: " Be off with you, Patsey Mitchell, you playboy." I mentioned my name, but he did not seemingly know it, as it had not been spoken of in the house, although I had been staying there some weeks. He cursed me fluently, ending up with the curse of the crows; I knocked again, but as he became more exasperated I gave it up, buttoned up my coat and went to sleep on the ground. One of the sons found me in the morning sleeping, white with hoar frost. The old man always bore this in mind and never ceased to blame himself whenever he met me.

In the night time I often sat opposite to him in the fire-place listening to his talk. He always wore an old hard hat, light green with sun, brown mottled in spots with a torn brim and a dint on the top. He had a hoar stubble of a beard. He slurred his words in English through gaps in his stained teeth, but Irish seemed to flow swiftly enough. He had a great friend who came often; then they spoke Irish all the evening; sometimes the old man would translate or begin a story in English with many pauses. He would hold a match in his broken clay pipe or a piece of glowing sod, then puff, hold the pipe in one hand, talk, draw on the pipe to find it had gone out. Time and again the pipe went out; intent on the story he used it to emphasize words. Refilling the pipe was a ceremony. The 'baccy was pared from a hard black piece of plug or twist, ground slowly between the palms and rammed down into the bowl; some of the last pipe's ashes were placed on top, then a tin cover with a hole in the top. The pipe was cleaned by sticking the bowl in the red turf glow.

Sometimes they'd laugh together and shake their heads with delight when speaking of Pedlar McGrath or Seán O'Twomey. Some poems he would not translate; they seemed to enjoy them all the more. " The ould fellow is worked up," Maurteen would say, when he began on Rafferty or Donnchadh Ruadh MacNamara. Then I regretted I had not studied Irish thoroughly. I knew next to nothing of these poets save in translation. But here the seventeenth and eighteenth centuries lived again, for these two men could tell story after story of the poets' pranks, drinkings and songs, and describe them as if they had lived in the same parish. They recited verses of men whose names I did not know. I think the only thing that left me with a shred of reputation was that I had a battered copy of the *Love Songs of Connacht*.

Old Devitt and his friends were like the others I had met in this stretch of Clare and in the Rosses. Their sense of literature was on the lips and in their faultless memory. In craggy Carren an old man recited the whole of *The Midnight Court* for me. They were not literary nor had they any pretence to learning. The extension of their knowledge made them simple; they were not conscious of it, but they knew more of poetry as a living feeling than had anybody else I had met save poets themselves. They could curse hard and long mostly for emphasis and the sound of words, but also in anger.

What I liked most about him and others was their independence, their air of being true to themselves. In the towns people conformed their suppressed selves to an outward convention; here they created their own environment in and through themselves. They had no feeling of equality or inequality, but a definite reality, and it would be a long time, I knew, before I could ever hope to have anything as real in myself as they had.

They had a sense of life that made them fresh and interesting to listen to and the flavour of a life of the open air was in their words and thought. They were starkly real like chunks of their own earth when they spoke of the land, its irritable uncertainty and its aching sweat, but a feeling for words and phrasing would lift a talk about manure.

Old women screwed with rheumatism, their faces like ploughed fields, took snuff or a draw of the pipe in the corner while they fingered their beads. These were the obvious signs of outward realism and the harsh background of their lives; but there was a deep content, an ease in life and a depth in themselves that could well up nourishment. They were able to entertain and amuse themselves easily. Song was a definite expression as natural as talk, and they all sang. They sang at the end of a hard day's work and were refreshed or musicioners used fiddle or melodeon in a manner peculiar to themselves. In spite of aching land work they had the leisure of the wealthy and they made use of it simply and fully. Gentleness and fierceness, lack of sentimentality and a definite concreteness merged with poetry and sharp realism in speech; kind towards suffering and callous towards cattle and dogs and their burden-bearer the skinny ass.

*   *   *   *

On Sundays we manoeuvred one battalion against another, companies marched eight or nine miles to the mobilisation centre. Officers and men wore what uniforms and kit they had. Police and military followed us; we carried out tactical exercises whilst both our parties watched for and avoided the real enemy. The numbers gave the men more solidarity and confidence. During a practice attack I once watched an officer from Milltown Malbay, who had been in the Irish Guards, train his men to advance under cover. He carried a haversack full of clay balls and from behind belaboured his men when they did not keep close to earth.

I gave military books to the officers and typewritten notes, lectured to them and endeavoured to make field work and study interesting. It was a difficult task. All day they worked hard at their farms or in the towns; when evening came there was an added task. It "put years on them," it was "cruel hard" to study. To get reports was like drawing teeth; they hated "the pen in the fist."

In the day time Peadar and I, sometimes Maurteen Devitt, worked out schemes on our maps. We studied the country carefully, night found us far away from where we had set out that morning. From Spanish Point to the Cliffs of Moher, or we worked up inland from Mullagh Mór to Burren where the hills were terraced in solid limestone rock.

The jet blackness of the rocks near Black Head changed to blue and grey as we went inland. The mountains were moulded in stone and shaped in recessive curves or, angled like pyramids; in the valleys rock masses were piled like worn out cities and small stretches of plain had the breadth of desert. The bare impact of curve and line was very satisfying and opened up a sense of infinite distance. Light played strange tricks at dawn and dusk slanting colours across great stone tables where crevices spouted out a glare of wild flowers. Through Burren there is little soil; the dull grey surface is broken by the light-torn walls of a cannonaded castle, gutted early churches or the massive walls of stone forts. Hither Cromwell had forced the first batch of de-landed Irish from other provinces. They found " not enough wood to hang a man, enough water to dround him or earth to bury him." Up there we often made a wild rush for the door when we heard the noise of a lorry; but it was always the sound of a separator working in an outhouse or room.

Memories of the bitter land war in Clare remained. My guides at night told me bloodthirsty tales as we crossed the country; they knew what happened at each cross roads. Here a peeler, land-grabber, agent or landlord had been attacked or killed. Houses yet kept steel shutters from the days when a landlord's house was held in a state of siege, and when they wore suits of mail. Police in huts still guarded land-grabbers.

Peadar was a fine companion, alert, alive, his blue eyes like the sea beyond Moher, with a touch of green. Very steady eyes, an enveloping smile which took one under its protection. His cheeks dropped sheer from slightly prominent cheek bones; his jaws were long. He had big, strong hands which crushed each other when he was excited. Both he and Maurteen could change in anger; Peadar with a deep furrow and a glinting eye; Maurteen with a rattle of words and a white tenseness. Peadar loved growing things, and had a passion for cattle, stopping to chat about beasts and discuss their points on the road, with workers in the field or in the house. Once we went to Gort, where he was unknown and at ease, to buy sheep. He must have handled quarter of the sheep at the fair before he spat on his hand and gave a hard smack to the seller's hand to settle the bargain of black mountainy sheep,

and those almond-eyed devils for clearing fences, horny
ewes. He raddled their necks afterwards. " Let's have a
few more bars of that bucko," he'd say. That bucko meant
François Villon whom I translated whilst Peadar listened
or tried to put my words into Irish.

I saw Clare through Peadar. In the east of the Brigade
I did not have the same contact. Ennis was Brigade
Headquarters, but in name only as the resources of a large
town were not being used to slowly build up a centre from
which strength could radiate.

We visited the Aran Islands and around the fire at
night we talked sitting on very low stools, on the floor, or
with backs to the wall. And when it was my turn to tell
a story, Peadar and some of the boys who spoke English
helped me out in translation. Some of their stories seemed
to have had no beginning or end. They seemed mostly to
like smartness in the hero, a kind of cleverness bordering
on trickery; their tales of Fionn were such; accounts of
people on the mainland with a stress on meanness, or some
fantastic tale so elaborate that one could sense improvised
embroidery. Stories that were direct or that had much
concrete description, I thought, they would like. I told
them of Tyll Ulenspiegel, some of Hakluyt's sea tales,
Bricriú's Feast and Burnt Njal. Tyll Ulenspiegel and
Bricriú were favourites; they rocked with delight, and I
had to repeat them often and eventually hear their own
versions; but their greatest joy was in the story of Mac
Datho's Boar.

Everyday conversation and small events were dwelt on ;
states of the tide, weather, puffins, sea birds, clouds, fish
and the behaviour of animals all received weighty attention.
They had a medieval quality of wonder that came when a
world was unexplored ; beyond the small known horizon
there lay Cathay, the Seven Cities of Cibola, or the Land
of Promise. Some of the men and girls had been in
America. Their stories were strange enough. Boston and
Philadelphia took colour ; American families and their
ways were made as humorous as the stories of Americans
about Irish maids, but often it would seem that they
believed their fantastic additions more than the actual
happenings. I wondered what it would be like to live
always on the island, would stories become threadbare and

comment boring, and would their jealousy of each other and their secretiveness affect us?

* * * *

Peadar went north to get particulars about police huts which we intended to attack later. Near Ennis was a police hut, an armed patrol guarded stretches of the road at night. With two Volunteers I waited for the patrol. They passed us, rifles on their shoulders, as we were crossing a road in the dark; my men had blackened faces but the police did not halt us. After a time we heard the police returning. They were talking. My companions put the barrels of their shot guns across the ditch, waiting. Then I felt that if the police would not put up their hands at my shout, or if they tried to use their rifles my men would shoot. When the police came nearer I could hear their words which seemed to be important and out of all proportion to their sentence. But I did not call on them to put up their hands. I knew my men would shoot to kill. When the police passed one said: " That was a good chance, why didn't you shout? " But I had no reply. I could not give the order; shooting like that did not seem fair. There was no moral element in my thoughts. We waited until the patrol repassed, and again I let them go, cursing myself for the second irresolution. " We'll leave them be," I said, in gloomy silence. The men went as far as the house I was to sleep in. I did not explain to them; but I knew they were disgusted.

I went to West Clare. Here was a gentleness and out-of-the-worldness that Mid Clare had not. The land was sodden, tufted and low lying. A long triangle with the apex at Loop Head ran two sides into water, the Shannon formed one side, the Atlantic another. The tide came fifty miles up the river which was seven miles wide at the mouth. Inland from rising ground I could see the wooded edges of the river across on the Limerick and Kerry shores, far away the rounded breasts of the Paps and the higher mountain beyond Killarney.

I listened to stories at the firesides. I was told again of the *cóiste bodhar*, the death coach with its headless horses, the drivers carried their own heads under their arms. People were strayed at night in certain places, often on the unseen path between earthen forts, although they knew the ground as well as they knew the palm of their own hands, but they wandered around all night. They could be strayed crossing one of their own fields, almost within sight of the house. The cure was to turn one's coat and cap inside out It was bad to build on a path between forts; " they " always had their revenge; things were moved about in the house; the foundations shook. The priest might say a Mass in the place, but that sometimes did not make any change.

On the road to Kilrush was a figure with a long hand eight feet long. It followed travellers at night stretching out this long hand as it tried to grasp them by the back of the neck. On dark nights cycling without a light so as not to warn police patrols of my approach, I instinctively turned my head at times to ensure that the long clammy hand was not reaching out, whilst again I searched the darkness for the forms of the patrol. One incarnation seemed as real as the other in this country. But all I ever saw was a white ass lying on the road. Once I ran into one ; its colours merged in that of the moonlight.

" God help the creatures," said an old man near Kilkee one night as we were talking of the many ways and plans of England to settle us. " Musha, they haven't much sense. They'd best set their hand to Balor's advice." Then he told us of Balor of the Evil Eye. He sent his men to fight the Ildana, Lugh of the Long Arm ; when the people in Ireland were beaten, his warriors were to tie their cable round the Island of Erin which gave him so much trouble, attach it to the sterns of their long ships, sail home and place it to the north of Lochlann, where none of the Irishmen will ever follow. " And if I could ever meet that foxy schemer, Lloyd George, I'd tell him that."

In West Clare a butterfly appeared with green, white and yellow stripes. We called it the Republican Butterfly ; the people said that they had not put much heed on it before and it was looked upon as an omen. Dogs seemed to sense that we had the same beliefs as their owners. At night when I had to pass through backways and haggards of farm buildings the dogs seldom or ever barked ; though some were reputed to be wicked, I could approach them in the darkness. The constant feeling of danger saved my senses from being blurred and made for wonder in what I might otherwise accept. Tired out at night when I came to a house I felt the gift of shelter ; when I stirred the covering

of white ash and added sods or used the bellows the
expected glow seemed as mysterious as the first fire.   And
when I had made tea for myself in the quiet and empty
kitchen and had stretched my muddy boots to the blaze I
could smoke a pipe in contented peace.   If I stayed for any
length in a house I would be known by my step or whistle.

One night I was going across country from the Shannon
shore to O'Donnell's of Tullycrine.   Art, the eldest boy,
formerly a school teacher, was the Brigadier.   There was
a full moon ;   I could see the glint of the moon's path on
the waters of the Shannon.   As I crossed a field, gun in
hand and approached a loose stone wall, I saw a figure
move up along the wall ;   a crouching figure.   I halted ;
lay down ;   the figure disappeared.   I moved on slowly,
crossed the wall and again I saw the figure moving down
the wall of the next field ;   it carried something in its hand.
I took cover ;   faced it ;   the figure disappeared. I went
towards the wall, but I could see no movement.   I was near
the house.   I had to be careful for police might have
received information ;   they might be waiting in ambush.
At the next wall I found out what it was.   The moon had
thrown my shadow on the wall ;   I was trailing myself.

I fought a six-shot duel with a police sergeant whilst
Volunteers tried to disarm constables.   The rifles taken
were recaptured by police and seven arrests were made,
amongst them Art O'Donnell, the Brigadier, whom I had
made keep out of our raid.   He got two years' hard labour.
I was in disgrace.   The police put out the report that I was
a spy.   I had, they said, pretended to shoot at the sergeant
and, being a good shot, I had put a bullet through the
peak of his cap.   They made it appear as a good joke
against the local Volunteers.   Some of the men evidently
believed the police account, and that did not tend to make
things pleasant, nor did it prevent police from raiding for
me.

I had arranged with Mid-Clare to attack some police
patrol, posts and huts ;   East Clare, without my knowledge,
had been asked for the loan of rifles.   The attacks were
to take place at the same time, but three days before the
night agreed on I was told that some of the East Clare men
had made arrangements to tear up the railway lines,
destroy communications and carry out an operation on an

extensive scale, and that the police through random talk knew of the undertaking. The Bishop of Killaloe had been advised. I countermanded all preparations.

The men were inclined to talk somewhat loosely; the people gossiped and chatted in their homes, at fairs and markets with the result that the enemy intelligence system was enabled to collect information, sift and co-ordinate it. It proved to us that it would be impossible to carry out operations on any comparatively large scale and that, for the present, isolated attacks would be sufficient. We had thought in terms of a general, simultaneous rebellion throughout the country; now Headquarters endeavoured to teach us to train, arm and equip and to carry out minor operations for the seizure of arms. *An t-Óglach*, the Irish Volunteer paper, printed monthly on a handpress in Dublin was sent to all brigades. The British raided ceaselessly for it and tried hard to find the way in which it was distributed. When one was found with it a stiff sentence was given. Articles in it outlined Volunteer policy and point of view.

Dick Mulcahy had come to Limerick with Frank P. Walsh and Edward Dunne of the American delegation, elected at an Irish Race Convention in Philadelphia, to recommend to President Wilson Ireland's case for representation on the Peace Conference. I was instructed to bring the Clare senior officers to the city.

Limerick was tense with excitement. A volunteer, Byrne, who had been on hunger strike had been removed to hospital under a police guard. An attempt at rescue failed. A policeman on duty, acting on his instructions, shot the prisoner dead. He, himself, was killed and another policeman wounded. As a result Limerick was proclaimed a military area; a kind of curfew operated; workmen could not cross the Shannon without a permit. Refusing to ask for permits, workers outwitted the patrol and pickets daily. Armoured cars ran swiftly up and down or moved slowly and truculently; their machine guns swung from turrets on the people, barbed wire entanglements guarded all approaches, tanks threaded their massive way, patrols marched up and down in full war equipment. It looked as if a stage scene had been prepared for the visitors, in which business men and workers lost trade and wages whilst the military played at being soldiers. I paraded and introduced groups of officers

to the Assistant Chief after a public meeting.   He told me
to go to North Tipperary next day.

*   *   *   *

THE MAN FROM THE "DAILY MAIL"

The country is a mass of seething passion, 'tis Sinn Féin through and through
The peelers they are joining the Dalcassions and their password *Thiggin Tu*.
Every dog has a tricoloured ribbon attached firmly to his tail
And it wouldn't be surprising if we had another rising
         Says the man from the *Daily Mail*.

The other day I rambled down to Clare, boys, and in an old boreen
I saw a squad of bold and busy ganders dressed in orange, white and green
They practised the German goose-step as they warbled Granuaile
The country is all shaken or I'm very much mistaken
         Says the man from the *Daily Mail*.

Every bird, upon my word, is singing treble I'm a rebel
The hens and the jades are laying hand grenades over there now, 'tis quare
     now
Every cock in the farmyard stock crows the triumph of the Gael
If ever I try to hold them, sure they'd shoot me as a yeoman,
         Says the man from the *Daily Mail*.

CHAPTER NINE

MAY 1919—APRIL 1920

★

I HAD A NEW sense strongly developed and I relied on it
at times as I would on my sight.   On the roads at night
in North Tipperary I would turn back with the feeling that
something was going to happen.   Next day I would find
that soldiers had been holding a cross roads in front of
me or that the house I was going to had been raided in the
night.   The sense of danger threw out its warning signals
which could be disputed, but not argued away.   I would
sit by a hedge to discuss the new situation with myself,
but I would act on the warning.   Night manoeuvres of our
battalions under the drum of a harvest moon made the
enemy more active; cycling back from them or from
classes I felt my way in the dark slowly working through
their outposts or slept out till dawn.

Collins sent me north to Inishowen to raid for 200 Ulster Volunteer rifles. The Ulstermen had their rifles hidden, but the police did not raid for them. I was to draw men from Tyrone and the Finn Valley. Frank Aiken from South Armagh was to be sent to help me. On the strength of bad shooting with the stiff trigger of my thirty-eight I was given a Webley forty-five. " Now get the rifles," Collins said, " and for Christ's sake, Earnán, learn to shoot straight or I'll lose you one of these days."

My new gun helped me to cut my way through police at a station in Tyrone. I attended a meeting of Ulster Volunteers in Derry hoping to get information about arms. But beyond the experience of sitting with sturdy men whom I liked and who would have given me little mercy if they found out what I really represented, I did not gain anything. The Derry Irish Volunteers had a hazy knowledge of garrisons and wireless stations in the peninsula. Derry commanded the narrow neck of lowland that cut off Inishowen from the rest of Donegal. Troops if warned could with ease hold this neck and keep us from getting through. Cycling with a boy from Carndonagh I explored the iron-bound east coast and chatted for information at bars with British ex-officers. The raid came off in a wild storm ; our procession of cars blundered through, but we found no rifles. It was dawn before we passed through Derry.

Collins put me to work on organization with Seoirse Plunkett in the dug-out. We arranged card-indexes, checked lists of officers, read reports and filled in maps. I could not understand why G.H.Q. kept lists down to company officers. It would seem enough for them to have the names of brigade staffs and to note outstanding men. In the case of a raid the British would be able to supplement their extensive police reports and surmises with evidence. For a while I worked on home communications endeavouring to speed up our delivery of dispatches throughout the country. I dealt with foreign communications through which touch was kept with England, the Continent and America ; that work meant some knowledge of the underground by which men were sent quietly from Ireland and back again. I learned about the devious ways of getting in our small amounts of arms and ammunition from abroad.

The intelligence system had organized the Post Office, made use of friendly warders for communication with prisoners in gaols and collected information through detectives in the " G " division and the R.I.C. Police and military codes were changed often now, the information in their messages had frequently to be acted on at once and it was essential for us to have their key words. Well-planned gaol escapes had released important prisoners from English and Irish prisons. The prison system itself suffered, gaolers found it difficult to adjust their regulative minds to the disrespect of prisoners for their rules.

I stayed with Count Plunkett. He was erudite; he could talk with ease on any subject save contemporary art. Moderns could not paint he thought. For hours he would sit talking about some unexpected aspect of a little known writer, and when I tried to test him by looking up abstruse details for my further questions in an encyclopedia, I found he could change the bare facts by radiating life. Eoin Plunkett was attached to the Engineering department, his chief was Rory O'Connor. A discussion beginning with an Italian primitive would criss-cross and end in an elaborate analysis of a new type of light machine gun or the mechanism of an imaginary weapon which we could use.

*   *   *

I could see the various movements as a whole now and watch development. Officers and men from Sinn Féin clubs came to see Brugha, Mulcahy or Collins. Mulcahy probed and asked questions. Collins seemed to establish his personality quickly in the mind of his visitor; he was hearty, boisterous or quiet by turn ; he was uncouth, as judged by my early standards. He had a habit of baiting Tom Cullen, the assistant quartermaster, and a few of the Dublin men. That I hated. I could understand, take or make use of a tell-off, but the prodding got on my nerves. One day I told Collins I could not stand it and I left the room in a rage. He never baited anyone in my presence afterwards. He always backed up an energetic man, and would stand firmly by him in difficulties, especially those due to excess of zeal. I told him I was tired fiddling with files. "All right, Earnán, straighten out North County Dublin ; it's a hopeless area, but you won't mind that." He laughed at my disgusted face. He stood to attention and clicked his heels when I saluted.

Sinn Féin and all separatist organizations with their weekly papers had been suppressed; later, organizations were proclaimed. A one-day raid took place by the British all over Ireland. Courts martial sentences increased to five years; political prisoners were now classed as criminals. Markets and fairs were prohibited in Tipperary and other counties.

There were changes in the H.Q. Staff. Diarmuid O Hegarthy, whom I had stood in awe of in " F " Company, left Communications to be Director of Organization; Collins organized the Intelligence service as Director. Hegarthy's long cow's lick fell over his right eye; he had an untidy collar, an angled tie and a dishevelled appearance. He seemed to take life easy but he worked hard. He had a muttered rapid speech; his mind worked quickly, shrewdly and surely. There was purpose and a kind of amused kindliness when I dealt with him on army matters, but he dismissed my loose-leaf sheet suggestions and brain waves, which I had carefully thought over, to a drawer. He used clear, clever imagery, often biting. I admired his type of quick intellect, often disguised by a surface implication of casualness.

Gearóid O'Sullivan, the Adjutant-General, was neatly trim and a contrast in clothes to the rest of the staff. He was bouncing and alert, his teeth came together and his jaws stuck out as if he was being resolute when he talked of unimportant things. He managed his office well. I had heard him being smart at the expense of officers from the country whom I knew; he did not suspect their worth and judged them by their sloppy clothes and deferential willingness. He was a pale reflection of Mick Collins, he said " bloody bowsy " as Mick did, and shook his chin in a similar way.

Collins decided to stop smoking; he smoked thirty Greencastles a day. He drank, but I never saw signs of drink on him, except in 1917. Now he neither drank nor smoked. He showed me a copy of the oath of allegiance; members of the Dáil were to take it. The Volunteers were to become the Irish Republican Army and they would take the oath to the Republic. Up to this Volunteers had been responsible to their Executive of sixteen elected in convention. It would need another convention to change their constitution, but the Staff would not take that risk, although a Sinn Féin convention had been held secretly in Dublin. " That will give us more status," he said, " and it'll help some to realize that they're not joining for fun ; what do you think of it? "

That night I inspected a company in Santry. I read the oath to the men. It sounded significant in the small bare room.

" I [*A B*] do solemnly swear, or affirm that I do not and shall not yield a voluntary support to any pretended Government, Authority or Power, within Ireland hostile or inimical thereto ; and I do further swear or affirm, that to the best of my knowledge and ability I shall support and defend the Irish Republic, and the Government of the Irish Republic, which is Dáil Eireann, against all enemies foreign and domestic, and that I will bear true faith and allegiance to the same and that I take this obligation freely without any mental reservation or purpose of evasion. So help me God."

Officers and men came to attention ; one by one in front of the company they took the oath. The fourth began " I, A.B., . . . I, A.B. . . . then paused whilst he groped for his name, overcome by the solemnity; his throat moved, then he repeated the words. Collins read my week-end report. " Who the bloody hell gave you permission to administer the oath? I never told you, and it hasn't even been ratified by the brigades."

I wandered for months through the small lakes and little hills of Monaghan. I saw sieges of heron in the reeds and waited for bat-tailed otters near Carrickmacross where they are said to pass through when going from one lake to another. I was able to disprove the lines :

" From Carrickmacross to Crossmaglen
You meet more rogues than honest men."

I was at the taking of Ballytrain barracks—the first barracks taken north of the Boyne—with Eoin O'Duffy, the Brigadier; a policeman who had been praying during the attack was blown by the explosion of our gelignite through a partition wall without injury. There were, I think, nine police and that meant nine bright carbines, bayonets revolvers, hand grenades, Verey lights and ammunition.

O'Duffy was energetic and commanding. I had seen his typewritten reports at G.H.Q.—very few reports were typewritten. His area was fair, but no command could be managed with anything like efficiency until at least two of the brigade staff gave all their time to the work. Men continued to earn their living and carry on army duties after working hours until the British made them go on the run.

The Táin nearly brought me to trouble near Ardee. The name meant the Ford of Ferdia ; here he had been buried, after death at the weapons of his friend and enemy, Cuchulain. I cycled to look at the burial mound close to the stream in the town, but I ran into police who tried to halt me in the street. I back-kicked one in the face with the studded strength of a heavy boot, then drawing my gun on his partner, who was trying to open a holster flap, I cycled out of sight. Later I found that the grave had been cut away during a deepening of the stream.

*　　*　　*　　*

ASHTOWN ROAD
(*Attack on Lord French*)

On a cold December's day a motor ploughed its way
Mid bullet splash and spray on the Ashtown Road
In that car the living tool of England's hatred rule
And there began the duel on Ashtown Road.

Young Savage undismayed with bombs and hand grenade
Attacked them unafraid on the Ashtown Road.
But a bullet laid him low from the rifles of the foe
Yet another debt we owe for the Ashtown Road.

CHAPTER TEN

*

I RECEIVED NO guidance or instructions when sent out to organize a county or a brigade. Collins would hand me a pile of copies of the organization scheme, add some type-written notes reminding officers that their reports were long overdue; then I was left to myself. Usually I received the names and addresses of a few senior officers, the names of likely men to approach in an unorganized part of the country, and an introduction in writing from Collins in his clear legible hand.

The Irish Volunteers were organized by counties at first; each of the thirty-two counties was a prospective brigade area, but often there was but a skeleton of a brigade, later on there might be three brigades in some counties. The organization scheme had to be elastic. A company contained one hundred and twenty men, four sections and eight squads; in practice the number varied from full strength in some city companies to an average of thirty or thirty-five, but the parade strength would be twenty or twenty-five. Officers were elected by the company on parade; captain, lieutenant, and second lieutenant; the voting was by ballot. Section and squad commanders were appointed by the captain at a company council of his lieutenants. When there were enough companies, five to eight, according to regulations, to form a battalion, officers met to elect a Commandant, Vice-Commandant, Adjutant and Quartermaster. The lieutenants of the Special Service were appointed by the Commandant. In like manner the battalions elected a brigade staff. The average parade strength of a Brigade in spring of 1920 was close on nine hundred men.

Each battalion was expected to have self-contained special services: Engineering, Signals, Communications, First Aid, Transport and Supply, Intelligence. Each section was supposed to supply men to these services. On paper special service officers were appointed, but there they stayed. To make them function it would need classes for instruction in the different branches and a class for officers and section commanders, but such classes were to be found only in the cities.

Owing to the unwieldy natural configuration of the counties, brigades, as time went on, often took slices from adjoining counties, or valley s determined on what battalion of the slope a company would lie. Strategical considerations were given a little more attention. A battalion formed on a town as a nucleus from which to expand; but, except for the cities, the main Volunteer strength was in the country-men. The battalion was built around a source of enemy strength; there was a definite objective in the military or police barracks. In the country, sections were expected to have a tangible operation in mind; railway bridges, stretches of road, or a river crossing. In general all such organization depended upon a general, simultaneous rising of the whole country.

The point of view had been changed with the stress on guerilla warfare; but the operations' organization around a definite objective was the same. Each brigade was not again considered as a unit in itself ready to co-operate in a general scheme; but with stress on minute attention to its sporadic efforts at developing a fight. An important town was often of no more importance than the headquarters of a country section of ten men. A decent operation survey of the country would have shown the importance of certain cities, towns and localities; these might have been organized at once before the British occupied them in force and were able to overawe later attempts. There was no operations branch at General Headquarters; there were two or three untrained organizers for the whole country. They had to diffuse themselves, take on all developing departments of G.H.Q. without advice from any of them. The organization department followed too much along the lines of a political party. A meeting was called to discuss the formation of a company, officers were elected; names were forwarded to Dublin and a company or battalion existed on paper and worked out its own salvation after that.

The chief trouble, as I saw it, was in changing this paper basis. Officers would first have to think in terms of organization, then operations, and the advantages or short-comings of their commands. They would need administrative and then tactical training. Organization applied to the skeleton of a brigade, or to strategical and tactical considerations based on possible operations, or on the enemy's intentions, as shown by the positions held by him, could be worked out without professional knowledge. The officers brought some enthusiasm to the new work, offset by a sense of dependence upon authority for guidance in what they considered a new unknown and difficult element. Otherwise intelligent men could not think in terms of their medium; they created their own difficulties. Military work had always been looked upon as a marvel, something remote and other world like.

A stranger was always listened to with seeming respect. He might settle or walk upon a difficulty which would perhaps result in hostility or jealousy if a local man tried to fix it. A man of outstanding character in the neighbourhood would be listened to, but there were cross currents difficult to find. Generally it was best to make judgments independent of local feeling.

I found the country strange. Life had been very sheltered at home. We had been well clothed and cared for; neatness had always been insisted on. I did not understand the people. As a boy, I knew the islanders in Clew Bay; I had gone on visits to my uncle's farm in Roscommon but that did not give me understanding. The people laughed at pranks for which they would have punished their sons. Races, full tilt in asses and carts on narrow country roads, games of Indians in the bottom lands riding naked on the backs of tearing hunters after a swim in the Suck.

The food was good, but rough and badly cooked. Bulk seemed to matter most. Tea, eggs, bacon, stirabout, potatoes and cabbage were the usual food; tomatoes, lettuce, celery, beans, and fruit in general were unknown. The lack of green vegetables was said to be due to the famine years when the people ate nettles and grass. Mangels and turnips went to the horses, pigs and cattle, they bubbled and smelled with cabbage in cast iron cauldrons. Herbs, tansy, mint, and wild garlic were used sparingly. I gave a tomato to a man I knew at a fair. He eyed the shining scarlet. " What kind of a thing is this? " He bit into it, then spat out the pulp in disgust. " Man dear, do you want to poison me? "

In some places there would be apple cake, but the fruit would have made the outside soppy. Eggs were almost always, boiled—scrambled eggs were unknown. Once when I explained about scrambled eggs there came loud laughs : " Turkey-food," a girl giggled. Later came the soft liquid mass that young turkeys liked. I liked milk squirted hot to bubbly froth from the teat. Baker's bread and bullocks' meat they bought on market days. I enjoyed large oven cakes, slidderjacks, potato and griddle cakes. The oven cakes were divided into thick white cuts, the smaller ones were split into farls along the line of the cross always made in the dough, and then eaten hot, dripping with freshly-churned butter.

Soon I learned to dread bacon and cabbage. The bacon was often home cured. It hung in long narrow flitches from hooks in the smoke-blackened ceiling where it seasoned. It was fat—and I did not like fat. At home I was told it was good for me and I had tried to hide it under potato skins, cover it with bones, or get it into a piece of paper in my pocket. The cabbage was boiled a long time, and it was not strained. I ate the mate—as it was called—because I did not like to offend the people. They were kind, they had taken more care with my food, and they would consider me stuck-up. They were very sensitive, as a rule. For two years I ate bacon and cabbage or, if I had the option, changed to tea and an egg. Sometimes the tea was stewed. The pot " took a heat " by the fire from the early breakfast, or was allowed to draw too long. Strong tea that a mouse could trot on. Stewed tea took away hunger.

There was no organized hygiene and sanitation was of the sheltered hedges. They did not take care of teeth, they were careless of health. Wettings went unnoticed, umbrellas were not carried, even in the towns they would be thought unmanly. Goloshes or light overshoes were a genteel monopoly. Lack of general regard for health and personal comfort had become close to affectation with us. It was a sign of manliness. A similar disregard was echoed in the carelessness of faulty agricultural method, a reaper and binder blocking a gap in a hedge through the winter, decaying teeth, and a shame about disease as if it were a personal blemish.

I slept in huge four-posters with canopies; often there was a series of feather mattresses and a covering of reddish quilts, whole or patch-worked, with an oppressive sense of weight. Often I was given the best room in the house, but generally I slept with some of the family, or lay on a settle, in a warm kitchen. In places the boys dressed in front of their mothers and sisters. This to me was an ordeal. I had not their natural outlook. Furtive attempts to pull on my shirt and trousers, hasty dives back to bed, whilst the women of the house or the girls, without concern, went about their business filling huge black pots with vegetables and mash for the pigs and hens, or baking cakes in the round, flat-bottomed ovens.

I was given a small basin with less than two inches of water to wash in. The family did not wash daily. The basin was placed on a stool in the kitchen with a piece of washing soap. I was expected to wash before the women folk. Later I was able to take the soft rain water from the barrel beneath the eaves and wash in the open.

The girls wore rough, heavy boots for farm work, laces often untied, dresses to the ankles, many petticoats and dishevelled blouses. Sunday was the day for a real clean up. Sunday clothes were worn; all turned out rosy from soap and excitement on their way to Mass on an outside car or trap, mostly in asses and carts, or on foot by the short cut of the Mass path.

I did not play cards. In my spare time I read my military books or wrote essays and instructions. In the night time after parades or councils, I sat in " the room." It had curtains, a sideboard, an ornamented tea cosy, and a few books, old school books, *Moore's Almanac,* a religious monthly, sometimes a collection of sound books which had been read, studied and pondered on. The family bible would be used only to insert the dates of the birth and death of children. There were coloured post cards, family portraits, one or two sententious religious oleographs, hideous in mawkish colour, artificial flowers, and an auto-graph book; a picture of Robert Emmet, Parnell or Daniel O'Connell, or post cards of the Easter Week leaders. There were St. Patrick's Day cards from friends and relatives in the States: Paddy and his Pig, a shillelagh like a bludgeon waved in the air, corduroy knee breeches and colleens in costumes never seen on land or sea. The 17th of March must be thought of there as a sentimental orgy in which everything related to Irish life is carefully eliminated.

The Room was seldom used. The family ate, sat and talked in the kitchen, the main door led into it. The Room had a dank smell, and though a fire would be lighted it could not draw the unlived-in dampness and lack of cheer out from the wooden floor or the heavy tablecloth.

More than often I sat in the kitchen on a súgán chair; my back to the lamp which stood on the window sill. I could then listen to the talk when I tired of reading. I joined the groups around the fire. Talk and stories were punctuated by draws from clay pipes and by spits. The pipes had once been white; but use had turned them a shiny brown black, and their stems had broken off; sometimes just the bowl and a short toothy stump remained. They smoked heavy strong cut plug tobacco; it was pleasant when one got used to it. Baccy during the European War was scarce and precious. The blasts out of the pipe were a great solace after the day's work; they were lost without a good draw. The pipe might pass from mouth to mouth around the fireplace. Once in a smithy I saw a blacksmith hand his pipe to a man who had asked for a draw ; he cracked off the tip with his red hot pincers when the pipe was handed back.

From the nook alongside the fire I watched the turf blaze and glow. Shadows and patches of light were thrown up on to faces. Often I stared into the rosy red core of the embers watching the figures ; and traced them running from one fantastic form to another.

The life was hard and close to the soil; up early ploughing, harrowing, cutting turf, mowing, weeding. Footing turf and draining was about the hardest work. At its worst there was variety; change in the type of work and unending vagaries in the greatest of talk causers, the weather. There was the uncertainty of farm work and the waverings of market prices.

On the roads one said " Good-day " to everybody met with; " A soft day "; " A soft day, surely, thanks be to God." A chat over a hedge: " God bless the work." Older men and women were called by their Christian names.

In some districts where there were many of the same surname there would be handles on the houses, Michael Nora's, Andy John's, and the sons might be John Mary Ruadh.

The house that took in a daily paper would be the teacher's—the Master's, Mr. So-and-so, or the Big House; mostly the people were content with the *Weekly Freeman*, or the weekly local papers from the nearest big town. Around the fire the people talked of daily events, the weather, crops, letters from friends and relations in America or foreign parts; here was their paper; a living warp and weft spun of their own thoughts, fancies and doings. Now and again a biting turn of phrase for in their nature was the old Gaelic satire; sharp and direct or twisted endlessly like a súgán being made across the door into the cobbled street. Malice and spleen might burst forth suddenly or heavy hearty cursing. Words were often used as a club, a means, not an end in themselves.

There was a love of discussion and argument that would take up a subject casually without belief and in a searching way develop it. That might mean a pleasant joking or an ornate, shrewd and enjoyable development for him who sustained his unbelief and heated words from his opponents; or anger from all in the end as the baiter was drawn into the net of his own words. Anger they played on often as on fiddle strings. Deferential to a stranger, they evoked in themselves a sympathetic mood, changing gears in conversation to suit his beliefs and half believing then through sympathy whilst he was present. Afterwards when they checked up on themselves it might be different; they would laugh at the stranger's outlandish opinions when their mood had hardened.

Always for me there was the relish of a phrase; they were conscious of it also. Acute, natural observation was converted into shades of meaning; some improvised as they talked, they became more extravagant, and delighted listeners helped them over appreciative stiles. Proverbs were many, even in the English-speaking districts, but the Gaeltacht alone kept the richer anthology, remembered from old literature; quotations from poets and stories, sayings of ollaimh, and their apt use.

At a wake, turf spreading, hay gathering, threshing or

a *meitheal* to help a widow woman or neighbour in difficulties, I could enjoy their co-operative sense; hard work
together was a relaxation; bantering jokes, songs, a racing
competition in individual work and a natural place for
match-making.

The weekly market was a break in routine. The men
were able to drink double or triple porter to their hearts'
content. Then the boisterous drive home, often without
lights, careering along the country roads in a bone-shaking
cart.

The countryman to himself was worth what he had in
his pocket at any given moment. The land was his wealth;
unlike the townsman, he had few ornate possessions. He
would look with envy at the many knick-knacks and
furniture of town house. His total wealth would be greater,
but his living was simpler. He had no useless possessions.
He had not to keep up appearances like the townsfolk, he
had not their mannerisms, fashions, or interest in superficial
values. Yet the countryman would think of the townsman in
terms of the prosperity that his own sons might strive for.

The boys worked into manhood without pay. If they
were given a sixpence or a shilling on a fair day it would
mean a deal, but the sons of a house had their own means
of getting money. A bag of 'praties sold on the sly, the
hansel money when a beast was sold and the readjusted
sales price, or a gathered dozen of eggs. The girls had less
say. Even their marriages were arranged. The parish
matchmaker, I often listened to, as he wound his sinuous
conversational way amongst the tussocks of the parental
bog: " A fine upstanding man with five milch cows, two
springers and ten fine head of cattle." The parish priest
might carry out the deal: " It's well to have the children
settled early." From the fortune that came in with a girl,
the husband would be able to have his next eldest sister
married off. If there was not enough to fortune her to the
satisfaction of her boy's parents, it meant a runaway match,
if she had spirit—and America.

The Jansenistic older priests, hard, austere, some more
human as they grew into age bore on the people: sermons,
advice and the-to-be-feared calling from the altar sun-
merged them in a facile but unreal submission. Some priests
were hostile to dancing and gatherings; they interfered

in every aspect of life. The lack of organized social inter-
course made the young discontented, especially in the towns.
The wise domination of age, to some hard and harsh in the
soul as the cancer of foreign rule, made volunteering an
adventure and a relief. Parish priests were managers of
national schools. They had the power to appoint and remove teachers. Some, hostile to the movement, dismissed
young men and women who were separatists. They found
work in England or turned their hand to anything they
could find or joined our export of youth to America. We
had other exports: priests to the mission fields of the
British Empire, artists and writers to London because our
nation did not support them.

There were certain hide-bound conventions within which
the people moved and solved problems by formula. To them
there was a normal in life and in individual human conduct.
Life was simple, as it were, between good and bad, easy to
classify, accept or reject: anything outside of this was not
to be tolerated, sympathised with or understood. Life was
to be lived in compartments, but some disputed in their
hearts though they accepted the outward interpretation.
Advice on life, action and procedure in terms of observed
normality was always forthcoming.

The movement had created for me as for others a code
of ethics that disciplined. There were no affairs; the
nearest approach to them were the furtive hole-and-corner
meetings that took place. I did not drink now because
I was too active, and partly because it was easy to slip into
heavy drinking in the country. Drink meant an open
mouth, talk and rumour. It was easier to discourage drink
among the men if one did not drink oneself.

The people were conservative; they had a hatred of
change. They had been driven in on themselves too
long, clinging for centuries to Gaelic usage in land and
law, and suspicious of changes that had been forced on
them by the conquerors. What was good enough for their
fathers would be good enough for them.

I had left home with suits neatly pressed and cleansed,
an ample supply of ties, collars and shirts. In time my
store disappeared. A spare shirt and a few socks were all
the clothes I needed. I was glad to leave aside a collar.
It was a badge of distinction seldom worn by countrymen

save on Sundays and Fair days. At night the shirt and socks or suit beside my bed would be taken away to be sewn, darned or washed, and clean clothes left in their place; if I stayed two nights my socks and shirt would be back at my bedside. All this often without a word.

My clothes were now a composite collection from many counties. I had my coat from Donegal, my waistcoat from Dublin, my trousers, very voluminous, formerly belonged to Michael Murray of Newmarket-on-Fergus, and he was somewhat rotund; my shirts and socks generally belonged to the county I happened to be in at the time. My trousers billowed around my legs in folds, the waist had to be folded and refolded beneath a belt. Michael Murray had girth.

My hat I seldom wore when passing through towns and villages; when I was given it I do not remember; it was a faded green. Sun and rain had each in turn touched it strongly. There was a bullet hole on either side of the crown near the top. Once in Clare, Peadar, Maurteen and myself were cycling from Ennis to Kilfenora. At a cross road we saw police with carbines; at the same time came a command "Halt there!" We drew our revolvers and fired, running for cover. The police used their carbines. It was near sunset. We had carried our bicycles over the ditch. When twilight came Peadar brought our bicycles across the next field whilst we replied slowly to the ragged police firing. Then we crawled away, reached our bicycles and cycled into the welcome friendly darkness. When I arrived at Maurteen's house I found the bullet hole in the hat. The most obvious sign of my light-headedness in the eyes of the old people was my not wearing a cap or hat; the men usually wore their hats, even in the house, and they always thought I would catch cold in my bare head.

My boots reaching to the knees were my own; they were heavy, but being well oiled, kept out rain. They were conspicuous, however, and when worn about Dublin must have attracted some comment for few, save the Plunketts, wore them. At night when moving across country and jumping ditches filled with water my long boots brought me into difficulties. I had not the agility of the countrymen in jumping with heavy kit. When we crossed country at night with a local guard we endeavoured to avoid the honour of taking the lead, for one profited by the leader's stumbles and splashes. We made use of a long length of stick to probe our way when the darkness was intense. I had a good sense of direction and was able to retrace my way at night after I had once crossed country, but I went astray occasionally and blundered around. Fixing a landscape was often like remembering a face.

I was on the outside. I felt it in many ways by a diffidence, by an extra courtesy, by a silence. Some were hostile in their minds; others in speech; often the mother would think I was leading her son astray or the father would not approve of what the boys were doing. We of the Volunteers were talked of at first: "Musha, God help them, but they haven't a stim of sinse". Yet there was a tradition of armed resistence, dimly felt; it would flare up when we carried out some small successful raid or made a capture. Around the fire it would be discussed; it would heighten the imagination of those who were hostile. In their minds a simple thing became heroic and epical. Perhaps the sense of glory in the people was stirred, and the legend that had been created about myself, whom they did not know, helped them to accept me as part of it.

I felt that I should be able to fuse with my material, the people, so that I could make better use of it; yet look at them dispassionately, as if from a distance. My approach to teaching and training of the men was impersonal; they would have to learn to do without me, to depend on themselves and avoid too much trust in what they considered leadership. This often meant a cold quality creeping in, but few could mingle with them without gaining warmth.

At the beginning it was the poor who stood by us in the country, and with them mostly I stayed; in some parts the standard of comfort was better, as in North Tipp, or when I was in a town house; but food, irregular meals or conditions did not matter to me whilst I was busy trying to improve a command. The life of the people was hard enough, but money or comfort were not standards that interrupted their content; above all they were alive and personal. The struggle with the soil rarely ground them down.

At home gatherings I sometimes felt the people withdraw their already partly granted family intimacy; the eddy that had taken me in would fling me out again. I would be like a hole in the wall then. That was all right, I thought later. They had their own dignity and aloofness; there was a seemingly unconscious boundary beyond which I could not get.

In time I learned to judge men by a look, bearing, intensity or deliberateness of speech. I had to make quick decisions about them for the time I remained in any area was short. Each county was different; the very map boundaries in many places seemed to make a distinction. The land seemed to determine the nature of the people often enough; whether pasture, grazing, tillage; good or bad; nearness to the sea; whether remote from towns and cities; hilly, mountainous, or undulating. Sometimes I came to a townland where there was a company of twenty or thirty men and boys. Tall, well set up or lanky, eager, lithe, willing to learn and anxious to take risks. Six miles away across the barony the people were cowed; the men had no initiative. They were irresolute. The Captain of the Company sometimes made the difference, sometimes the men themselves, but in parts it was the nature of the land and the long struggle against odds that had told.

Areas of country had a habit of going to sleep. They would wake up after a century or more and step into a gap. This unexpected quality was there in what I knew to be a bad area. It might awaken of itself: the times and situation might start the spark.

The selection of their own officers by the men was a difficulty. Election was traditional. Had they not elected their Tanists? but then the selection had been limited to a caste. Often at first I felt the choice was faulty; the men must know in their hearts that the new commander was no bloody good. He was chosen because he was from the town, a strong farmer, or a neat hurler. I knew that another candidate would not be put forward when a name had been proposed. After the meeting men would speak their thoughts on the way home. It would be too late then. A disposition to please rather than to be direct; a desire of not wishing to start ill-feeling or to begin trouble; irresoluteness, or not thinking things through were at the root of it; a moral cowardice with extenuating undercurrents of a candidate's influence, position or power.

The clan spirit as such, deeper than the isolation and accent of individual counties, had to be overcome or switched to rivalry in organisation and action with those across the border. Distrust and jealousy had to be fought by fostering their own development in command; the dead weight of tradition grinding us between millstones had to be diverted to a new outlook and in a new hold on the present.

I grew a moustache to change my appearance in the towns. Some of the officers were elderly as judged by my age. They might be 35 or 40, and I felt a diffidence in giving orders. In a short time this wore off. The men had learned to judge of themselves. Hard work, zeal, ability, driving force, eagerness and enthusiasm; all these in their eyes contributed. Sometimes the man who would have made a good Volunteer, if left in the ranks, was now neither a good officer nor a good Volunteer. The responsibility of fighting the empire with his untrained men must have changed him. Later I set the election system aside. I picked an eager boy and appointed him captain.

I was lonely. It was hard work, this constant supervision, insisting on work being done. Often in an area where the spirit was poor one seldom or ever met with boys who could influence the others or whose eagerness would give warmth and cheer. Then life seemed as if I was wearing damp clothes on my skin, and the light and colour went out of the landscape; yet I would be caught up by a silver mercurial sun-glint on water or by the peace of twilight.

That was heartbreaking when I felt I had to keep driving; but when I met a keen boy or man the day became brighter; I could lift my mind from drudgery and responsibility. In bad areas senior officers did not come round with me. As they did not know even the physical nature of their command they would have to rely on me for information. They would have very little personal contact outside of their headquarters town or battalion. I felt then more than ever isolated. I could not do much good. I knew the random threads of my work would not be gathered up; in time the instructions, orders, notes would be forgotten. I felt that I was a burden imposing on the people's hospitality. The people would be indifferent if the officers were dispirited. Conversation would become hushed when I appeared. Often I slept out under a hedge or rolled up in hay which I had pulled down from a rick or cock. On rainy nights I was wet through.

I ate hedgehog in late winter or stewed hare with wind red tinkers in their camp on the sheltered side of a hedge. They accepted the length of strong cut plug I usually carried with me for other people's emergency smokes. They were curious for they knew there was something strange; but I would lead their few questions away to their own activities and likings. Many of the men had been reservists, but their great foes were the police who interfered with their frenzy of drink and stick-walloping in the towns.

There was always the solace of the men in the ranks; why did they turn up week after week for the same monotonous minor movements? They must have felt the lack of imagination of their officers. They were not being trained in the use of arms; two or three men in a company would have held a rifle in their hands, and their drill was too ragged to give them a composite sense so that in danger they would feel each other and act together. Anyhow they would seldom have to fight in large bodies, but they were not being trained to any decent squad or section sense. Yet there was a certain co-operative value in meeting boys who thought as they did. During the European War the English found that the platoons of a company had to be self-contained for trench warfare. We would have to think in terms of the quarter company, the section.

To effect any change I would have to remain four months in an area and insist that some of the senior officers remain with me. My temper was ready to fly when I found that men had shirked duties and responsibilities. I did not remember that they had been working hard all day. Only for a short time in the day could they think in terms of military work. On parade I would curse, tell off sharply the absent ones, but that lash-stinging would affect the relations between myself and the individual men in front of me. Before council meetings or parades I lectured myself, composed my mind and was perfectly at peace. Then I would go up in smoke at some unexpected stupidity, prevarication or neglect and time passed before harmony was restored. They might get a certain satisfaction when I sprawled over a rabbit hole, tripped in a hedge, or fell in a dyke of water weighed down by heavy knee-boots when jumping in the dark, or when after long shouting my crisp-enough voice broke and trailed to a falsetto squeak.

By degrees the stern parental discipline was broken, and youth learned a certain independence. Dispatch riders had to leave their work, ride off on horseback, bicycle, or walk on foot across the fields. A raid by police or soldiers on a house meant the threat of another raid, and arrests broke up the family circle. In gaol, boys learned to carry on a gaol war; they mixed with men from other provinces and widened their national horizon. Men had to leave home to avoid arrest, then they were "on the run." Girls in Cumann na mBan had First Aid Classes and weekly meetings to attend; their officers had to cycle to meet others at the District Council. Gradually sons and daughters built up a small life of their own. Now fathers might attend the village Sinn Féin Clubs to discuss the situation or to debate and carry out instructions forwarded by the County Secretaries.

One had to fight against unpunctuality, lack of method, carelessness. Time did not matter to a countryman who judged time by the sun or his stomach. Dawn, breakfast, noon, dinner, afternoon, tea. One tried to make them appear neat on parade; boots brushed, coats buttoned up, but the outward discipline would be nullified at home. Inward discipline, the urge from men themselves to do what each considered his duty, was hard to build up. That was a thing of the spirit.

There were so many shades and half shades. The force of a flame like spirit; the owner had never to be reprimanded. One knew that he would always do more than he should; with him one was at once closely knit. Something jumped across the gap of personality and made a contact. He was indeed a friend; a comrade with whom one could travel at ease. Talk was not necessary; an understanding had been firmly set. There were others whose spirit was not strong; they joined from mixed motives, or because their girls egged them on. It was hard for them. They created their own difficulties. They saw the land ahead too much; they questioned themselves at every new departure; they were inclined to count the cost. Talking to some made me feel how inadequate speech could be: you said things that meant nothing

unless a man was attuned, and in the conversation there
would be two languages. I would fence for an opening,
slowly or quickly follow with words that might or might
not have a common value. At times one came across a
man who had been born free. There was no explaining it.
One just accepted and thanked God in wonder.

It had been difficult to avoid comment and observation
moving from one place to another. I had to remain in a
town or scattered village in bad areas. Any gossip would
be sure to get to the police barracks. I had to study the
layout of the town or village closely, its streets, by-paths
and back gardens. The neighbours would not know that a
stranger was near them; often the children of the house
did not know I was living with them, or they had to be
kept from school whilst I remained. It was hard to sneak
about from place to place, but as part of the game it was
interesting. It would keep the eyes and ears alert. I had
to learn to efface myself, to merge into the customs, speech
and dress; to withdraw myself from my own work in such
a way that my movements and talk would seem natural.
Almost by steady ignoring of the fact that I had to move
cautiously was I able to make others think that my movements were not out of the way.

This alertness could be annoying. I felt that it might
undermine courage and interfere with outlook. I would
like to stride down the town street rattling my hob nails
knowing that my gun could be quickly pulled if challenged
by the police; sometimes I did rattle past the open door
of the barracks. Perhaps the strain told in time; there
was a constant watchfulness, a training in observation and
minute detail, but also, at times, was the sense of being
pursued. My first few fights left me unafraid, anxious to
close at once, less inclined to carry out our plan of running
to fight another day. Later we avoided towns and villages
altogether; avoided the danger without making it the less.

My visits to Dublin were at intervals of every three
months or more, there I remained two or three days, and
was able to walk around leisurely and enjoy my leave,
when not detained at the office of the Adjutant-General.
At Eileen McGrane's flat I was always welcome; it was
difficult at first to get a place to sleep in as I did not know
many Dublin people in the movement; but after a few

visits I was always assured of a welcome by the Joyces at St. Ita's School, Count Plunkett, and by Mr. Sears who was a T.D. At times I slept in his bed when, owing to suspected enemy raids, he could not sleep at home. It was good to visit my friends, to sit with others in the flat in Dawson Street, yarn, talk, or read or listen to the latest Dublin gossip of which there was always plenty, and discuss the endless permutations and combinations of the situation till dawn broke. I occasionally slept with Frank Gallagher whom I had first met in the flat. I had found him covered with a rug pretending to be a bear, his back to the door; he evidently thought I was some member of the household as he continued his impersonations. There was silence; then he turned to find me looking rather startled; we both laughed and that served as our introduction.

In his room we talked far into the night. He was attached to publicity where his imagination was restricted. He worked out various fantastic inventions to outwit the British, and I supplemented by others. An injection of the concentrated essence of Irish freedom to be given to Lloyd George who would then become violently Republican, and would startle the House of Commons assembled to hear his budget scheme by delivering a speech advocating Irish Independence; a machine on the vacuum cleaner principle to be placed in position near Dublin Castle; when operated, it would suck all the anti-Irish element out of the seat of government; a patent for flattening out members of our intelligence service, so that they could remain behind furniture in a room or under a carpet in government offices; and the organisation of a Suicide Club, the members to use rifles, automatics or revolvers and inform the secretary, who would be either Frank or myself, when the self-execution was to take place. We would then collect the weapons. I described the different counties I had been in since last we met. I took them in battalion areas, related the doings and sayings of the people, our adventures and misadventures; the many amusing or grim incidents that had occurred. What had been once misery now in time was an experience, something to be broken up and reformed as a laugh.

Eoin Plunkett of the Engineers would branch into

technical abstractions at the slightest provocation. Seoirse discussed the inner discipline as opposed to the mass automation of regular armies. Rory O'Connor talked with a sense of humour, the grooves tightening his cheek muscles while his eyes smiled. He always had what I called an interior look. One could become worn down with the continued banter and chaff, the intimacy of this life which apparently did not leave one shred of one's own. There was no such thing as a swelled head in such companionship; it could never stand the isolated and mass attacks of kindly malicious or wry humour.

*   *   *   *

Two years had passed since I had left home. I had to carry all my belongings on a bicycle when I moved, and what clothes to discard and what books to bring was often a problem. In winter I wore a heavy trench coat which clung to my back and sides with rain, sweat or heavy misery, my clothes splashed with mud and water; cycling up and down hills with a pumping throb or down hill in the night with a swish, my boot on the front tyre as a brake, cycling in the dark with the help of my maps, mending punctures in match or candle light, making the best of borrowed bicycles, some smooth running; faulty ones with tight jibbering brakes, uneven camel-humped saddles and slightly buckled rims. Cycling without lights trying to follow the road from dim curving hedges, or looking up at an indefinite streak of sky between dark lanes of branches on nights aroar with wind, when only the missel thrush, the storm cock, sang into the biting blast. Robins and larks lifted rounded and clear song at evening and the bird chorus of banded winter flocks came in day time. Orange berries of the black thorn, dark purple elm flowers, silver willow catkins and the tiny crimson flowering of hazel stood out against masses of bluish willow thickets, darkened boles and leafless branches. Kestrels struck at tiny finches and small wrens made thin points of sound in the furze.

I looked forward to Spring: broken land, brown, umber, upturned, earth smells awakened by the rain. The wild daffodil quivering on pliant stem, purple-frittered wild iris, the delicate cream of the primrose backed by its crimpled leaf and the rich golden glory of the sedate crocus. Wych-elms would have a leaf-like bloom, the larch furry catkins and rosy blossoms, the hazel a pink flower and willow wrens sang above purple ash bloom.

March was a harsh month: April showery and uncertain, but flowers increased, sedgy meadow lands were becoming lush, buds thrust upwards into leaves, and in the orchards the trees petalled. Then there was the cowslip in short grass, the singing strength of blue-tit, thrush, yellow hammer and finch; the yellow bill of the blackbird pecked at the haws, and bees hummed over fragrant willow catkins.

May brought the first assurance of dryness and a regular stretch of sun, the cuckoo called softly in the distance and the yellow water lily, known as the drowned leaf, spread its floating coolness. Near the coast the light was pearly and luminous and scents were stronger. I could leave my bicycle one side and lie on my back on the grassy edge of the road now to read Blake or Villon at my ease, or shout them aloud to the surprise of interrupters, listen for varied bird notes and follow the unexpected swoops of swallows as they dived and dipped, wondering if they would ever strike each other. Passing an old house or castle I could hear the rooks cawing and watch them tilt in squadrons as they followed their leader, all performing their aerial evolutions simultaneously with a carrying noise of wing swish. At dusk the sound of them and crows in the beech trees brought a sense of peace and of long settled habitation. Out in the bogs in the day time men were working at the turf banks, cutting chocolate rectangles with their gleaming loys ; all hoped for fine weather as they footed, spread, gathered and ricked the fuel. The rich drying smell of it blew out on to better land. The yellow, amber bog water shone below the heather clumps, bog cotton waved its white tufts and foxglove blushed on yellow clay banks. June brought the scent of wild burnet roses and yellow broom and long, delicate evening light.

Summer came, my clothes stuck to my back, riding breeches chafed, heavy boots wrinkled and dust worked up to my fuzzy hair, but there were white and pink blossoms of the rigid hawthorn and the rose of wild crab huddled for company with matted tops, and their sweet fragrance across the fields, with smells of mint, thyme and sweet briar. Berries in the hedges, poppies bright glossing pages of corn, sweet scent from the trams of hay in the air and a lingering waft of wild woodbine on the roadside hedges. I would be offered a large glass of fresh buttermilk from the churn when I stopped for a drink of water, or sometimes get a shout of welcome to drink from a can of tea, and back it with the soft buttered delight of a hot farl of cake or a slidder jack. There were nests of strong, rich, dark, wild honey to be searched for in the clipped meadow lands; I watched hunts for frightened rabbits or a hare gathered in trembling fright in the standing islands of large hay fields. The glint and sparkle of leaves and the contrast of their lighter undersides swaying in the breeze, the fur-fur of weeds startled into movement on the banks of a quiet stream or lake, the scarlet flick of a kingfisher or a bittern trailing slowly across a lonely marsh. Running water to be looked at from bridges. I watched it ripple over stones in the bed and, listening to its sound, was drawn slowly out of myself into its rhythm; tracing the eddies I followed a bank until at a bend the water became deep and quiet near one side. Water was always fascinating to watch, running with the light touch of reflected sun on its surface or sullen from the ruffle of wind gusts.

Up amongst the heather were mountain lakes, deep, old and knowing, with the serenity of old age; removed from the cares of the world, a prelude to the hills beyond. Mountains rounded or irregular, bare of wood, showing a recession of curve or a chain mass thrusting out in a drizzling rain separate echelons of its blended strength; hills, hazy, purple, mauve and lavender in the distance, changing colour as the day advanced; aloof or personal. Clouds forming, reforming, hanging still, drifting leisurely or moving swiftly with darkened menace, bog water with seemingly unfathomable depths, quiet, mysterious, the bare black wall of clean cut turf overhanging. Rosemary and the delicate smell of the thorny wild rose too easily wasted by the breeze, ferny larch leaves and willows taking solace near a pool, the quick skid of a wild duck taking water or the startled warning as the drake thrust forward into a swift feathery beat, wind like a cloud shadow tipping the barley ears and hairy rye, the duck's egg splash of lupin in un-expected ease and the glistening white of mushrooms, *fás na h-oidche*, growth of a night, against verdant grass after rain.

The cold spell before dawn, the morning star that often told us our watch was over as we lay under the ferns, and that the sun and not our sense of direction would be our guide, then the massed clouds and the first cold, faint streaks, rabbits jerking their white scuts among the weeds and grasses, the undulating form of a weasel slipping by or the shrill scream as the death cry of a rabbit rang out, the thin squeal of a field mouse and birds worming. A hum of insects as they tuned up for the day's orchestra, the harsh rattle of the corn crake or his hurried trot in the meadows, the chirp of young birds, meadow larks soaring higher in sound and space making the air thrill, grass-hoppers noising, tweets of a zig-zagging snipe in bottom lands and the tall stilted grey-blue form of a heron in the distance holding himself in dignified slimness.

Twilight, restful ease, the clear cut views of trees on skylines and the blurring of shapes, the thickening of the hazy plum-skin dusk, a swollen sun dropping quickly over the edge of sight, soft lowing cows driven homeward to be milked, house swallows diving from the eaves, the rattle of a cart in the distance, sometimes the honk of wild geese swift flying in a " V," and a wrench as I thought of the split wasted lives of our Wild Geese in foreign armies.

Night noises; rustles in the bushes and tall grass followed by silence that seems more hushed, the curlew with its sound of mournful remembrance echoing to die away slowly, the barking of dogs disturbed by something, which I could not see, or their attempts at conversation across the uplands, the drift of words coming out of the distance. The strong smell of turf, a homely smell that left its tang in the air, light shining warm and rosy from a window ledge out of the darkness, the murmur of the Rosary deepening as the family answered the response, the low furring of the owls in a startled ground flight, a hedgehog crossing the road. Trees thrusting upwards with added power or bulking sideways; they were arrogant at night, they filled the mind and they ruled the dark. Trees, shrubs, bushes and woods took possession and through them old nature showed its untamed strength and freshness and made us see how small we were, stars helped them to widen the external world. Familiar landscapes changed, hills played tricks in the moonlight and roads became mysterious.

Around the turf fires when the family had gone to bed I could hear the chirping of crickets as I sat on a low stool or settled back in the whitewashed seat inside the wide fireplace : were they not lucky even though they did eat socks hung out to dry—but only the socks of strangers. Beetles crawled across the flagstones, you'd be let off a year in purgatory if you stepped on one. Flitches of fat bacon hung from hooks in the ceiling, rows of delph mugs on the dresser reflected the turf light; then the covering of the glowing sods by fresh turf and white ashes so that the fire would itself slumber till morning.

Corn and hay cocks, chestnut flowers, the dripping mustard of locust trees shared the flaxen or gold hue with yellow rag weed and the heavy gold of meadow sweet. Lilac scented blue near tufted clusters of mauve rhododendron, oak leaves in a now startling green twisted their paler backed powder, tall avenues of beeches burnished smooth stems and brown twigs.

Autumn : grey still, placid days, windy skies and a whiff of yellow death in the air, the first cold leaves dropping to dance in form and pattern of their own, whins yellow on the hillsides glowing after rain against deep green luminous after-grass, rowan trees with the scarlet lips of their berries, and brambles of the blackberry bush torn when the soft fruit was reached for. The big bellied harvest moon floating heavily on still clear nights when one walked around anxious to avoid bed; the symphony of subdued colour on stacked oat sheaves, corn and cocks of hay, on meadow land and trees and hedges. The jagged branches of the sloe, almost black from underneath, showed the powdered blue dust of its berries, so did the damson and wild plum. Green linnets shot through thick leaf clusters in the orchards, golden-crested wrens pecked and thieving blackbirds chortled on the glossy, brown red boles of cherry trees. Starlings suddenly swooped on to a field in the evening to rest. Heather was thick on the mountain sides and moors; it was fine to stretch down on the earth and watch its mooded colours near by and see it merging into the clear cut blueness of distant, soft folded mountains. There was a stillness in the air as the evenings began to close in ; beech woods were leafy gold, delicate branches of the maidenly birch waved with a shivering nervous

stammer against velvety white bark ; oaks twisted their bare
limbs and fallen chestnut foliage rustled in a deep leaf whirl
underneath the stretching spread of the branches ; the wych-
hazel sprawled indolently proud of its yellow streamers.

October with its lash in the air, the snap of frost made
one feel extra strength and take deep virile breaths.   On
hardy nights I often fell from the bicycle trying to guide
myself and look up at the crackling stars.   Wet days when
soft, gentle rain fell unnoticed until one realized that
clothes had become sodden ; stinging rain that whipped
the face and stung, teeming on the land, but with a taut
challenge that one accepted.   Hands became blue on the
handlebars and, it was hard to draw a gun quickly, gloves
were in the way of a grip.   November brought more
stillness and the delicate softness of late autumn sky, with
its nonchalant disturbance by wind.   The bare strength of
the country showed lean and hardy, form was more emphasized with the dropping of the more eye-filling beauty
of colour and covering.   The austerity was softened by
wispy branches, slim grace, or the fantastic knarled,
twisted boles and out-thrusts of crab apple, oak and the
water-loving elm.

There was always a memory to help when I became
despondent ; the roads I mucked through had been
followed by many another trying to do what I was
attempting ; the hill I climbed or the townland I crossed
at night with a company at my heels had been named over
two thousand years ago and the tradition remained.   Ruins
in plenty ; ornamented stone crosses, a castle battered by
cannon or a shell from the torch, a gaping Romanesque
abbey or monastery, grave stones of an ancient university
centre ; a grass-ringed dún or lios, a dolmen, stone circle, gal-
láin, moat or stone fort, earlier monuments that took one
back.   Living Ireland was always present to strengthen with
its beauty when we became tired of it all and doubting, to
comfort us in despair and misfortune.

Winter again : looked forward to by some of the
people for its long evenings and chats around the fire or
dances, but dreaded by me for its long journeys in rain and
mud, draggled clothes clinging to the skin and drying as
one moved on the dreaded bicycle.   Always in the end,
however, there was the pleasant soothing of dead weariness

and utter exhaustion when one went to bed seemingly too
tired to sleep.

*   *   *   *

Through the country military were taking over work-
houses and courthouses for their troops, sand-bagged posts
commanded roads and the people farmed the land and
traded in the towns.

CHAPTER ELEVEN

MAY—JULY, 1920

★

DETECTIVES FROM the " G " Division had been shot on the
Dublin streets. Soon this important political intelligence
branch was reduced. They had always followed at the
heels of our men ; they knew all the important officers,
T.D.'s, and prominent men in other national organizations.
Now they moved about at bullets' risk.   I met Seán
Tracey's grin as he cycled past on a bicycle. He had grown
a thin moustache since I had met him with Breen and
Robinson in North Tipp. Séamus Robinson was given
to pedalling also. Both were on intelligence work ; they
were helping to reduce the number of detectives.

" We asked Michael Collins to send you to South Tipp.,"
said Seán. " He told us that Kerry had asked for you, but
we'll wear him down and we'll go back with you."

Collins now had another office in Dawson Street, in
Eileen McGrane's flat, where I often sheltered. He was
very busy. He was raising the Internal Loan, de Valera was
pushing the foreign loan in the United States ; but it
would be necessary to prove that the people at home were
willing to subscribe. I was due for Kerry, he said. We
went over a map of the county ; whilst he talked of the
names of battalion officers. " He's a good man, bloody
good, you know ; and he's a louser, but it'll be hard to get
rid of him." Later, in the dug-out he told me I was to
go to South Tipp. Raids were expected in Dublin. I had
seen men who looked like detectives near the dug-out.
Collins laughed : " We'll know when a raid is coming and
we'll have everything packed up."

Seán Tracey was Vice-Commandant and Seamus Robinson was Brigadier. They met me in Tipperary town where I held an officers' class. They had run into police at Goold's Cross on their way down but had fought through. The Brigade ran from East Limerick to the Kilkenny border beyond Carrick-on-Suir. On the South it was cut off by the Knockmealdown, Monavullagh and Comeragh mountains ; on the north were the hills above Hollyford, the plain of the Golden Vale and the Slieveardagh hills beyond Killenaule. There were eight battalions. South Tipperary lay across communications with the lower Shannon and the south-west. The land was fertile, there was hardly any bog and roads were numerous. Mountains rose sheer out of the plain as massives and the land close to the mountains, unlike that in Donegal or North Tipp., was good.

There were strong military barracks at Tipperary, Cahir, Clonmel, Cashel and Fethard. There were independent posts as well and police barracks. Tipperary town had over 1,000 troops between the barracks, rifle range and hutments, and Royal Irish Constabulary. The Sinn Féin Hall was our usual meeting place ; scouts watched the barracks, the movement of military and police, and guarded the approaches to our class. Men on the run carried side arms. We were never interrupted, though exciting reports came in at times, and there was an added intensity in my listeners.

We worked hard to build up a good intelligence system. On our knowledge of enemy movements and routine would depend largely the element of surprise in attack. We sent memoranda and suggestions to officers and men to help them to analyze, sift and rebuild information ; but reports were not forwarded : information had to be dragged out of the men. Often we sent them information of the strength and movements of garrisons in their areas. The officers could now see what force was pitted against the Volunteer strength in each locality. In the Tipp. battalion we would find ten of our rifles and thirty shotguns opposed to eleven hundred and fifty of the military and police ; in the next battalion three rifles and fifteen shotguns to eighty police carbines. There would be less excuse for lack of action in a battalion not held in strength by the enemy.

It was a satisfaction to have with me two who could think and act for themselves, and who were prepared to fight it out. They were good shots and without fear. We discussed the nature of the country, training and operations continuously, as we walked or cycled. I wanted to visit each battalion first, then plan operations for the Brigade.

Three was an ideal combination; two could always combine to attack the ideas of one or to poke fun. Seamus was pudgy and took short steps, which were hard on my long stride. Brown eyes helped a grin when he played on words; he liked to pun even to the limit of our groans. He had a slight clipping speech which came from Belfast, a stout stubborn underlip, sparse hair on a high round forehead. Seán was taller, an easy smile or a long grin showed his teeth. Glasses gave him a quiet appearance; he had a good strong-thrusting chin. His humour was dry enough.. He dealt with men quietly. I envied him his ease; yet he never allowed slackness to pass by.

Seamus had little sense of direction even in day time, and in country he had travelled through many times. He believed he had a good memory for country. At cross-roads there would be a discussion varying in degree of banter, helplessness or annoyance. Seamus would assert that this particular road was the way or short cut. He was always ready to debate the rightness of his way. The result was usually the same. Seán and I sat on a bank or lay hidden to watch his short form walk out of sight. We knew he would return when he had discovered his mistake to advance extenuating circumstances, or we might not meet him till night time.

During the day we eased the springs of our automatic magazines in turn by withdrawing cartridges. Automatics would have the hammer cocked with safety catch on; rifles, if we carried them, had a bullet in the breech. If we met trouble it would mean sudden, quick action in which every second counted. At night, revolvers or automatics in hand, we moved in file on foot along lanes and roads walking quietly; the collars of our coats buttoned up to cover the white of our throats.

When we were hungry we spoke of the good feeds we could have at certain houses. Seamus and Seán talked

lovingly of bacon and cabbage. Seán would smack his lips;
they both knew I hated the dish; the thought of it would
make a stretch of road bleak for me.

Our ancestors must have turned in their graves as they
listened to us. Why hadn't they fought as they should and
have ended the struggle? In the light of our experience
we cross-examined the dead, stripped them bone-bare of
romantic gloss and put ourselves in their places trying to
get the background of their times so that they could be
judged.

Why should we wear ourselves out we asked on wet
streaks of days or when we had finished a battalion class
at which most of the officers were absent without explanation or excuse? The idea of freedom would crop up
as we carefully studied the microscope of our maps and saw
the possibilities of the counties before us. Séamus was in
advance of us in thinking things out. We tried to peer
into the future.

Our fight was a beginning not an end we knew, but in
what direction would it go? We could not say. In the
country the small farmers and labourers were our main
support, and in cities the workers with a middle-class
sprinkling; towns we could not count on. The countryman, sympathetic enough where a land revolution was
concerned, was hostile to the revolution of organized
labour. The farm labourer could understand the city
workman, and was organized in labour unions with him.
The movement as a whole was hostile to labour claims even
though labour had helped to prevent conscription, had not
contested the last election, and was now refusing to carry
armed troops. In our minds Seán and I left the building
up to the Irish Republic to others. They might be hostile to
us we sensed; but we knew where our sympathies were:
with the labourer and small farmer in the country, the
workers in the city; but that definite belief would be again
covered by my latent gentility. I could feel my annoyance
at the convictions of purely revolutionary workers who
stood outside of the nationalist movement and a certain
amusement at their arguments. The "scrap," however,
kept us busy getting ready for action. Our generation we
often told each other would have to see this fight through,
release this dammed-up energy and our warped nationalistic

strivings and divert them to work out the direction that control of our own country would mean.

I was to administer the oath of allegiance to the Brigade officers ; they would then visit the battalions. I had never been asked to take the oath ; that would be a matter for someone on H.Q. Staff. Séamus was opposed to it. Why doesn't the Volunteer Executive call a convention to consider such an important step? Headquarters had no authority to hand over the control of the Army to Dáil Éireann ; the Executive is responsible to us. "To the Irish Republic and the Government of the Irish Republic which is Dáil Éireann"; "the Dáil might go wrong," he said, "it might accept less than a Republic. That clause should be omitted."

Seán and I laughed.

"I suppose the H.Q. Staff might go wrong also?" asked Seán.

"Yes, it might."

We laughed again. He looked at us somberly with a dour expression in his brown eyes and a pursing of his stubborn lip. He dissected things too much, we thought. He analysed orders, sought for motives. Mulcahy and Collins admired him, but they did not like him.

We sang old songs together, or whistled them when objections became too numerous. Séamus was trying to find a marching song for the Brigade. He would try out the notes. Seán's cracked spindle of a voice would join in and I would help the discord.

Sé do bheatha, a bhean ba léanmhar,
Do b'é ár gcreach thú bheith i ngéibhinn
Ár ndúthaigh bhreágh i seilbh méirleach
Díolta leis na Gallaibh.

Oró ! Sé do bheatha 'bhaile !
Bhfearr liom thú ná céad bó bainne
Oró ! Sé do bheatha 'bhaile !
Anois ar theacht a' tsamhraidh.

Tá Gráinne Mhaoil ag triall thar sáile,
Oglaigh armtha léi mar ghárda.
Gaedhil iad-féin, ní Gaill ná Spáinnigh
'S cuirfid ruaig ar Ghallaibh.

K

Welcome back woman of sorrow
We grieved for you in chains,
Our fair land controlled by robbers ;
Betrayed to the foreigner.

Ho there ! Welcome home !
Better you than a hundred cows.
Ho there ! Welcome home !
Now our summer comes to us.

Grace O Malley sails the sea
Guarded by armed youth,
Gaels are they, not English nor Spaniards
And they will rout the foreigner.

We sat to watch a stretch of country, to pick out a
distant hill with my field glasses and follow the undulations
of the land across hedge rows, clumps of trees and rises.
We listened to the song of a bird, throaty, unconcerned
with war or peace. We looked long from a height, then
studied our maps. Place names in Irish we attempted to
translate, or used the Joyce in my haversack when in doubt
about a proposed signalling or look-out station.

Séamus had not studied training, but he would take
nothing for granted. That meant long discussions about
points which had been gained by study, thought or experience. Seán and I handed him the more detailed
organization of the intelligence service. He could draw
up circulars and forms to his heart's content. We two went
together now to battalion councils and to discussions on
training and operations with staffs.

We distributed one-inch contoured maps. The battalions
had first to define their areas and dispute the overlapping
parishes next, then companies would fill in their maps, and
finally the sections. We listened to many hard fights over a
stretch of road or a piece of a river. The officers had now
in concentrated form the extent and condition of their areas;
they could read into them the possibility of development.
I set map problems for them and tried to make them believe
a map was one of their most important military aids.

Our dispatches were carried on trains by guards, firemen,
enginemen; by road through travellers and vans, from
brigade to battalion headquarters, and from company to
company by our dispatch riders. The British had control

of telegraphic and telephonic communications, the postal service and, indirectly, the press. They used codes and ciphers in army or police messages. Lorries and aeroplanes carried their dispatches; there were wireless sets in the barracks. We could never hope to compete with their communication system. We could tap telephones on the roadsides or through friendly operators get copies of code messages, but the decoding would have to wait until a policeman gave us the changing codeword or our own Headquarters sent it to us.

We inspected positions that might prove useful in attack or defence, noted sniping, signalling and good ambush places, took ranges. I brought officers on staff rides and tactical tours. I tried to make them familiar with the country they knew, from the angle of possible action.

Training they were interested in. It was something new and it gave them more confidence. The applied use of weapons was not difficult for me to impart, but with rifles and machine guns there was a deal of musketry theory to be taught. The use of ground in relation to movement and formation was easy, especially in scouting and reconnaissance. The applied tactics of weapons in relation to protective formation, ground and movement was harder.

The officers were not accustomed to handling men; only by actual fighting would some of them gain assurance. In their mind I knew they thought guerilla warfare should be waged without any regular army groundwork in technique applied to their own organization and mentality; thus they would not know how the unit opposed to them would be prepared to act. Some small idea of actuality was induced by tactical exercises or manoeuvres with an objective in mind close to what we could expect in our type of fighting. Men would realize for the first time as they crawled through wet grass or tried a night advance on a town that the time for easy going drill nights was over and that parade routine had another aspect.

The trouble began when they attempted to train their men. They were eager to learn, but officers lost confidence in themselves when they began to teach. They did not continue to read their notes or to meet together to clear up difficulties. Often, I listened in anguish to officers run a series of progressive lectures of mine into one rapid sketch of packed sentences.

There was a great contempt for the English as fighting men. It helped untrained boys to operate against opponents who had been maintained in the profession of arms, but experience would train them to estimate enemy courage and efficiency in their future appreciations of situation.

We handled our weapons constantly to get the feel of of them, and practised at odd moments with empty guns, a used cartridge case prevented abuse of the hammer action. We learned to disarm one another when suddenly held up, practised snapping at moving objects and at sounds or flashes in the dark. We made wooden grenades of the same size as the hand grenades used by the British, small ones like the egg grenades of the police, and large ones like our own G.H.Q. grenades. We weighted them with lead and taught officers and men to throw with some kind of accuracy.

Moving across country, we studied patrol formations, the use of cover, learned visual training and judging distances, worked out the various forms of fire that might be brought to bear on imaginary enemies in different formations ; we learned to run with full kit and to advance without losing breadth. We were often accompanied by officers from battalions through which we moved and we taught them what we knew.

We were attempting to instruct our people, who, with the brief exception of the Cromwellian and Williamite wars, had been disarmed since the time of Elizabeth. Most of them had never had rifles or revolvers in their hands ; hardly any had seen hand grenades. A number knew the shot gun, but since 1916 there was not much ammunition ; a few had used explosives in quarry work. There was not enough miniature ammunition to allow the men to practise. It would be difficult to build up confidence in a weapon unless a man was thoroughly familiar with it or believed in it.

The uncertainty of raids by police and military made houses unsafe to hide weapons in. Floors were now torn up, drawers turned upside down ; mattresses, thatch, ricks and oats were stabbed with bayonets. The country was damp from outside rains. It was hard to get proper arm dumps built, and harder still to have the quartermasters inspect weapons regula-ly to prevent rust and ill care. Few knew the mechanism of the collection of weapons to be found within one of our Brigade areas. British long and short Lee-Enfields, police carbines, Lee-Metfords, single shot Martini-Henris, Sniders, Remingtons, Winchesters, German, Turkish or Spanish Mausers, French Lebels, American Springfields, Japanese patterns, Austrian Steyers and Mannlichers, old flint muskets, muzzle-loading Queen Annes. Revolvers: the Webley, Colt, Smith and Wesson, Harrison Richardson, bulldog patterns. Automatics: the Naval Webley-Scott, Colt, Browning, German Mauser or Parabellum, Steyer. Machine guns were rare: Parabellum, Vickers and the German Spandau, the French Hotchkiss, the Lewis gun. There was gunpowder, gelignite, dynamite, blasting powder and odd slabs of guncotton. All these had been bought, captured in action or taken in raids on private houses. It was impossible to extract a reliable list of names, arms and stuff from a brigade Q.M. Companies were afraid the battalion wanted to distribute some of their arms to other companies; the battalion was afraid the brigade would transfer stuff to other battalions. The brigade always made the poor mouth to G.H.Q. to extract more arms. Short of being a very competent fortune teller I could not assess a brigade's armament.

We had to fight against carelessness, faulty method, sloppiness, lack of confidence and bad schooling. In rural schools boys had been taught to be good clerks or civil servants. They had not been trained to solve the living problems of their agricultural settings. Men did as their grandfathers had done, thinking in brawn: " fine, upstanding men they were, God bless them, eating nothing but praties and buttermilk, and they could mow or swing a flail the live long day." Often they were cocksure and bombastic; they had nothing to learn and they suspected all ideas.

I was a captain on Headquarter's Staff, impressed with my own energy and snappishly eager to pass on my approach to military procedure and technique which I had studied, and then resolved in my mind. The reality of the fight was covered in their minds, they thought in terms of the land, blurring their sense of responsibility with slipshod attendance at councils and classes. There was an inability to become aware of the extent of their resources in people, in the nature of the countryside and in their men. I knew well they thought I was a bloody nuisance and a red-headed bastard—this out of ear range; my periodic swoops could be smoothed out by an after lull.

In Tipp., landlords' estates had been broken up and there were many small holdings. The men were more independent; the houses neater and better built than in other counties I had visited. The men were tall and quiet; they had a deal of purpose and were dependable.

* * * *

We moved into the hilly country near Glenough where the people were sound. They were aloof from the towns and they did not talk. I called up men for a two-days' course of training. I intended to form them into a reserve to be used later as a small column. Now we had six men armed with rifles. We cycled around the hills. People came to the half-doors to look at us in wonder, but they would have to get used to the open bearing of arms. It was strange for us to have rifles slung across our shoulders and khaki ammunition slings slanted on our chests.

There was a police barracks on a pass in the hills at the village of Hollyford. The Hollyford captain described the barracks, but I had no clear picture in my mind. I walked to the pass. The road below ran with a stream through a cut; above and below the village the hill slopes were steep. Houses straggled on either side of the road; the barracks looked down on thatched roofs and zinc outhouses. It was a high two-storied, white-washed building, larger than the usual barracks and long. There were many windows protected by steel shutters; loopholes were cut in the walls. In front a porch jutted out with slits for rifles. The gable-end near the road had a window high up and loopholes on the ground floor; a lean-to building about fourteen feet high, loopholed, ran from the gable-end to the rear. On the far side of the road was a rugged stone wall. It would give us a little cover. The gable-end might be blown in with explosives.

Séamus, Seán and I talked with the Hollyford captain that evening in a small slated house a mile from the village.

He had close on a half-hundred of gelignite, a little blasting powder, a few pound of gunpowder, a good supply of fuze and two boxes of detonators.

"Is the gelignite in good condition?" I asked the captain.

"I don't know but I'll see."

"And bring all the fuze and explosives you have," said Séamus.

We looked at my map, picking out the police and military barracks marked in coloured inks. My note book gave their strengths. Within nine miles were four barracks; within less than fourteen miles were Shevry, Kilcommon, Annacarty, Cappaghwhite, Doon, Dundrum and Rearcross. Pallas, a large barracks, was twenty miles away, Goold's Cross and Tipperary twenty, and Newport twenty-seven. There were military garrisons also at Dundrum, Tipperary and Newport. Newport and Tipperary were the chief danger. We pencilled places where the roads had best be blocked to hold up their reinforcements.

The gelignite was frozen. Two men put on pots of water in the kitchen to thaw it whilst we talked in another room. There were eight rifles in the battalion; ours made thirteen; about twenty rounds for each rifle and four hand grenades. There were ten or twelve police in Hollyford.

The woman of the house made tea and potato cakes for us. We sat at the kitchen fire. Jim Gorman, lieutenant of Hollyford, blinked the rain from his eyebrows as he shook himself on the flagstones.

"The ground floor of the barracks is six feet higher than the ground outside; you might as well try to shift the Rock of Cashel," he said. Gorman had leathern jaws tight with lines, and blue eyes glinting out of a tanned face. He was an Irish-Australian. He had fought through the world war and was a crack shot. He had assurance. He could curse better than any man in the hills. We decided to burn out the garrison by an attack from the roof. We had, none of us, tried to burn out a garrison before.

Next day we cut time-fuse in lengths, crimped them into detonators and made improvised grenades from tin cans packed with scrap iron around a stick of gelignite. I made "bursting charges" by filling mustard tins with explosives. They would, if tied to a stick, blow off slates and be effective when dropped close to men. We cleaned shot guns, rifles and ammunition, took Mills' grenades apart and oiled the springers. Ladders were collected but none were tall enough. The gable end was forty feet high. Two long ladders were made by splicing two shorter ones together. A mason, who had been a sailor, saw to that. I trained a group of men in ladder-drill in the evening and after dark by making them hoist the long ladders perpendicularly and place them against the high gable of a house near by. Soon they were reasonably proficient; every man knew his place.

At 11 o'clock cyclists told us that Volunteers on the outposts had begun to fell trees and to put stone barricades across roads. They would cut telegraph and telephone wires at midnight. As I inspected outposts in the Kilcommon direction I met Jim Gorman. There was a good position in the pass, but no stones or trees near.

"Can you block the way quickly?" I asked.

"Yes," he said, kicking a pile of picks and shovels with his foot. "I can have them throw the road over the ditch."

Séamus and I were to climb the ladders. Seán Tracey would take charge of the attacking party below, seven riflemen and five shotguns. We walked quietly towards the village, picked men carried the ladders, others had zinc buckets of paraffin oil. We halted close to the barracks. There would be a night guard on duty. There were lights in a few houses.

Séamus and I had two revolvers each, grenades, bursting charges, supplies of fuse, detonators and hammers to smash the slates. On our backs a tin of petrol was tied, sods of turf which had been soaked in oil hung around our necks from cords. The oil sopped into our clothes. The men with the ladders took off their boots; they tied them around their necks. When Seán's men had found positions that commanded the windows we moved towards the gable. The ladders were placed in position. Séamus's was to one side, mine against the chimney. I intended to sit on top of it so that I could fire through the roof. I hoped the peelers would not use their rifles through the flue. Buckets of paraffin and petrol were placed on the ground near the ladders. I told the men to get back as we began to climb slowly, weighed down by our supplies. They refused; not until we were on the roof. They were in danger. They had no cover. The loopholes looked down on them.

We crawled on to the roof, smashed slates with hammers, poured in petrol from our tins. We lighted sods of turf and threw them through gaps. Flames came with a yellow roar. We crawled further along the roof banging with hammers. I lighted the fuzes of two bursting charges. We lay flat on the roof. Then came two loud explosions, bits of slates flew; a piece hit me on the head. Police fired rifles and revolvers. We poured in more petrol.

Flames flaunted out of the darkness. We got back to the edge of the roof. Below I saw flashes through the loopholes; police grenades burst. I climbed to the chimney; the top was cemented over. I sat dangling my legs. Shots were fired from the partition walls of the barracks. I used up both revolvers, reloaded and emptied again. The police fired through the roof of the lean-to building. I lay flat on the chimney. We emptied our tins of petrol. There were great holes in the slate roof; smoke and flames were blown by the wind against, and away from us. Our hands were burnt. Séamus brought up buckets from below. I helped to carry them up and we poured them in. Jim Gorman dashed across with two rattling bucketsful. I flung in grenades; the second rolled and caught in the eaves. As I gripped the hot slates I shouted to Séamus who was coming up the ladder; his head was on a level with the roof when the grenade exploded. It deafened him. I had told the man below not to shout. A silent attack would make the defenders feel the unknown quality of it; it would unsteady their nerves and make them more uncertain in the darkness of what was to come next. Below now I heard men taunt the police and shout. My language out-coloured the flames, but the shouting continued.

I went down for a rifle. Police had been firing at us through the roof; splinters of slate had been splashed about by bullets. I fired a few clipfuls through the roof of the lean-to from the top of the chimney and down into the building itself. That must have driven them out beyond the partition wall.

The remainder of the building would not catch. We tried to get across by the eaves but the heat drove us back. We splashed in our last two buckets of petrol. Flames rushed up suddenly and cut across the ladders. I got to the chimney. I could see Séamus on his ladder clinging to the ledge. My hands and face were burning hot, my hair caught fire; I rubbed my hands through it. My coat was alight. I could not get down the ladder through the fire; neither could Séamus. This looks like the end, I thought, as I lay flat on the chimney whilst the flames waved and thrust forward with the wind. I fired quickly into the roof, the rifle was hot. "Good-bye Séamus," I shouted. "*Slán leat*," he said.

I could see a snatch of hills near by and the thatched roofs of houses. Above them was light across the racing clouds. I began the chorus of "The Soldiers' Song," but I changed the words:

"The barracks now is burning slow
See in the East a silvery glow."

The flames went down. Séamus and I met on our ladders. "O golly," he said, "I'm all burnt."

Dawn came slowly. Towards the rear there was steady shooting. I climbed down and crawled to the back of the barracks. One of our men from Kilcommon was firing ecstatically at a loophole in a steel shutter. There was a pile of empty cases beside him. Stammering through a whirl of curses in my mind I stopped. He looked too pleased for me to let fly, but he knew what I felt from my face. "Don't fire again until you see a peeler's head," I said. "You know damn well how scarce amm. is."

At the beginning of the attack the police had sent up rockets and Verey lights. Séamus was nervous about military reinforcements. Seán and I argued with him. Our outposts, he said, would not be able to hold up an attack now that it was day. Reluctantly we went up the hill. When we reached a crest we looked back. Smoke drifted slowly in the cool early morning wind; the police still drove off imaginary attackers.

Séamus and I looked at each other. The hair was burnt off his head, his face was black, red and blistered; he had no eyebrows. My face felt strange. My eyelashes and eyebrows had gone; there were raised ridges on my face and head and on the back of my neck; my hands stung most of all. Our clothes were burnt in patches, and soaked with oil and petrol. We laughed at each other whilst we wrung our hands in pain. We had failed to capture any rifles, but we had driven in that post.

Séamus, Seán and I cycled in the wide valley between the Galtees and Knockmealdowns. We had been refused a bed in two houses. Seán and Séamus meant trouble people knew. Police and military had often combed the South Riding for them; there were two nooses waiting. "Let's try Tincurry," Seán said. Mrs. Tobin greeted Seán and Séamus with both of her hands. "How is every bit of you," she said, "you're heartily welcome; but Glory be to God, what happened to your faces?"

Séamus, Seán, the battalion commandant and I waited for half an hour for the Burnfort Company at Rehill; it was to burn the rifle range. We walked up the slope carrying picks and shovels. The night was cold. We turned up the collars of our coats. "Maybe they have forgotten," said Seán, in quiet disgust "or there's a dance somewhere."

"We'd best start," I said, " and do as much damage as we can." We cut up and buckled the wire of moveable figures, smashed targets, broke up posts. As we went towards the trenches higher up we heard voices singing " The Soldiers' Song."

" Go down to the road, and bring up those songsters at the double," I said.

Seán walked into the darkness. Later we heard a sharp "Halt," then two shots and scattered firing. A pause, and then controlled volley firing. The bullets whizzed up the hill. We lay close to earth. That's strange, I thought, what are they firing at? Our men couldn't have that number of rifles.

" I hope nothing has happened to Seán," said Séamus. " But why should the men sing " The Soldiers' Song?" It must be the military and they'll come up the hill. We'll cross to The Glen."

I watched Séamus and the commandant go up the mountain. I was anxious about Seán, but I did not know what to do. I did not know the mountains well. If I got close to the road I might find out something.

Later I heard horses trotting up and down, then the sharp snap of an order. Cavalry from Cahir Barracks. I lay amongst ferns trying to keep myself warm.

The dawn was slow in coming, ferns rustled with a cold ground breeze and clouds like muffled glass were lighted from overhead in the East. Near me a tawny hare slowly stood up its long ears like a wooden toy, a quiver ran along its flank; a vixen played with three brown cubs and rolled them on the grass; she barked with delight. Edges of plantations and tops of evergreen stood out; mist rolled away in the valley, and I could see hedge enclosures and houses. I crossed the road. If I could pick out the bronze-red sheen on the copper beech in the front lawn of Tin-curry it would be easy to cross country towards it; but I was too far away to see it. I crossed a by-road. Two cavalry men on rising ground beyond a bend in the road saw me as I got to the hedge. They galloped down, shouting. I ran back across the bohereen and lay down behind the stump of a fallen tree within fifty yards of the road. I gripped my revolver with both hands for distant fire. I heard the crash of their horses through the hedge on the far side of the road. Like Brer Rabbit, of our childhood books, I lay low. I heard them gallop away.

Smoke was rising from a chimney in Tincurry. Mrs. Tobin came out when I shouted from beyond the stream. "Glory be to God, it's you," she said. "Well . . . well . . . well! Come in and warm yourself; you must be perished with the hunger. I'll ready the breakfast." She swung a black kettle on a crane above the embers. "When you left the house last night I knew something would happen, so I took your books and papers off the carrier on the back of your bicycle and hid them. It was well I did. Two hours later police and military from Cahir brought me out of my bed. They searched the house upside down and they asked me about the bicycle, but I said it belonged to some of the workmen. They were hardly gone when in comes Seán. 'Did Ernie or Séamus come?' says he. 'No,' says I. Then he told me the whole story. You remember the time you sent him down to the road? Well, he heard the men singing and when he got close, he shouted to them 'Shut up,' and then 'Halt,' for they were marching towards Cahir. He ran after them and there he saw tin hats; Tommies, he said to himself, and he opened fire. The soldiers threw themselves down in all directions and they fired all round them." She stopped for breath, her cheeks shone with eagerness. "But that isn't the best of it. When Seán was making for Tincurry across the fields, who did he meet but two of the Burnforts trying to smash their handcuffs with a stone and they spancelled like two goats, God help them; then they told *their* story.

"They were late for the drilling and whilst they waited for the rest of the men to come, up marched the soldiers from Cahir and took them all prisoners—about thirty of them. They handcuffed them arm to arm, then the soldiers, if you please, stood round and sang ' The Soldiers' Song,' and they knew it, too. Seán, as I told you fired, the soldiers were thinking of their sweet selves and the boys got away, all save two. And that's my story from start to finish. Did you ever hear the like of it? Wasn't it grand? " She beamed as she poured out tea. Twelve-year old, fuzzy-haired Eva, who had often scouted the neighbouring roads on her bicycle, came down stairs. She had to hear the story too. Her speckled grey eyes lit up with joy: " Oh, show me your revolver," she begged. She tramped about the house in my Sam Brown and imitated the accents of the raiding officers from the barracks. Two days after there was a heading in the paper: " Two Hundred Armed Men Attack Military Patrol. Attack Beaten Off, Prisoners Captured."

I went to the towns to sketch the posts and check up on the routine of barrack life. I examined Clogheen workhouse which was held by military, and the police barracks. I made rough sketches, then cycled on to the next barracks, Ballyporeen. A girl driving a pony and trap halted me.

" Are you afraid of police? " she asked.

" No."

She drove on. That question was unusual, I thought, when she was out of sight. There might be a catch in it; but she might be all right. I cycled after her. I came up with the trap.

" Why did you ask me was I afraid of police? "

" I don't know. You're the first person I stopped."

" But, why? "

" There are police lying in ambush behind the walls outside of Ballyporeen barracks."

I thanked her and asked her name. She was from Mitchelstown, County Cork.

*   *   *   *

Ostracization of the Royal Irish Constabulary had been enforced for over a year. They would not be served with drink or food stuffs in many shops ; people would not speak to them. Their patrols were disarmed and barracks taken by surprise ; individual police who pointed out houses and men to the military were shot down. Many police resigned; there were not recruits enough to fill their places. Their Inspector-General had been given indefinite leave of absence. The Deputy Inspector-General had been *replaced* by an Advisor, a British General. Four Divisional Commissioners, military men, had been appointed to more thoroughly militarize the R.I.C. The commander of the troops, Shaw, was superseded by General Macready. Shaw had asked for more troops. He wanted to impose martial law through Ireland, but it was not the policy of the British Government to admit that there was a serious situation in Ireland. They had another trick in the bag.

Macready at a Cabinet meeting was assured of full support for his campaign. A Divisional Commissioner, Smyth, had put it up to police in Kerry to shoot Republicans. Some threw off their uniform tunics. Smyth had to seek protection in another room of the barracks. All the Royal Irish were not thoroughly dependable now. Later Smyth was shot dead in his club in Cork City. In England ex-service men were recruited for service in Ireland by advertisements in the paper. Brigadier-General Tudor, who had reorganized and improved police transport was responsible for recruiting. A knowledge of modern warfare was their chief contribution to the maintenance of law and order. They wore khaki tunics and black-green trousers whilst awaiting their R.I.C. uniforms. The people called them the " Black and Tans." That also was the name of a hunting pack of beagles in County Tipperary. It was felt that they would quickly suppress what was known as " disorder." They had burnt and bombed some shops and houses in County Tipperary.

*   *   *   *

Séamus, Seán and I were in the pleasant valleys of the Comeragh mountains on the Waterford side of the river

Suir. We were busy annexing a strip of another county, forming companies and strengthening our position on the northern mountain watershed before the Waterford Brigade would wake up. Strategically, this area should belong to South Tipperary, but the Waterford men would have less cause for complaint if it was organized before they knew of its possibilities.

Séamus and I cycled past military road posts and fortified barracks in East Clare; we left Seán behind to prepare an attack on Drangan barracks which would take place three days later. Mick Brennan intended to blow in an end wall of Sixmilebridge barracks; he wanted our advice about the demolition.

Brennan, and visiting officers from across the yellow Shannon, thawed out gelignite whilst we lay out on the thick green of the dykes above the carcas grass. Near by, Brigadier-General Lucas, who had been captured by Liam Lynch in North Cork, was a prisoner.

The Buffs and the Flying Corps had broken loose in Fermoy after his capture. They had the honour of being the first to seriously destroy property and wreck shops. In his honour a song " Can anybody tell me where the Blarney Roses Grow? " had been changed :

" Can anybody tell me where did General Lucas go,
He may be down in Mitchelstown or over in Mayo? "

We had warned the officers about the poisonous fumes which nitroglycerine exudes; they gave what we called " gelignite head," a terrible roof-splitting pain. When we came back to the house we found a number of the men yellow green ; their stomachs heaved in dry spasms, but others kept at the thawing.

I was in charge of the attack now. There was not enough gelignite thawed out and local men who could have helped me, were at a distance ready to block roads and carry out feint attacks on other posts to divert reinforcements. I had to send dispatch riders to call off the men moving up to Sixmilebridge. I knew that an attack was due on Kilmallock in East Limerick that night, but Séamus and I would have to cross the yellow Shannon by boat and we would find difficulty in getting through our own outposts in the night. We cursed Mick Brennan and his lack of thought. We would have had to work our way up to the shop beside the barracks where I had meant to detonate petrol tins with the gelignite. The explosion might have been as serious for Séamus and me as for the police, I thought, as I went to bed.

Next day Séamus and I hurried back to be in time for Drangan close to the Kilkenny border. On the Limerick road three lorries of Tans and R.I.C. came up. They were shouting, singing and shooting off their rifles. There was no cover nearby; we would have to draw quickly if they halted us. The lorries kept the middle of the road; red flags were tied to some of the rifles. Near the sandbagged road post at Pallas a man told us about the attack on Kilmallock in East Limerick the night before. The barracks had been completely destroyed. Police had retreated to a bomb-proof shelter; some of them had been killed. A punitive expedition from Limerick had just burned the co-operative creamery and many houses. They had shot up and bombed the town.

Late in the evening we found Seán in a house close to the small town of Drangan. He had incendiary mixtures and a supply of yellow clay, "yallow ouy," it was called. The clay when thrown against a vertical wall would adhere. By moulding it around a half stick of gelignite with detonator and fuze attached, it became a grenade which would stick to a steel place. We had used mud bombs on the roofs of deserted farms. They blew off a great patch of slates.

Seán had seen the barracks; next door was a one-story house commanded by the loopholes. We could smash through that roof, put up a ladder, climb it, break the police roof and use a pump attached to a barrel of inflammable material.

Seán had no plan of the village; by the time we were ready to move up there were no local men to guide us. I set off with four men from another battalion to see if it was possible to use the houses opposite the barracks. We carried picks and jumpers. We blundered in the dark across fields and ditches until we reached a high wall. It was opposite the barracks. The men took off their boots. They could find the best places on the wall to loophole later; I told them not to talk. As I left a house I heard voices roaring "Surrender," followed by a rattle of revolver shots. I was run into by one of our men who was rushing away in panic. I opened fire at the flashes and followed up until I ran into barbed wire which dug into my face.

A police patrol had heard our men talking and had surprised them from behind. One man was wounded; I bandaged him under a flashlight, and gave him a tabloid of morphia to ease the pain. There would be no element of surprise in the attack now. We moved cautiously up the street. We had reached the small house beside the barracks when the police threw grenades and used their rifles. We smashed the roof of the small house, climbed through the hole and concentrated automatic fire on the loopholes above us whilst we hauled up the ladder and a barrel of oil. We threw mud bombs on to the police roof and used tubing which was tied to a length of wood to make it firm. Soon the roof caught fire.

We could hear ammunition exploding inside as the flames got to it and we cursed hard. Séamus wanted to ask the police to surrender. I was against that. They should not be asked until we had an alternative in case they would not. As we collected jumpers and picks to make a hole through the wall on the first story, I heard "Hello, hello, there."

"What do you want?"

"We want to talk with you."

"All right. Put out a flag and I'll stop our fire."

A shirt tied to a rifle was stuck out a front window. Séamus called me back as I started to walk over to the barracks. "It may be a trap. I wouldn't trust them. They might shoot you."

"If they do, rush the place when you make an opening and shoot what's left of them."

I talked through the slit in a steel plate. The police were afraid we would shoot them, they said. "We won't shoot you; but come out quick before any more of the ammunition explodes." They asked for ten minutes to talk it over amongst themselves. At the end of five minutes they walked out; one was in khaki. Their names were taken. It would go hard with them if they were captured a second time, they were told. They were ordered to march in single file down the road out of the village and warned, like Lot's family, on no account to look back.

The barracks was raked for equipment, ammunition and papers. We handled the shining carbines and long Lee-Enfields and compared them with some of our worn rifles; several large boxes of ammunition had been set off by the flames. A *History of Ireland* in a green cover specially written for the Royal Irish was found; one boy going through letters for information came upon a girl's letter to the sergeant. She had signed herself " Your little lump of love." The men sat down on the sandbags swaying with joy. The fat peeler and his little lump of love. A doctor bandaged two other boys and myself who had been burnt; the rest of the wounded had already been cared for.

We cycled away. The military should be due now. People who had listened to the firing were waiting outside their houses on the roadside. They gave us milk; they wanted us to stop for a sup of tea. We waited at several cross-roads for enemy reinforcements; then we went on to get through the net.

> At Sologbeg the war began,
> And next was heard the song
> Of the rescue of Seán Hogan
> At the station of Knocklong.
>
> Soon after Hunt, the bully, fell,
> Races day in Thurles town.
> It broke the hearts of peelers
> For miles the country round.
>
> From Thurles town to Galtees brow
> All peelers turned pale
> When the boys attacked the barracks
> At the call of Graine Ua Uaile.
>
> From hill to hill that winter's night
> Did speed the rifles ball;
> We won at Rea and Hollyford
> But failed at Drumbane Hall.
>
> The Rag we need not mention,
> There we lost a comrade true;
> They may trample on his body,
> But his spirit ne'er subdue.
>
> By peelers' hands MacCarthy fell;
> In sainted ground he sleeps,
> 'Neath the ancient walls of Holy Cross
> Where Suir's bright water creeps.

All true men miss them sorely
And their death they do deplore
Three hirelings for them suffered
In the groves of Lackamore.

We'll drink a health to every man
Who treads in death's pathway;
Drink up my boys, get ready,
'Tis the rising of the day.

CHAPTER TWELVE

★

DÁIL ÉIREANN functioned slowly. It appointed consuls, floated a foreign loan which was increased to £1,000,000, and closed the home loan of £250,000 with a surplus of £40,000. Twenty papers were suppressed for publishing the loan prospectus. People were arrested for having a copy of it. A commission of inquiry sat to probe the resources and industries of Ireland with Darrell Figgis as secretary; committees inquired into fisheries, dairying and the meat industry. The Commission played hide and seek with the police. British troops held approaches to the building where the meeting was advertised to be held whilst it sat quietly in another part of the city. The results of its investigation were not allowed to be published in the Press by the British Censor, and its industrial exhibitions were suppressed. Daily news bulletins were sent to the foreign press from the Publicity department; attempts were made to open direct trading with Irish ports. A Land Bank was organized. The members of the Dáil took an oath of allegiance to the Irish Republic; the Dáil was proclaimed.

" Whereas, as by special proclamation dated July 3, 1918, in pursuance and by virtue of the Criminal Law Procedure of Ireland Act of 1887, be declared from the date thereof certain associations in Ireland known by the names of Sinn Fein organization, Sinn Fein clubs, Irish Volunteers, Cumann na Ban and Gaelic League to be dangerous. And whereas the association known by the name of Dail Eireann appears to us to be a dangerous association and to have been after the date of said special proclamation employed for all purposes of the association known by the names of Sinn Fein organization, Sinn Fein Clubs, Irish Volunteers and Cumann na Ban, now we, the Lord Lieutenant-General and General Governor of Ireland, by and with the advice of the Privy Council in Ireland, by virtue of the Criminal Law and Procedure of Ireland Act of 1887, and of every power and authority in this behalf, do hereby, by this our order, prohibit and suppress within the several districts specified and named in the schedule the association known by the name of Dail Eireann."

In December, Lord French, the Lord Lieutenant, and his armed escort was attacked, but he managed to get through unwounded. Tracey, Robinson, Hogan and Dan Breen, all from South Tipperary, had been amongst the attacking-party.

In January of 1920 there were municipal and urban elections; eleven out of twelve cities and boroughs and ninety-two out of one hundred and sixteen towns returned majorities for the Republic. From now on the British had a new objective in public bodies. Thomas MacCurtain, Lord Mayor of Cork, was murdered by R.I.C.; other mayors received death notices. Later the Mayor of Limerick was murdered. Lloyd George sheltered those responsible for " unofficial " reprisals. Two Republicans were to be shot for every soldier, spy or policeman killed. It was hoped that this policy would break down resistance. Police and military gangs killed Irishmen to produce an effect on the people; they selected victims who were in many cases inoffensive. Irish Volunteers, now known as the Irish Republican Army, shot down police who pointed out houses for gangs and raiding parties, high police and military officials, and people who were trying to seize Dáil moneys deposited in banks. The I.R.A. stood over their shootings: the British did not.

Wilson, Chief of the Imperial General Staff, wanted to double the police force and throw on it the burden of trying to restore order. The use of police would make the outside world believe they were suppressing crime. Wilson was not in favour of unofficial reprisals or shootings. He wanted " shooting by rooster," and demolitions carried out officially by the military.

In April the British prepared for another Easter rising ; on the eve of Easter Sunday the I.R.A. destroyed three hundred and fifty evacuated barracks, burnt court houses, and Customs' offices, raided Customs and Revenue and Income Tax offices for papers. Practically no income tax was collected from this on. County Councils refused to help surveyors to assess the tax and later in the cities corporations would not give the required information.

R.I.C. and military burnt five co-operative creameries, four of them in Mid-Tipperary. There was a hunger strike of prisoners in Mountjoy; Greenwood, the Chief Secretary, said they could starve; there would be no release. Irish Labour ordered a one-day general strike; next day, the eighth day of hunger strike, workers' committees organized food supplies for the general public, but the prisoners were freed.

In May dock labourers and transport union men refused to handle munitions; English labour would not ship munitions to Poland for use against Russia; it shipped them to Ireland. Drivers of railway trains refused to carry armed police, soldiers or munitions. They were dismissed; their successors were dismissed. By July two thousand had been given notice; their resistance continued for eight months.

Justices of the Peace resigned; there was no one to replace them at Petty Sessions Courts; magistrates resigned, though not in numbers. Republican Parish Courts had three justices elected by representatives of local bodies, I.R.A. and Sinn Féin clubs; Parish Courts corresponded to the Petty Sessions Courts; District Courts corresponded to British county courts. There were five District Judges; elected by the men who presided at Parish courts. Within four days the Parish court could appeal to the District; their decrees were enforced by the I.R.A., and later by Republican Police attached to companies. The Republican Minister of Justice had standardized organization and procedure. In a period of thirteen days forty-one courts were held, and eighty-four arrests made by the I.R.A.

The arresting of criminals meant additional work for the I.R.A. which had to select men in each area for public duties, but the people actively helped them to track down wrong-doers. The people were our intelligence system in this respect, and our public opinion. Republican Police raided for and smashed poteen stills, made public-houses

observe licensing laws, kept order at racecourses and carried
out patrol duty.

These prisoners were a drain on us; they had to be kept
on islands or in boggy and remote parts; they were, in the
newspaper phrase, "removed to an unknown destination."
The local company had to feed them, use their arms to guard
them and send out scouts to protect the guards from raiding
parties who would release the prisoners and arrest the guards;
but often enough the prisoners would again surrender.

Guards never thought of themselves as jailers; there was
an old sympathy with the hunted. They played cards
with them, smoked, chatted and swapped stories. The
officers responsible had to watch their own men as well as
their prisoners and protect both from surprise. None of us
liked to have to keep or guard prisoners. Once I found the
guard asleep in a deserted house whilst their prisoners were
out on sentry duty with shot guns.

British county courts were practically deserted; cases
listed for appeal to the Judges who made visits at the
assizes were withdrawn. They had already been dealt with
by Republican courts. Men listed for jury duty would
not attend the assizes or inquests held in military barracks.
Witnesses and magistrates were kidnapped and held until
the court was over. Courthouses were protected by sandbags, barbed wire and garrisons. The decrees of the
British courts too often needed a small expeditionary force.
In the country scouts guarded Republican courts; imperialists, reporters and solicitors who attended were
committing a criminal offence; the armed scouts were
protecting imperialists from the soldiers.

Parish and District courts settled cases quickly on their
merits; there was no forensic eloquence; common sense
and good will replaced involuted legal formulas. Justice
was elemental, strict, but impartial and human; costs
were low. Sentences varied from fines and a shake hands
to parading culprits outside chapel gates on Sunday with
their offences and sentences tied around their necks on
cardboard, or banishment from Ireland. Sentences were
read at chapel gates or posted up.

Elections were held for county and district councils and
boards of guardians; twenty-nine out of thirty-three county
councils and one hundred and seventy-two rural district

councils were for the Irish Republic; ten followed the Irish Parliamentary Party, five were evenly divided and nineteen were Unionist. Dáil Éireann could now use the greater part of the Local Government system, which, however, collected and forwarded taxes to the British Income Tax Department; a proportion of the money was returned in grants to county councils. It was more dangerous now to be a member of a public body that had given allegiance than to be one of the I.R.A.; the former were known, they had to work in public and were an easy mark for raiding parties; soon they had to go on the run. Seven fresh British infantry battalions came over.

In July the Auxiliaries were organised as a *corps d'élite* of ex-officers in fifteen companies of one hundred men. Three fresh infantry battalions and a Divisional Staff landed. Marines were shipped to the South to reinforce the armed garrisons of Coast Guard stations. Their stations had been attacked and burnt, and lighthouses raided for detonators and explosives.

Emigration was prohibited by the Dáil; two hundred and twenty-three public bodies had now pledged allegiance to it. There was land trouble in the South and West. The Dáil, afraid of the spread of land hunger, used the I.R.A. to protect land owners; the I.R.A. who were in sympathy with those who wanted to break up estates carried out the orders of the Minister of Defence.

A Partition Act was being discussed by the English Cabinet as a settlement, but Ulster was not satisfied at the terms. In the North riots were generally staged during a time of surplus labour or when the English political situation in its approach to an Irish settlement demanded it. Fighting began in Derry between armed Orangemen and poorly armed Nationalists; I.R.A. filtered in. The Orangemen were driven back with loss, British military, who had stood by, now took notice and troops were used. Twenty-eight people were killed and fifty-five wounded. In July Belfast took up the rifle. British troops evidently found it difficult to use troops in a loyalist stronghold.

Lord Grey had discovered a feeling for Ireland in America; it prevented closer English-speaking relationship there. In August Lord Curzon was insistent about pleasing America by an Irish settlement. But that month saw a

Restoration of Order in Ireland Act, weighty in words and possibilities, put into force. The military absorbed more of the function of civil authority.

The increasing attacks on barracks had resulted in their capture or partial destruction; the burning of evacuated posts had driven garrisons into the towns. The police, " the eyes " of the military, could not now supply information about certain areas; many country districts and the mountains were controlled by the I.R.A. The R.I.C. had ceased to be a police force; they pointed out houses, localities and short cuts to the Tans and soldiers; they identified wanted men from arrested suspects and they guided punitive expeditions. Some of the older R.I.C. were near their retiring pensionable age. If they retired before the pension was due they would lose it. In divided mind they remained on. Police had to give a month's notice before they resigned; a few who had left the force had been killed or beaten up by Tans.

CHAPTER THIRTEEN

JULY—AUGUST, 1920

★

I ATTENDED A meeting in Dublin where the G.H.Q. Staff met senior officers from all commands. I saw Liam Lynch and Terence MacSweeney of Cork, and many others who had been names to me. The officers pressed for a campaign in England to counteract the destruction of creameries and houses by the military and police; they offered to send over picked men. Our final instructions were to slow down the guerilla campaign and allow civil administration to develop.

*   *   *   *

I brought eight boys from South Tipperary up the slopes of Slievenamuck, which looked down on the military barracks and the town. A military wagon left a post in the Glen of Aherlow every Saturday for supplies; an escort of from twelve to fifteen soldiers went with it. Up in the heather and long grass we waited, scouts watched the road up from The Glen and the country beneath us on the other side. Rifle shots would be heard below by the guard on the rifle range and at the strongly held barracks; we would have to capture the escort at the first volley, then get away quickly across The Glen to the Galtees which overlooked us.

I watched the barracks through my glasses, then swung them to the rising ground towards Lattin, and Emly in the East Limerick area. North were the hills I knew, jutting out below Hollyford, and beyond, a dim mass, Maugherslieve; to the north-west a misty haze of blue height, Slievefelim.

Saturday was market day in Tipperary; as the sun went overhead we heard the noise of traps and carts being pulled up the hill road by horses and asses. Animals tugged, harness creaked and jerked, wood whined, and whips cracked. We lay spread out behind a steep bank at a sharp turn. We could hear the drivers : " Get on, get on up . . . get on up out a that," followed by a lash or " bad cess to you," " pull you divil you—pull." Some of the boys knew the drivers : " here's old Patsy Walsh from Lisvernane, wait till you hear him let go, he's a sour old crab . . . and here's herself the widow Quinn." We tried to stifle our gurgles of laughter as we kept our mouths deep in the heather. They told me of the drivers' histories in flamboyant extravagance before they came to our position. As we reached the low land a lark lifted his clear song to the indigo hills in the dusk.

I left on foot for East Limerick; passing lorries of troops halted to search passersby and the roads were not safe. I was glad to walk; it was better than the necessary evil of a bicycle. I could follow my liking now when the influence of a hill or mountain drew me to climb; it was good to have my boots on the grass and to feel the hill power drawing my feet over the land.

I had overhauled my kit and books. I carried two guns ; one was a Mauser automatic. Steel waistcoats often worn by police and officers could turn most bullets, but the Peter bullet, with its high initial velocity, would go through. I had a prismatic compass, prismatic binoculars around my neck, a map case, ammunition pouches and haversacks, a series of wrist straps for a fill of cartridges, a whistle, and a luminous watch. I had a book sewn together, and bound in soft leather, of selections from

English training manuals with my written notes and sketches; I carried it in a waterproof case. My coat was burnt, torn and scratched. It had been darned with coloured wools, patched with odd cloth, and the pockets, its most important part, were lined with moleskin. They could support the weight of notebooks, books, maps, pencils and medical supplies. I was my own base, and I looked it. I had books and accoutrements in triplicate: one set in Dublin, one in the area in which I happened to be, and a selection on myself.

Jerry Kieley, who had been above on Slievenamuck, came with me. He carried my Winchester rifle, an ammunition sling, haversacks, and his own Webley revolver. We walked through East Limerick, from the wooded glens beyond Doon, through the low, scattered, sharp hills of the central ridge, to the narrow Southern passes beyond Ardfinnan in the Ballyhoura mountains.

This was a rich land with a good standard of comfort; there were many creameries. Some of the houses sent a boy to Maynooth to the priesthood and a girl to the University to get a teacher's degree. The area was cut up by roads which gave easy communication to the activities of closely linked posts and barracks. There was the difficulty of three different times for councils and classes. Summer time was kept by cities, some towns and the railway; new time was an increase of twenty-five minutes on old Irish time to synchronise with English time; as yet punctual time had not come.

I was president of the first land court held in the area; two brigade officers sat with me. The courtroom was a low, slated cottage. It had trailing vine on the front wall and a small well-kept garden bounded by a bright blue fence. A strong after-rain smell came from mauve lavender and the yew across the road, surrounded by heavy topped grey willows; behind in the apple trees goldfinches bubbled over with songs, and a grey wagtail beat time with his tail. The people of the house wished us a good hearing. They set off to visit the neighbours so as to be out of the way, as they said. We sat in the kitchen on three brown wooden chairs with our backs to the small oblong panes of a window. A grandfather clock ticked heavily; the table in front of us was covered with green oil-cloth.

Seated opposite to us were the plaintiff and defendant, but as they made claims and counterclaims about trespass and right of way it was hard to make out which was which. They did not object to any of us three; they selected counsel from a group of officers, then signed a form that they would honour the court's decision.

The defendant was burly; he had a red beefy face, ragged moustache and long hairs curving out from his nostrils. He spoke with an even roughness when he addressed the court, but with an emphatic hoarse distaste when he turned towards his opponent: "this bloody fellow," he called him. I had to ask him to speak with more respect. The plaintiff was clean shaven and dark-skinned with black hair; his cheek bones ridged out, below them the cheek line caved in. He had a lean face, wind-red and scrawny at the neck. The beefy man looked a bully. Both sat with their knees wide angled, their hats revolved between the gaps as if the twirling helped speech.

On cross-examination of witnesses flaws were found in the burly man's evidence. We went into another room to consult. Both had to pay compensation and the slight costs of court. "Are you satisfied?" I asked them in turn. They both were. "Will you shake hands, now?" They shook hands with each other and with us. We made tea and drank together.

I was glad when I saw them walk away together. "No more courts for me," I said to the Vice-Com. "I feel like the woman who was called in to decide a quarrel: 'Faix you're right,' she said, 'and the other man is right, musha, you're both right in your own way.'"

Jerry and I came down the slopes of the Galtees to a house in Anglesborough; we were tired and very hungry. "You must have walked on the *féar gorta*," the woman of the house said, as she scalded the tea pot. I worked in a small sun-lit room that looked out on the mountain slopes. One of the girls came into the room. I was writing in my notebook; my revolver was on the table in front of me. She smiled. "Is it loaded?" "Yes, it is," I said, and wrote on. She picked up the gun. I tried to hide my temper as I continued to write. Inwardly I thought the fool! what the hell does she want meddling with a loaded gun? I hated anyone to touch my weapons. She pointed the gun at me and pressed on the trigger, the hammer rose and fell. She's trying to frighten me or annoy me, I thought. She pressed again, the trigger pressure swung the gun a little to one side as the muzzle went up. There was a report, a shriek and a smash of broken glass from a lamp behind my head. She trembled and became white : "O my God," she said, "when it didn't go off the first time I thought it wasn't loaded." Jerry rushed in with his Webley in his hand; her mother followed, her hands white with flour. I found a slight dinge on the cap of the cartridge which she had first touched with the hammer.

*   *   *   *

Enemy movement was prevented or restricted by continually pot-holing the road, digging holes in it at intervals, or by trenching and then covering the openings with soft earth so that an unsuspecting lorry would dash in. Trenches might be left open, then they had to be filled in by the British before an advance could be made. Walls were torn down and spread over a large area or piled up in cuttings where it would be more difficult to remove the stones. Heavy trees were felled across the road, barbed wire often wound around them and kept in position with staples to prevent or retard the use of cross-cuts. Our snipers delayed convoys or raiding parties ; they had to get down to attempt to outflank the attackers. The enemy moved more cautiously; raiding parties increased in strength, but night raids, save in towns and villages, were less frequent. Near Bruff we found that a gate-keeper and his wife had one night cut down two trees in the demesne, near the lodge, intending to use the wood for fuel. They thought the neighbours would believe that our men had cut down the timber. The obstructions were not at first taken seriously by the country people. They removed the trees and filled in the trenches, but heavy fines were imposed by our battalion officers. After the fines had been paid in money or cattle the people left obstacles alone. Alternate routes for carts and traps were made by cutting gaps in the hedges on either side of the obstruction.

Police barracks now had machine guns and rifle grenades, the approaches were protected with barbed wire and often mined. A barracks at Bruff was aroused one night, rifle and grenade fire was opened and a mine exploded. In the morning the dead body of a mule, which was picked off the barbed wire entanglements, constituted the attack. A few shots at night drew continuous fire, and rockets for reinforcements flared up; garrisons never felt themelves secure. At Hospital I was told that a lorry of troops held up their hands and shouted, "we surrender," because the lorry in front had backfired, and the rear ones thought it was the beginning of an attack.

Police and military shot prisoners; "shot dead whilst trying to escape," was their explanation. At inquests verdicts of wilful murder were returned against them. Raids became more destructive, and rings, watches, and valuables disappeared. Officers wore masks on their faces and Tans used blackened cork when they came at night to shoot men who were on their Black List; bloodhounds sniffed whilst the family cowered. The destruction of creameries continued. Police and tans were shot down on the streets by the I.R.A.; houses which police or military were about to turn into posts were burnt.

* * * *

Jerry Kieley, my orderly, was leaving for Tipperary. " I thought," he said, " I came to fight, not to walk my legs off during the day, look at officers being trained in the evening and take turns with you at sentry work during the night." We were crossing country near Knockainy. The Battalion Commandant, O'Keefe, was with us. He had sent two scouts with whistles some distance in advance. We walked through the small village, mounted the slight rise near the chapel, crossed a bank and walked abreast, separated from each other by three or four yards, across a large sloping field, the old racecourse. The scouts had crossed the road at the foot of the field and had disappeared from sight. We were within a hundred yards of the road when we saw a tender of police; it had made no noise. The tender halted near the low stone wall bordering the road. The police, about twelve of them, were seated back to back facing either side of the road. They all turned in our direction and trained their rifles on us. We flung ourselves down on the ground. I had a Winchester rifle. O'Keefe and Jerry had revolvers. I handed Jerry my Peter; it had a wooden holster that could be fitted as an adjustable stock and the long-range sights would make it a light rifle. There was no cover. The long field sloped gradually away from the road. " Run back," I said to the two, " I'll cover you and open fire when you begin to run." " I'm going to walk back," said O'Keefe, " but don't fire."

The police sat watching us. I moved my body and settled down closer to earth, my heels angled flat, and I had a good comfortable firing position. There was more cover in the bare field than I had thought, but the top of my body was completely exposed. The lanyard of yellow sash cord, which held my Winchester slung to my side when on the move, was of such length as to steady my aim when I shoved the butt in to my shoulder. I took a sight on a sergeant who sat in the front row. He'll give a fire order, I was thinking, and as he shouts I'll fire. I'll get him before I'm riddled. My finger was on the trigger, and the temptation to fire was strong. If the police used their rifles suddenly they would get me, and their bullets would jerk my body up before I could fire. That again made me want to fire first, and I began to squeeze on the trigger, but I stopped the pressure in time.

Another tender of police came up quickly and silently. It halted close to the first. I could hear voices, then the new arrivals brought up their rifles. I looked behind me. Jerry and O'Keefe were about 200 yards away; they were running now, but it would take them a little more time to make the bank. The silence was louder than any volley. The black green coats held their rifles with muzzles up and their caps tilted as they sighted. " Blast your souls ! can't you fire, can't you fire," I said aloud, but the rifles pointed accusing fingers. In the distance I heard like a mechanical corn crake the smothered rhythm of a mowing machine ; over the heads of the police, as I lifted my eyes from the sights, were small hills in front of a soft blue mass, the Galtees.

The other two were climbing the bank. I ran back up the slope, my breath came in great gasps though the strain was not from the running. I threw myself down often to get my breath and to steady my nerves, but my legs shook whenever I dropped down and spread myself out to sight on the sergeant. Nobody moved in the tenders, but the rifles pointed. One of my puttees began to work loose and trailed a long khaki serpent behind me. The bank was near me now; I walked towards it and climbed over. I lay breathless behind it, my heart sledged hard and my mouth was dry. Jerry and O'Keefe were watching the police. "Spread out a little and we'll move up the hill," I said. "What the hell do they think they're doing?" I called to Jerry. "There's no saying and they're not an ass's roar away." Our rush back, the immobility of the police and the terrible silence was too unbelievable to be real. We had no earthly chance of life, and yet, there were the two tenders below on the road, and here were we behind a bank. "Maybe there's a bunch of them beyond that hedge," I said to O'Keefe, "keep your eyes skinned." There was no one behind the hedge. "Bend low and let's rush it," I called. To our left there was a road running down at right angles to the police; they could easily outflank us if they used that road. We had to cross it for there was no cover on our right where the hill sloped down to the road.

Surely they would attempt to outflank us. After ten minutes the tenders drove off slowly, halting at intervals. We lay on the hill and wondered. A rather shaken trio re-entered the village, our eyes strayed more to the rear than to the front. Later we heard that the police had come from Bruff barracks; they reported they had met a decoy party at Knockainy which had attempted to lure them out of their lorries into an ambush, but they had not fallen into the trap.

I sent a dispatch to the Captain of Ballyneety Company; he was to forward my bag to Oola and hold a parade that night. I was on the road to Ballyneety the following day when I met an old woman coming towards me. She wore a black shawl. I said "Good-day," as I passed, but she did not reply. I thought her surly; everybody saluted on the country roads. After I had gone past I heard her shout, "Hi!" I walked back to her. "I thought you were a Tan," she said, "with all those trappings on you, but maybe you're one of the boys." "Yes," I said, "I am."

"You'd best cut out across the fields, soldiers in tin hats and Tans are raiding English's down the road, a few perches away, so be careful. God keep and save you." I thanked her and left the road. I had intended to call at English's on my way past.

I reached Ballyneety, less than a mile away, and sat down under cover to await developments. I looked down on to the plains towards Limerick city and over towards the hills on the left. Straight ahead beyond the plains were mountains rising higher as they receded into Mid-Tipperary, the Clare hills in the dim distance. Here Patrick Sarsfield had once, over two hundred and seventy years ago, surprised and fired the seige train of the Williamites on their way to powder the walls of Limerick. He had left the city at night, passed through those distant mountains, guided by rapparees to Donohill, then up to this hill by the old road. I waited until the lorries passed down the hill. I could see them through the branches of the hedge.

I inspected two companies that night. On parade I was told that English had been arrested. The Battalion Commandant came with me to the house I was to sleep in, a well-built house surrounded by trees and a high stone wall. I took some papers out of my bag, which had arrived, and then left it outside for safety. Two sentries were on guard—the sons of the house, armed with shotguns. I had a new holster, of which I was very proud, made to my design by the local cobbler, with straps to go round my leg. The holster remained firm when I practised a draw. I stripped the Peter the Painter, cleaned and oiled it, then cleaned my Smith and Wesson. I hung the two guns attached to my Sam Brown belt on a clothes hook. This was unusual; I always carried my guns with me in the daytime; in bed one was tied to my wrist with a lanyard. I wrote a training memorandum, and replied at the same time to the Commandant's many questions on tactics. He sprawled even when he stood up. He had large powerful hands which moved not in a nervous but in a powerful way. He twisted his mouth with eagerness and shifted his weight when he spoke. One thought of the hands rather than of his face. He was very strong, I had been told.

He stopped suddenly: " What's that? " he said.

" The wind, I suppose."

He listened again. " No, it's not."

" You had better go out and see," I said, continuing to write. He rushed back shouting: " They're coming . . . they're coming," as he came near the window. I could not hear any noise. "Go back again, and bring a clear report, the sentries have not opened fire." He went towards the gate, moving in the shadows. We had been accustomed to reports of excited scouts and men, who often rushed in to shout, "They're coming." Often that was the end of the incident. I wrote on. I'd hear a shot anyhow and then there'll be shooting, I said to myself. A form rushed past my window and shouted breathlessly, "Military on the avenue . . . coming," and disappeared. It was the Commandant.

I packed my books and papers into my haversack, put out the lamp, reached for and grabbed my Sam Brown belt in the darkness. I slung my haversack over my shoulder. I opened the door. I was in the kitchen. I found myself at the foot of the stairway. That's the wrong way, I thought, as I moved around feeling with my hands. I blundered against a door, it had a latch—the back door. I opened the door and rushed out. Fire was opened at me from all around the yard—revolver fire—I judged from the flashes and noise. I ran for the first two flashes; in my excitement I whirled my belt and flung it. I had lost my guns. Voices cursed and shouted, "Halt!" Where was the gate? The firing continued. I saw a light spot against the sky—the gate. I clambered over it and felt a stinging pain in my right thigh—I was hit. I jumped down and ran—no great pain—the bone had not been touched. I was in a muddy field, the clay hung to my boots and I fell heavily. The firing was indiscriminate, rifles and revolvers, then it became controlled. I heard volleys and whirring noises came down the field. I was as often on the ground as on my feet.

As I came near the corner of the field I saw a form rise out of the ditch. I flung myself at it and a voice said as I gripped his throat : " I surrender!" It was the Battalion Adjutant who thought I was one of the British. I laughed with relief. We crossed the hedge and ran for some distance. I threw myself down; I felt sick and if I ran I would only become panicky. The Adjutant lay down beside me. We spoke in whispers. " I've lost my guns," I said, " isn't it terrible? " " I have a gun," he said, handing me a revolver, "but the spring is broken ; it won't work." "Oh damn"; then I thanked him, " I think I'll try to get back to the yard,

M

perhaps they have not found my guns." "You're mad," he said, "they have the house surrounded." I was still thinking of the guns, the disgrace of losing them without firing a shot. A pain in my leg reminded me that I was wounded. In the darkness I cut a hole in my trousers. It had stuck to the skin and my trousers and hands were wet. I took lint and a bandage from my pocket and bound the wound up. The adjutant helped me to tie a knot. "We must get away as soon as possible across the main Limerick road; I know the country well," he said.

At Pallas there was a garrison of soldiers and police, and a barracks at Oola five miles away. We could cross the road between the two posts. There were bloodhounds at Pallas ; they had used them before, they would certainly use them now. We reached and crossed the main road. A few fields further on there were horses. "We'd better mount one to break the trail for the bloodhounds," I said. As we rounded the horses into a corner to catch them I thought of how to throw bloodhounds off the scent ; running water, pepper. I tried to remember how Pedro, the bloodhound in the Sexton Blake detective stories, published in *The Union Jack*, which we read at school, had been defeated by the master criminal, Plummer. I could not remember. We held two horses by the noses. "This is a good one," said the Adjutant, "he'll jump I'm sure." He mounted, I got up behind and put my hand on his shoulders. We crashed the horses through a hedge, jumped a small drain, over a gate into another field, then another hedge. We got down off the horse, walked a little, then lay down behind a hedge and waited for dawn. I was cold and stiff. The dew was deep on the long grass of the meadows.

We saw the few stars go out and the light drop slowly on to the country, a cold light that took the colour out of the land. As we crossed close to the ruin of an old castle the adjutant, who had been telling stories of the neighbourhood, said : "Do you see that old castle? well . . . " and he told me the story. In the land war when evictions were carried out with crowbars, battering rams and a parade strength of soldiers, an old man lived in the broken down castle; he refused to pay rent and threatened to hold his shelter at any cost with his friends. On the morning of the eviction the Coldstream Guards were told off to take the castle.

Guards regiments were seldom sent out of England. The neat guardsmen in waves charged up with fixed bayonets, but the castle was empty. " There was a song about it," said the adjutant; he sang some verses. As we laughed I wondered if that charge of the Coldstreams was in the regimental memory.

In Tipperary I had my wound dressed, my friends there laughed when they heard I had lost my guns; in mock pantomime they rehearsed the dash for my belt. English, I was told, had my dispatch, instructing him to forward my bag to Ballyfirran House, near Oola, in his pocket when he had been arrested in his own house; he had kept it in his pocket for a day instead of destroying it at once. The Tans and military from Pallas knew that I would probably sleep at the house that night. After I had escaped, the raiders searched the house thoroughly for my bag. They threatened to shoot the owner of the house and one of the sons unless they told where the bag was hidden, but they refused to give any information. After man-handling the two of them the raiders went away.

* * * *

In South Tipperary, men had been injured when using revolvers, some had lost fingers and portions of the hand. In other areas similar accidents had occurred. On investigation we found that the British had prepared revolver and rifle cartridges loaded with a powerful charge which blew the weapon to pieces when the cap was exploded.

Hand grenades picked up or bought from British soldiers had been converted into instantaneous instead of time grenades. When the pin was withdrawn the grenade exploded in his hand. The markings on the special ammunition was noted. Our G.H.Q. sent out warning to all brigades. We examined all ammunition carefully now. Some revolver ammunition which we captured from police had the cup-shaped base reversed. The suction of the air in the hollow base would inflict a lacerating wound. The issue of this type of revolver ammunition was not general, but it had been specially manufactured, yet grenade splinters were worse and carried in dirt; our refilled buckshot was as bad, and what of a jagged lump of a shell, the gunner's pride, which ambushed you from a distance? A trench mine, trench mortar bomb, percussion grenade, or a tank on one's stomach were equally unpleasant. Why there should be rules about killing as if it was a polite parlour game was hard to say ; the rules possibly made the game more noble and chivalrous. The British objected to our shotguns and repeating rifles but accepted the gashes of our grenades.

* * * *

I was making my way across country in the Limerick Junction direction. I wanted to see Seán Tracey to discuss attacks with him. As I came to a hedge I saw a glossy cap beyond a distant bank ; a police cap. I used my prismatic glasses which were slung around my neck. Police and soldiers were in the fields in front of me and to my left. They were moving slowly as if searching. I worked across to my right under cover and lay down behind a small rise of ground in the corner of a field. I heard someone give an order in the distance. I used my glasses, slowly sweeping the ground I intended to cross.

Suddenly I saw an officer cross a bank about a hundred yards away. He had a tin hat and his field glases were in his right hand. He walked slowly in the short aftergrass swinging his glasses, then turned and came towards my corner. He had not seen me, I knew. I lay closer to the grass. I gripped my Smith and Wesson and steadied my right wrist by gripping it with my left. He came closer. His tin hat was angled, the flap of his holster was closed. He had a captain's stars on his shoulders. He kicked the grass as he walked, probably thinking of something that had no relation to this field. He was over six feet in height.

I raised myself a little when he was about ten yards away and pointed my gun at the war ribbons on his left breast. He halted suddenly as he saw me, the hand that was swinging the glasses came to his right side. He looked startled, but he made no attempt to open his holster or to put up his hands. We looked at each other, there was a be-damned-to-you-and-shoot expression on his face.

I lowered my gun till it pointed to the ground and waved the back of my left hand in the opposite direction to the one by which he had approached me. He stood there. Then, as if he knew I would not fire, he turned quickly and walked in the direction I had indicated. Before he was halfway towards the bank I was in the next field. He did not look back.

Later in the day I heard that a lorry had been ambushed that morning on the road to The Junction, a second lorry had come up and police had rushed across the fields from Oola barracks. Seán Tracey retreated with his men. Two soldiers had been killed and some wounded. Brigadier-General Lucas had been in the first lorry. He had escaped from our men at Loch Gur in East Limerick and had crossed country to Pallas, where he had been given an escort to bring him to Tipperary barracks.

* * * *

When a carefully-planned operation failed through enemy preparedness or our own indecision I was at heart relieved. Often I was afraid of failure, but when fighting began I did not worry about the result. I tried to test myself as if I was not sure. I knew fear, and nameless terror would dog me, hovering and threatening; cold spinal fear that went down to trembling hands.

It was easy to be a coward; nobody would ever know except in action. There were classes to be held; staff and council meetings to attend, parades to inspect; enemy might hold the approaches or one could persuade oneself that the area was hopeless and that duty could sleep. Then a new surcease of strength would come from the mountains and hills, not obstacles but friends. It reached out from the land, our safest and best ally; courage came through the people who suffered and who were with us in our weakness, loneliness and strength. Was it not from them we had our moments of strength?

Silent struggles were fought in darkness and in plain day in the battle field of the mind. There was the communion of the recent dead and the long living memory of Ireland's dead to warn and advise. What would they do in such a case; would they have faltered? Then I would feel a change; head up, chin forward, and a rage at my own cowardice, I went forward. Sometimes an old woman as I left a house would say:"Good-bye, God save you and guard you *a' mhic*, and may you have the strength to fight well," and press a strong firm kiss on my mouth. For the moment I was her son whom she loved and was proud of. I could see the peaceful, quiet strength of her worn, serene face when I was on the road. It was as if Ireland herself An Shan Van Vocht, the Poor Old Woman, had saluted one who was fighting for her.

There was a strange passionate love of the land amongst the people. Material possessions were low or gone, the arts were a broken tradition, the ideal of beauty had gone into the soil and the physical body. Their eyes had long dwelt on the form, colour and structure of the landscape. It had become personal; its praise had been sung by joyous or despairing poets, and had been felt by the people. An old soil well loved had given much to them, and they had put much into it. They clung to this last treasure and solace with imagination and with physical senses.

*   *   *   *

Near Kilteely I heard that Rearcross in North Tipperary was to be attacked. It was late at night when I arrived, but arrangements were not complete, and the attack had to be postponed. Trenches had been dug and roads barricaded; next day was Sunday. The people helped to remove the stone outworks; they filled in trenches so that the peelers would not suspect an attack. The North Tipperary Brigadier had countermanded the attack for no reason that I could see; a barracks had never been attempted in his command. I undertook responsibility for the action. Men had come from South Tipperary and a few from Mid. We had no explosives.

The country near "Rea" was without trees; it was a lichened skull that dogs had once picked clean. The mountains were clouded all day and rain poured down; it was a dreary country. In the dark we blundered down from our meeting place, a grey stone dolmen on a hill top; the night was stormy and dark. We held to knotted ropes for guidance, but the noiseless advance became a series of rattles from buckets and sprawling stumbles from men weighted with ladders and petrol tins. A few of us went on ahead to get into the house next the barracks.

Out on the Newport road Seán Tracey, Dan Breen and a few South Tipperary men held a position, waiting for the soldiers from Newport. On the heights our scouts had sods of turf steeped in paraffin; the number and arrangement of flames would tell us of enemy strength, formation and direction. They had signalling flags to use when dawn came.

We attacked from the roof. The pump gave up. Wind blew the flames on to those of us on top, but we stifled them with a supply of wet sacks. Lieut. Jim Gorman was wounded by police rifle fire through the roof. A sortie of police were driven back, a cadet officer was killed. Seán Tracey and I flung bottles filled with petrol against the remains of the roof; the necks and bodies had been filed so as to break easily. I had placed some men behind a broken stone wall to cover the door and loopholes whilst we hurtled in the open; but, unknown to me, the men had gone away.

I was lifted up and came down with a crash; I had been hit by grenade splinters. I was dazed and shaken; my shoulder was numb with pain. I lay down with Jim Gorman. Later, a scout rushed by: " The soldiers . . . they're coming, . . . they're coming." " He won't stop till he reaches Nenagh," said Gorman. I waited for Seán Tracey's report. He was very angry when he came up. The soldiers were not coming and our men without orders had gone up the hill. The police who had been driven to a bomb-proof shelter could easily have surrounded what was left of us.

A number of police had been killed; there had been thirty-five of them before the attack, a North Tipperary man told me. I had been told there were fifteen of them. " We didn't want to give the men their number," he said, " for fear they wouldn't attack."

In Tipperary, P. J. Maloney, a member of the Dáil for South Tipperary, told me that Taylor, a Dublin surgeon was operating at the barracks. He knew Taylor; he asked him to look at my wound. Mud had splashed in with the splinters, I could not move my right shoulder. Taylor did not ask any questions, but he could see my muddied uniform trousers. He gave me an injection of anti-tetanic serum, and offered to take me with him to Dublin in his car, but I refused; doctors were expected to report all gunshot cases to the police. If I was stopped and questioned too closely I might endanger him.

Surgeon Taylor had arranged to operate on me in a private nursing home in Pembroke Street. " You will have to be X-rayed first," he said. I called at the nursing home and asked to see the matron. A stout, efficient lady in

stiff white appeared. " We have heard of you from Mr. Taylor," she said. " What is your name? " " O Malley."
" Your rank? "
Unconsciously I said " Captain.'
" Is it an old wound? "
" No, not very old."
She brought me upstairs to my room which looked out on the street. Next day she visited me as I lay in bed. Evidently she mistook me for a British officer. She talked, the conversation veered towards my wound. My replies were guarded. She smiled, " I suppose you do not wish to talk about it. Such terrible things are happening now. I suppose you are on special work." I smiled with an air of mystery, then she went away. She thought I was attached to their Intelligence Force. Nurses sat on the end of my bed ; they talked of the unsettled conditions and of the " Shinners "; they asked me if I knew officer friends of theirs. I was a nice boy, one said, when I got better I was not to forget my friends in Pembroke Street.

Two days later I walked down to the small operating theatre. " I must not talk," I said to myself; " I must not talk." I undressed and lay on the table. I was covered with a warm white cloth. Surgeon Taylor in a white coat, rubber gloves and a mask stood by the table. He smiled at me. " How is our patient? " he asked. " All right, thank you sir," I replied. The room smelt of iodoform. The anaesthesist placed a clip on my nose, a mask over my face. " Breathe deeply," he said. I took long breaths ; there was a sweetish smell of chloroform. Soon the breaths came without effort, they seemed to become deeper and deeper. I could hear a noise as if I was moaning. The assistant said, " He's going." He raised my eyelid. The words were drawn out, droning away into the distance. I tried to say, " No, I am not." I tried to struggle to make them realize that I still heard. " Go-ooing o-off." The words were drawn out. Would he ever finish them? My head expanded, it reached out and out. The words seemed to enter it, to buzz and sound. He was still drawling out " oooff." Flashes before my eyes—oooff nooow. Would he ever finish? Deep, deep breaths with a moaning sound. A flash and a point of red light. My head had burst.

I awoke when nurses were carrying me upstairs in a

sheet. I could hear myself singing in a low voice and I tried to stop my words, but they got away from me. I sang louder, the words ran into each other. "Stop, you fool," I said, but the words continued:

> "Soldiers are we whose lives are pledged to Ireland
> Some have come from a land beyond the wave,
> Sworn to be free . . . ."

In the evening I asked my pretty fair-haired nurse if I had cursed or used bad language on the operating theatre. "No," she said, "you were quite nice; you did not speak or even struggle."

"Some people do," I said, thankful that I had not mentioned names or talked about the fighting.

"Yes," she said, smiling, "we hear strange things at times; you'd be surprised."

I remained in bed for two weeks; nurses read the daily papers to me—shootings, arrests, attacks. They told me what they thought of the "cowardly Shinners," "shooting in the back from behind hedges." "Anything is good enough for them, the well-paid murderers." Some of my friends came to visit me; we laughed when the door was closed: "It's dreadful," they'd say in a loud voice, "dreadful. I wonder when the Government is going to put an end to the murder gang."

My visitors were an added danger as I had told only one of them myself about the operation, others had evidently been told by some one on our own G.H.Q. Staff. A slip in words would have made my position clear to this now friendly nursing home, which would most certainly inform the enemy.

CHAPTER FOURTEEN

AUGUST—OCTOBER, 1920

★

JERRY KIELEY and I were on our way to the hills beyond the Blackwater. I was trying to get to a Council of the North Cork Brigade in time. We had walked for a long time across low hills where branches of purple dogwood and crimson fuchsia hedges stood out against pale corn stubble and yellow hazel leaves. We crunched mauve heather and smelt the fragrance of yellow furze and bog myrtle; higher up were feathery green rowans behind their coral red berries. It was a clear still day.

Jerry had fine features; his face was brown under thick black hair which he carefully combed. He held his head to one side; there was something bird-like in the look of his light brown eyes. He spoke rapidly. He had a way with him that the girls as well as the boys liked; he was good company around a fireside, and could make up for my preoccupation with maps and pen. I could often hear his songs in the night time:

> " For I don't know it may be so,
> But a bachelor is easy and he's free
> For I've lots to look after
> And I'm living all alone
> And there's no one looking after me."

We halted near a bank. I had heard a starling mimic a disgruntled sparrow and then the clear whistle call of a black-bird. As we watched him feed on purple elder-berries there was an orange blue green flash and a petulent screech as a kingfisher slipped into yellow flags amongst the reeds at the bottom of the slope. Jerry gripped my arm: " look! . . . soldiers!" I saw two bits of khaki figures throw themselves down on the upper slope; bullets whizzed as we crossed through the thorn bushes on the bank. We spread out; rifle shots came from different directions. I saw tin-hatted soldiers rush towards a hedge. I used my Parabellum; I heard the loud dull sound of Jerry's Winchester. He had moved further up the slope.

Through my glasses I saw glimpses of khaki above him on higher ground; behind us was a rise of ground. I ran towards him: " they're outflanking us on the right, Jerry. Get back to the rise and cover me," I shouted. He ran back quickly with bent back. I lay on the bank and fired rapidly towards where I had seen the outflanking soldiers. I reached the rise where Jerry was. Heel to heel we angled our bodies and swivelled on the low aftergrass of the slope. There was a strong sweet smell from the clover.

We heard orders shouted from behind the bank which we had left. A rush of men came over with bayonets shining on their rifles. From above us came the quick mingled beat of rapid fire. There was something deadly about the rush though none of them fired. I emptied two magazines. Jerry pulled back and forward at the piston magazine of the Winchester as the tin hats clumped together, yelling. Five of them dropped, the others wavered, then ran for the hedge. "That's fine, captain," said Jerry, as another fell, shouting "Help!" Jerry gave me my rank on important occasions. We were kneeling; I felt a great warmth in my body and a rich joy as I filled my magazines. I rammed one in with a click. Jerry's face was a glowing brown. There was a soft light under the skin as if it would flower, his black shiny hair was tossed. The Winchester made the hell of a noise and the Parabellum sounded like a baby machine gun. Soldiers without rifles came through the blackthorns; they carried back five men, but the figure nearest us was spread out on his face. We heard the wounded cry in pain.

"My amm. is low, Jerry. Be careful." Soldiers came down the upper slope, but they ran back again. "Let's charge up whilst we have any stuff left," I said. We rushed up, shouting; bullets pelted by us, then the firing stopped. We halted for breath beyond a low bank; a few yards away was a soldier. He was lying on his side and his hands were full of grass. "He's dead," said Jerry. One bullet had torn open his rifle magazine and had blown three fingers off his right hand. He took up the rifle. "Leave it," I said, "it's only a single shot now; we'll find another." We dashed down the far slope under fire.

We lay down behind a row of smooth beech boles. "You're wounded," Jerry said, "does it hurt?" Blood was dripping down my coat. I had been nicked under the eye by a bullet. Arms linked and content we walked across corn stubble. Jerry looked back: "I wish now I had taken that rifle," he said, regretfully. There were two bullet holes in his haversack.

Liam Lynch had a high domed forehead. When he smiled I could see a row of large teeth; his face tightened quickly on his smile. He was quiet, but forceful and commanding. He tapped the table impatiently with his pencil at side issues and quickly worked through a long agenda. His eyes had large pupils which grew blacker and larger when he stammered in anger. He had a

clear, well organized mind.   He made frequent notes in a
loose-leaf note-book as we talked.

That night Liam told me about the capture of General
Lucas.   He had been with two officers on a fishing trip
when Liam and his officers came upon them.   Liam
did not like to tie their arms.   Lucas, and Danford, a
staff officer, were in the back of one car guarded by Paddy
Clancy who stood up to face them.   The officers spoke
to each other quickly in Arabic, then Danford made a dive
for Clancy's gun and Lucas jumped on Liam who was
in the front of the car.   Clancy was suffering from the
effects of a hunger strike in gaol, but he fought off Danford.
Lucas twisted round Liam's Parabellum till its muzzle
was against his chest, but the safety-catch was on.   Liam
slipped it off, twisted the gun and made Lucas put up his
hands, then Liam fired at Danford who was overpowering
Clancy.   The other officer, Tyrrell, was left behind with
the wounded Danford and a car.   " It was a near thing,"
Liam said, " Lucas nearly crushed my hand as we twisted
the gun every which way."   The prisoner had seen a good
deal of the country as he moved through North Cork to
West Limerick, Clare and back to East Limerick.   " He
must have learned a lot more about us than he should,"
I said.

The column or Active Service Unit—" A.S.U."—was
developing in the South.   East Limerick had organized
the first column, but it had kept away from me.   I had a
bad reputation for working men too hard.   The North
Cork column of twenty-four men was drawn from battalion
staffs; Liam had some brigade officers with him as well.   I
trained the column in field work for over three weeks, as
we moved around ; at night the men attended lectures that
I gave to officers of the local battalion.

There was great rivalry between the squads.   Nightly
they held councils to discuss the day's training and the
ground problems for the next day.   In the morning squad
commanders came to a column council where they made
suggestions and interpreted the complaints and difficulties
of their men ; an action council to discuss operations was
attended by the local battalion staff.   In two weeks' time
I felt that we could carry out attacks.   Liam was worried ;
if we were surrounded and beaten or surprised at night the

officers would be a great loss. Often an area depended on the personality of its commandant.

Paddy McCarthy, our Quartermaster, was stocky; he had a rosy, eager face. His cap was at an angle on his thick hair. He was very good humoured; that was unusual for a Q.M. who had too many worries through excessive demands on his small resources. He sang at unexpected times. He had a huge sack from which he could draw pencils, sticks of gelignite, a bull's eye card, a text book or cigarettes. He drew out the articles with a surprised flourish. A shortage of tobacco was hard on all of us except Liam. None of the men drank; drinking was discouraged by senior officers. They usually set the example. We had to keep our wits clear and to avoid random talk.

* * * *

Liam Lynch and I went off on foot to inspect the road from Mallow to Cork. Convoys passed along there frequently through a pass in the hills; armoured cars escorted lorries and two or three lorries often went together. We found two good positions. We looked at them from either side and from either end, and decided where we would place scouts, signallers and men. Whilst I was giving a lecture in a barn to officers that night, Liam was called outside. After the lecture he said: "The Mallow Commandant brought out a young lad named Bolster, but I thought I'd wait until you were finished. He's working in the military barracks, and says he thinks it can be taken."

The boy was seated in the kitchen of the house where we two slept. Liam brought him into another room and closed the door; we sat down at a table. The boy was tall, serious looking, a little nervous at first, but by degrees the nervousness wore off. He had a strong Cork accent and was eager to speak. He spoke evenly; we both eyed him closely as he talked. "Are you a Volunteer?" Liam asked.

"No, sir; but I want to help in any way I can."

"What do you know about the barracks?"

"I am a painter and I work there with another chap who will do anything you want him to. The arms are nearly all in the guardroom at certain times."

"How many men in the guardroom?"

"Four or five."

"How many sentries are there?"

"One inside the main gate during the daytime."

"How many officers?"

"One and a sergeant-major. The regiment is the Lancers—the 17th; they call themselves 'The Death or Glories,' and there are about forty or fifty men."

"Can you draw a rough plan?"

On a piece of paper he outlined buildings, sheds, the guardroom and the sentry. "In the morning-time horses are taken out for exercise, and about eight or nine men and the officer go with them."

Liam asked him to come out next evening; in the meantime he was to examine the guardroom without attracting attention.

"Well, what do you think of it?" said Liam.

"It looks simple enough," I replied. "We could take the barracks in the morning-time."

"Do you think Bolster can be trusted; perhaps it's a trap?"

"He gave his information steadily. Two machine guns and thirty rifles are worth a risk. We often have men killed trying to capture a rifle."

Next day we went into Mallow, walked around the military barracks and the side streets and had a look at the police barracks. The difficulty would be to bring in the column in the morning. They would be noticed, and the people of Mallow—long a garrison town—were not very friendly. The Town Hall stood high above the houses near it. "We could bring the men in at night and stay in the Town Hall till morning," I said.

"Yes, we could," said Liam. We looked at the back walls leading up to the Town Hall then we walked back to Burnfort. We decided to act at once, the garrisons might be strengthened at any moment or additional sentries might be posted. The plan was formed and reformed. Our Quartermaster, McCarthy, would next morning go to the barracks as an overseer to superintend the work of the two painters. Each would carry a revolver. When the troopers left to exercise the horses, I would knock at the barrack gate and say I had a letter for the officer. When had disarmed the sentry, the other three, who were to b working near the guardroom, would hold up the guard and wait for the rest of the column. Motor cars and drivers were to be ready outside the town waiting to move in when signalled to by our scouts.

In the evening Bolster came out. Liam asked: " Can another man go in with you to the barracks? "

" Yes, he can come in with me in the morning; the lancers won't notice anything."

" Can you use a gun? "

" No, nor can my pal; we've never handled guns before."

He was shown how to load and unload, how to grip, then our plan was explained to him. We watched McCarthy and Bolster disappear into the darkness with three revolvers; we hoped they would not be held up before they reached the town.

The column was drawn up. They smiled joyfully when they were told that we were going to seize the barracks. At two in the morning, behind our scouts, we moved into the town. The advance guard was told to make prisoners of everyone they met and blindfold them. There were no lights in the houses, no people on the streets. The men moved quietly and that was a comfort, each was part of the adventure. Our approach up to higher ground brought us through back yards, barbed wire and across high walls. We used ladders on the high walls. When I looked down on the houses I saw a toy town blurred and misty with half light and warm through changing shadow colour. The nerve straining to joy sense of danger increased until we were safe in the large Town Hall.

We had not disturbed the inhabitants or their dogs. Scattered throughout the rooms we lay on the floors and waited. For the first hour we were ready in position for a surprise attack. We might have been seen by someone who would report to the peelers or to the military. We're like the Greeks in the wooden horse, here in the belly of the town, I thought, and laughed. Dave Shinnock, the column adjutant, was with me in one of the front rooms as we peered out into the night through a window; he asked me why I laughed and I whispered to him the end of the seige of Troy. Later I heard him whisper it to the men in an inner room, and when I passed through, a boy slapped the wall, and said. " Now, girl, whoa girl, steady there," and made a wind purr with his mouth as if he were rubbing down a horse.

At dawn our scouts reported. Nothing unusual in the military or police barracks; our entry had not been noticed. Liam and I moved cautiously through the rooms of the Town Hall, a massive old building, and noted how it could be defended in case we were attacked.

Then we waited, impatiently. At nine o'clock the horses were usually exercised. At ten o'clock a scout to say that the horses and riders had left the barracks. Riflemen were placed in position to cover the police barracks and the approaches to it, and to hold up passing lorries; but we had few men for the work. Liam and I had already detailed off men and had questioned them until we felt that they knew what they had to do. The work had to be done quickly and there could be no bungling, but we had to make allowances for excitement.

I pulled my trousers out over my long boots, placed a Parabellum automatic in the breast pocket of my coat and borrowed an overcoat, which I put on. Liam shook hands with me as I left by the back door. " I hope nothing goes wrong with the timing," he said, " or you will find yourself holding up the barracks alone." I walked up to the gate of the barracks. Paddy O'Brien from the column was some distance behind. I knocked. A face with a tin hat on its head peered out through the iron grating. " What do you want?" said a voice.

" I've a letter for the officer commanding." He unbolted the door. I passed through. He closed it. He stood in a half on-guard position, the bayonet of his rifle pointed at me. About fifteen yards away was a group of lancers, others stood around the barracks yard. I held the letter in my left hand; as he stretched out for it, I bent down and put on the safety catch on his rifle so that he could not fire. I snatched the rifle from his hands, slipped off the safety-catch and shouted " Put up your hands! " He put them up quickly. I backed and opened the door ; our men rushed in. The guardroom had been held up as soon as I had disarmed the sentry.

Motor cars drove in. Rapidly, rifles, revolvers, lances, swords, ammuniiton and equipment were carried out to them. I heard a shot and saw a lancer fall as I rushed with two men for the officers' quarters, but I had no time to investigate. Upstairs we went, to find the officer's room locked. With a smash three of us broke in the door. Inside was a soldier—the officer's orderly. We searched for papers but did not find many. Later we discovered a large tin box full which was too heavy for us to carry. I sent down for two more men. On the officer's desk was an unfinished letter: . . . " Mallow is a very quiet town; nothing ever happens here . . . "

I saw motor cars move off, long lances stuck out and pennons waved. A wounded sergeant-major lay on the ground; some of his men were trying to stop the blood whilst I bandaged his stomach wound. I heard Liam order all men to leave the barracks. " But it hasn't been properly searched yet," I said, " and it hasn't been burned."

" We have no time," he said, hurriedly. I tried to stop the flow of blood whilst the comrades of the dying man stood around. I heard a shout from the gate. Jerry Kieley, a rifle slung on his back, ran towards me.

" I came back," he said, " when I heard you were alone; why didn't some of them stay? "

" Let's move those bales into the building," I said. There were compressed hay bundles in the yard. We tugged them towards the main building, loosened them inside and set fire to the hay, then we dashed through the gate and down the town. We caught up with some of the rear guard, seated on an ass and cart; their rifles covered the road behind them. One was playing a melodeon. The thin swirl of smoke from the barracks did not increase.

Above Burnfort we halted. Thirty rifles, two Hotchkiss guns, small arms and over four thousand rounds of ammunition had been captured, and had been brought by the motor cars to a safe place in the opposite direction. Sentries were thrown out while some of the men slept. Twelve miles away was Fermoy with a strong enemy garrison of about fifteen hundred men. Buttevant with its hutments and camps was eight miles away, and was a Battalion Headquarters. We could expect a concentration of troops in and around Mallow. The Mallow Commandant sent off dispatch-riders to mobilise some of the armed men in the battalion. After some time they came, poorly armed, mostly with shot guns, and reinforced our outposts.

"We must get away as soon as it gets dark," said Liam, "there will surely be a round-up, a big one, and they'll know that we've come in this direction."

Some of the column officers wanted to remain with me to help the local men defend the town against reprisal parties. "We must get away," Liam said, "the local men can easily avoid the round-up. We must get twenty-five or thirty miles away before morning." The Mallow Commandant received instructions. He said he would do his best to defend the town. "The Colonel from Buttevant has promised the parish priest and the minister that there won't be reprisals," he added.

"We cannot rely on such a promise," I said.

Bolster and his friend Willis, were now members of the column. We started off in ponies and traps, strung out at intervals. We lifted the cars across trenches and through gaps where the roads were blocked with heavy, fallen trees. We hauled and pushed them across streams where the bridges had been smashed, we removed heaps of stones or networks of boulders strewn over a long stretch of road. We bumped over filled-in trenches and lurched into deep pot-holes. This battalion had done its work well. Enemy would find it difficult to penetrate. The rear guard had to put back the obstacles.

We halted from time to time on rising ground to look towards the town ; at first we could see a faint haze, the lights of Mallow, then it dimmed as we moved on. Nothing had happened. Later we saw a dim glare; but as we watched it seemed to disappear. Could it be the town? The men would surely defend it. Some hours later we came to a high hill and as the ponies struggled on the bad road the men jumped out and ran up quickly. Away in the distance were flickers of light, separated by intervals of darkness. The flames leapt up as the wind increased. It was Mallow. "I hope to God it rains," said the adjutant. Another pointed to a big glare in the centre. "What's that?" he said. "It must be the creamery; that means about three hundred out of work."

Bolster looked at the leaping stabs of flame. "I think it's the Town Hall." There was silence for a time as we watched, helpless. The sheltering belly of our horse had paid for harbouring us.

"Damn it, it's terrible," said Liam, " to think of the women and children in there and the Tans and soldiers sprawling around drunk, setting fire to the houses." The enemy had revenged the capture of the barracks on the townspeople. Our elation at success ebbed away; we felt cowardly and miserable; in silence we journeyed on amongst the hills.

Next morning we learned that an aeroplane from the Fermoy direction had circled around Mallow barracks, some time after the colonel had given his promise, and had dropped a message. It had flown towards Buttevant and had then returned to Fermoy. Some of the people felt secure, others nailed up galvanized zinc in front of their glass windows so as not to expose the glass to temptation. In the night the soldiers from Buttevant and Fermoy had come in lorries, equipped with sprays and incendiary grenades. The local lancers joined them; they had burnt the creamery, the second largest in the South of the country, the Town Hall and ten houses. A volunteer fire brigade had confined the flames although they had been fired upon repeatedly. The police from the barracks and the few Tans there had given shelter to some women and children who had fled from their homes ; an expectant mother and a woman, who had spent the night in a graveyard, died of exposure.

We painted our tin hats green. Some replaced their homemade haversacks with captured khaki ones; webbing took the place of rain-warped leather. The men wore police badges and those of the various regiments they had fought against, in the lapels of their coats ; the skull and crossbones of the lancers was the most original. Once in the hills we passed through a village after twilight. There was a hurried scampering of men and women. Doors opened cautiously and a sound of wailing reached us; women cried whilst shadows in the rear of the houses meant that some of the men were escaping in the darkness. We laughed at first. A man said, " They saw our tin hats, they think we're Tommies on a raiding party." Then we realized what such a raid meant for them. Remote from a town, seldom visited, a raid here meant terror. Houses ransacked, women and children shouted at, men searched and interrogated, the amount of violence to be used depending on the individual officer in charge. The departure leaving the women nervous or vociferous in indignation, the men silent, the troops taking a few suspects with them away into the darkness. We began an old marching song in Irish, "*Oro! sé do bheatha 'bhaile,*" and the column joined in the chorus. The doors remained closed.

The column had become gayer now, work was taken more eagerly. Coughlan, who spoke slowly and deliberately, helped to keep all in good humour, and his droll sayings were repeated. He had been billeted in a house which had a reputation for being stingy. One morning the woman of the house asked him how he would like his egg boiled. "With a couple of others, Ma'am," he replied. "The column," he said, "is a great cure for rheumatism; divil an old man of seventy who is so crippled with rheumatics that he can scarcely walk, but makes for the door in fine fettle when we enter with the rifles on our backs." "Coughlan's cure for rheumatism," it was called.

Jerry Kieley left for Tipperary. He would not be given a rifle by the Corkmen. He felt he deserved one after Mallow, but rifles were rifles; they belonged to the brigade in which they were captured, and Jerry, angry with me because I would not insist on his claim, went off in disgust. It was hard to keep men outside their own counties; in the column some men made excuses to get home on leave. Mountainy men were the worst; their girls or the mountains made them unsettled when far away.

Close to the County Kerry border we waited for convoys but none came our way. We crossed into West Limerick to co-operate in an attack on a barracks; we were to await the Auxiliary Cadets who would probably send reinforcements from Newcastle West. We were anxious to meet the Cadets. They were a new force organized in special companies; they ranked from generals to second lieutenants who had seen service during and since the World War. They wore officers' tunics, carried revolvers and automatics on their thighs. They were equipped with rifles, repeating shotguns and machine guns. Their transport was of the best, the fastest tenders and cars. We wondered what would be the result of a fight with the Auxies. It was night when we arrived close to the barracks. A dispatch rider met us. The Commandant had postponed the attack; he was afraid it would interfere with other plans for an attack on a larger post. The officer himself did not appear. He was not anxious for fight. We tramped back singing improvised rhymes about the West Limerick men.

A hail of bullets one day announced to the scattered members of the A.S.U. that I had learned to work a Hotchkiss gun by experimenting with it. We inspected positions and awaited troops. Beyond Liscarroll, where there was a cavalry post, we encamped one night; sentries were posted and outlying scouts had instructions to ring the chapel bell in case of enemy approach. At three in the morning the bell went, a scout reported at our headquarters that cavalry had advanced at a gallop down the road and had halted. We made for our clothes. As I dressed in the darkness I was fumbling in my mind for the details of our defence scheme and while I cursed the narrow legs of my riding breeches our course of action came clear.

Liam went across to the appointed action position whilst I went to the section headquarters to reinforce whatever house was first attacked. I met one group which had very nearly fired on me. They heard me moving up the road and had seen my tin hat and the shape of my trench coat against the sky. They had taken me for a British officer and were ready to fire, but one, who had served in the war, told them to wait as the officer was bound to be followed by some of his men. By this time I was on top of them and they had recognized me. I visited a house which had received the alarm later than the others. I found two men struggling in the dark in their room; they had each a leg in the same trousers. The attack was a false alarm. The horses had stampeded from a travelling circus which was in a neighbouring village, and the sentries, thinking they were cavalry from Liscarroll castle, had rung the alarm.

*   *   *   *

The Brigade area was wide; it ran from Araglen to the Kerry border. First the foothills of Tipperary; the winding valley of the Blackwater, rolling country, then hills, passes near Mallow with plains beyond; mountains near Millstreet stretching into County Kerry, and long defiles running down toward Macroom backed by steeper mountains. A wilder country than South Tipperary, the soil less easily cultivated, larger areas without towns, and few roads.

In North Cork we were well protected by scouts. Officers were quicker, more excitable; they partook better of discipline, and personality did not outgrow organization but enhanced it. There was more natural talent, a better type of officer, but one more inclined to work on the crest of a wave. As a boy on my uncle's farm I had heard the men laugh at what they called " the Dublin Jackeen." They imitated his speech and his conscious air of superiority when in the country. Later in the Midlands, in 1918, I had met a travelling tailor who had worked in every county. When he spoke of Cork he spat with an air of contempt. No, he did not like them, they were too clannish and aggressive. Now, Dublin was remembered as giving birth to the new spirit during the Easter Week fighting and Cork was producing fighting men. There was a bumptiousness in the Cork temperament. They resembled the Gascons; quick and volatile, but they seemed too conscious of their qualities ; as if they were surprised at possessing them.

One morning we ambushed a lorry and captured the rifles of the escort whom we outnumbered ; we had been expecting three lorries and were disappointed. We were sprayed with machine gun fire from the Vickers' guns of the garrison in the nearby town as we retired through wooded country. Some goats and a donkey were killed by the fire. The Tommies had fought well ; our Hotchkiss gun had jammed as the gunner began to use it, grenades were thrown with the pins in and they could not explode, our riflemen owing to the close nature of the country lay down at revolver range. Only the shot guns had worked properly and faith in them was restored for rifles were beginning to make some of the men look down on the shotgun. I saw again the effect of buckshot on a dead young soldier's face ; it made a wound, sickening to look at.

We tramped in towards Kanturk in the darkness to wait for reprisal parties of troops which we expected would be sent to burn up parts of the town. By midnight we were in the streets, testing out between communication by lanes, and looking for good positions. Quietly the men were scattered in threes and fours. There was a British garrison in the military barracks and police in their own barracks. At about two o'clock scouts reported that soldiers had come in from Buttevant. We had white stripes down the backs of our coats and squares in our caps to recognize each other in the darkness. Reprisal parties often wore civilian clothes. The men were excited; night and expectancy made us warmly tense. We had determined to make up for our desertion of Mallow; our squads had orders not to retreat. I was with a Hotchkiss gun crew in a front garden half way up a hill. The night got colder. We waited until it was close to dawn then, upset at our bad luck, we marched into the clearing sky towards the border.

Commandant Seán Moylan, in whose area we were, was the proud owner of an old cannon. Once it had, with two brother cannon, adorned Ross castle in Killarney. Ross had been the last castle to surrender in the Cromwellian wars. The Kerrymen had taken all three and had moved this cannon slowly towards the Cork border. His engineers had drilled away the rust, polished it until it shone, although there were little pits of a darker colour where the rust had eaten its way into the metal. Springs from Ford cars had been used to take the recoil of the gun in action. The gun was mounted on small iron wheels. Next day before dawn a pony and cart pulled the gun towards a deserted house. The gun was loaded and tamped with powder, a cannon ball was placed in the muzzle. Wires, running back to a battery three yards away, were attached to the touch hole. Two boys lay down beside me; we pointed the muzzle of the gun towards the house a hundred yards away.

I was thinking of Pierce Ferriter whose poems I had in my pocket. He had been hanged in Killarney with a safe conduct in his pocket; perhaps he had once handled or directed this cannon. " I wonder when the old gun was last fired," said one. " Cromwell's time or before," I said. Liam Lynch, Seán Moylan and others lay down behind a bank a long distance in rear. " You three had better get back further," Liam shouted. We lengthened the wires and moved back a few yards. I pressed the switch key; there was a roar and a whirr of metal over our heads; smoke blown by a faint breeze covered us. We could not see the gun nor the house; where the gun had been was a broken jagged piece of metal sticking up on end out of the earth. The others behind us had heard pieces of metal whirl over them. The visions of barracks crumbling

before the attack of our cannon faded away. The
engineers who had spent their time in making a recoil
system looked in silence at the wreck. " It would have
made a good land mine," Seán Moylan said, when he
had ceased to curse.

A land mine was a tin or metal container of explosive
buried in the roadway and covered over; hidden wires led
from it to an operator who sat on a slope. He had an
electric battery. When the lorry or armoured car passed a
mark which he had selected in line with the mine he pressed
the switch. We could not leave the mines in position for
long; rain would injure them.

Near Millstreet we lay near a cutting to watch a train go
by. We meant to attack a train when we would be told
there were troops on board, but we did not get word that
day. We heard like a great heart the rhythmic threshing
stab of the piston and saw the snappy white blast. A
moving train was always exciting as it shoved its way into
space and time. The shining rail arteries connected me
with my other life in Dublin, and the men perhaps with
nearer memories—the platform excitement of a country
when the " here she is " meant the daily paper and eager
glances at the people who would again pull out of their
lives. Cheered by the sight of the train we returned to
field work. That other life I had thrown over my shoulder
and it seldom intruded. I used to have regrets about the
dissecting room, the clean, bare precision of muscle and the
structural design of the body, the club life of pipe smoking,
stories and ballads, and the interest of clinics.

The column moved into the hilly district, the threshold
of the mountains. The hills stretching towards West
Cork were naked as fear and the desolate stretch of them as
wide as hunger. Further in from us was an old megalithic
centre which I had explored. Liam and I had a day off
to work at our maps and to discuss the Brigade in detail,
whilst the section and squad commanders took their men
for reconnaissance work in the direction of the mountains.
We were in a small thatched cottage on a hillside. Small
window panes cut into oblongs, the rough edges of the
putty unpainted, low doors where one had to remember to
bend one's head. In the kitchen, which had been newly
whitewashed, were low súgán chairs and stools. In the

corner a curved skiv of turf, an old spinning wheel hung on the wall above the door. From hooks on the ceiling were slung flitches of bacon with thick outer fat sides. A round high pot-oven was on the edge of the fire. It had a lid on it covered with turf embers crusted white, piled around the sides were more embers. The girl of the house, a strong-bodied, rosy cheeked, handsome girl was baking a cake. She wore heavy boots. Robert Emmet faced Daniel O'Connell on the walls. I had often met the combination. I wondered what they would say to each other if they could speak.

Liam and I sat at a table facing a window; we watched the men through our field glasses advancing slowly in patrol formation. The man of the house was old, a long grey beard reached to his chest. Age had tamed his clear blue eyes, they had lost some of their lustre, but they still shone. He wore his hat in the house. He had been an old Fenian, he said. "Out there on yon hills I've drilled with the boys in me time, fine boys they were, God bless them. Tall and limber, they could use a scythe the live long day, not like some of the maneens these times."

"But the Fenians did not do much," I said, "why didn't they fight?" He looked at me a moment as if he was going to say something strong.

"They were willing and ready, always waiting for the word to rise." He looked at our automatics and rifles. "They'd be powerful yokes," he said. "I wish we had them in our time." Then he walked away, praying in a whisper, "Jesus, Mary and Joseph help and protect us . . . Mother of God, Mother of God, protect us." At dinner he first crumbled the soft flowery potatoes. His teeth were bad, only a few remained; he stopped between bites to pray: "Sweet Heart of Jesus be Thou my Love." Then he became the old Fenian again. He talked of the fighting. "Do ye think ye'll beat them? How long will it last?"

"We don't know," said Liam, "a long time, but we'll win."

"I'd like to see ould Ireland free before I die," said the old man, "many's the time we sat here discoursing about her, drawing down prophecies and wondering what kind of a country it would be at all."

All my assertive youth left me as I eyed the old man. We had a good chance of finishing this fight now; but the Fenians in spite of their own lack of training, hard labour

sentences of from five to twenty-five years, wavering
leaders, and a brutal landlord system that ground courage
from the people, had been willing to sacrifice themselves.
Perhaps we, too, might one day attempt to tell younger men
how willing the I.R.A. had been to see this fight through.
"The Fenians were fine men," I said, "and only for them
we might not have had our chance to fight like this."

Before the old man went to bed we knelt down and said
the Rosary, the five of us, the son having returned from
the mountains where he had been all day with the column.
The additional prayers at the end were long, the stone
flags were hard on the knees. We finished with Three
Hail Marys for Ireland.

There were three beds in the house. The girl slept in
one, the father and son in another, Liam and I slept
together. The door of the old man's room was open. We
could hear him saying the Litany of our Lady, his voice
rising, falling, portions of words coming to us:

> "Tower of . . .
> House of Gold
> Ark of . . . Covenant."

Then a pause. "Move up in the bed, Patsy." No reply.
"Patsy, move up I tell ye." No reply.
"Patsy, take in your fat arse out of that." Then:

> "Morning Star
> Help of . . .
> Refuge of Sinners
> Comforter . . . the afflicted."

Liam and I pulled the blankets into our mouths to prevent our laughter being heard. We shook and gurgled
in the bed.

* * * *

After some hesitation Liam Lynch agreed to divide the
column into fours. Working as a patrol they would move
through a battalion area for a week by themselves. We
would first give the battalion a week's notice so that the
intelligence system of their companies would be thoroughly
organized. By dividing the column I thought the enemy
would receive additional obstruction; the men would
develop initiative, learn to co-operate with local units, and
companies would learn that a patrol of four, well led and

energetically directed, could inflict much damage. The
intention was to disband the A.S.U. after a further two
weeks' training and send back the officers to organize
columns in every battalion. Liam was more apprehensive
than I was; he would have the responsibility of replacing
casualties.

I received a dispatch telling me to report to G.H.Q.
I went back by train and changed at Mallow Junction,
where I spent an uncomfortable quarter of an hour, for
some of the 17th Lancers were on the platform. Many
redheaded people had been recently arrested in connection
with the Mallow attack.

In Cork I had read of a British raid on a Dublin house
in which a British Major and a Captain had been killed.
Dan Breen and Seán Tracey had fought their way through
the raiding party; three days later Seán was killed by
machine gun bullets as his trigger finger sent his reply
towards a lorry of troops.

*   *   *   *

SEÁN TRACEY

We often heard our fathers tell
How in the Fenian times
The noblest of Tipperary's sons
Imprisoned spent their lives.

Those tales we can hear daily
And deeds of valiant men
As the war goes on right merrily
Through valley, hill and glen.

They searched for Seán at midnight
His comrade with him slept
Macready's murdering bloodhounds
In silence on them crept.

Our heroes fought as brave men should
And made a gallant fight
With bullet food they did conclude
The lives of Smith and White.

In a crowded Dublin Street he died
On a dim October day
The story will be told with pride
While men in Erin stay.

With trusty pistol in his hand
Two sleuth hounds he laid low;
'Twas well they knew this island through
They had no braver foe.

When the soldiers saw the battle
They shook with fear and dread
A machine gun did rattle
And our hero bold lay dead.

Seán Tracey killed! Seán Tracey killed!
Was borne on the breeze.
No bells were rung, no *caoin* was sung
He died for Ireland free.

While grass grows green in Erin
We'll think of you dear Seán
We'll sing your praise o'er hill and vale
When grief and gloom are gone.

And when the dawn of freedom's sun
Shines out on Erin's skies;
In Gaelic tongues we'll tell our sons
How brave Seán Tracey died.

ROMANESQUE

CHAPTER FIFTEEN

(OCTOBER—NOVEMBER, 1920)

★

CURFEW NOW LASTED in Dublin from midnight till five in the morning; one could not be out of doors without a permit during those hours. Hold-ups by armed soldiers on the streets increased, more houses were raided at night. Curfew made me keep respectable hours. I had always looked forward to the long talks which lasted till morning while I sat on the floor. Long acrimonious discussions, games of mental ping-pong in which ideas were clarified or hammered into shape, or became molten and fluid at our next meeting. Often enough our oblique imps would switch us away, or one left in despair with a sense of frustration. I was not asked since I was last in town where I had been in the interval. Walks in the night on rainy pavements luminous from street lamps when talk continued at a street corner or hall door. We found it as difficult to go to bed as to get up. Intimate beaks of banter which picked one thoroughly, yet an aloofness that left personal life alone. Books to be read and discussed, calls on friends at unexpected hours; throughout the intimate warmth of friendly Dublin life with an escape to the mountains for a long walk if one got fed up and wanted to be alone.

It was real to sit in St. Stephen's Green watching patterned flower beds around the walloping Clydesdalish bronze horse supporting George the Second, or the delight of ruffled glint in the leafy trees. Grey blue and steel grey skies, patched and streaked with slashes of dark and white clouds, moved slowly to mix to fleeting satisfaction; they brought a cold wind that spiraled worn dead leaves along the path. Children from Cuffe Street stretched on the grass, knarled men from the slums with bitter faces and undersized bodies sat on wooden seats, women gossiped, small girls in bare feet, or with one boot and stocking, carried young brothers half their size, mothering. Nurse-maids pushed prams to and fro as they flirted with the red-faced keeper. In the National Gallery there were a few good pictures to be looked at, and books to be read hard in the National Library.

Wind was dull in the city; it was more like a draught save when a gale swept in. The night sky and the moving moon had nothing to do with city life. I had the taste of the country firmly in my teeth. There was a definite friendliness and ease about Dublin, but also an air of polite helplessness. It was more tolerant. A quiet aloofness lingered round the mellow austerity of its eighteenth-century houses in a number of large squares, but the mood became strident and frowsy in the blight of the slums. Dignified wealth and open-mouthed poverty alternated their strophe and antistrophe in the capital.

The city's breweries, distilleries and biscuits were not much of an economic asset; unskilled labour predominated, and was quickly affected by trade conditions. A walk through by-streets to St. Patrick's Cathedral and the Coombe, by Thomas Street to the duplicated forms in Guinness's Brewery brought one more in touch with the haphazard life and trade of Dublin.

The new Cadet Force could be seen, moving swiftly in open Crossley tenders, seated on each side with rifles held across their knees. Wearing officers' khaki tunics, Glengarry bonnets angled, they had a dashing neat appearance. They were conscious of their power and soldierly snap. They felt impressive. People stopped to look at them. "Why aren't they attacked?" I asked Diarmuid O Hegarty; "it would be easy to lob an egg."

"That will come, don't fear," he said.

Four months ago cadets had been sent out as defence officers to instruct the R.I.C. in the defence of barracks and to strengthen *morale*. Then they had been formed into an Auxiliary Police Division, commanded by a divisional staff. Individual companies were moved from place to place throughout Ireland and were controlled directly by the Police Adviser through their divisional staff.

In the evening time I did Grafton Street between four and six. Cadets and officers were in mufti or uniform; it was easy to pick them out when they wore civies. We passed each other or sat drinking tea at nearby tables in Mitchell's café or the Grafton Street Picture House. That was stupid, I would admit to myself, as I drank my solitary tea, for a cup of tea was not worth fighting for; but Dublin was my city and I would not admit the right of foreign troops to deprive me of a habit.

Some of their hip pockets jutted out in rigid lines; all would be armed. I carried a Smith and Wesson forty-five and a Parabellum underneath my coat; the revolver seemed to follow the contour of my iliac bone, the automatic was strapped over my heart. I could reach it in a quick draw as if I were fixing my tie. Daily I practised quick draws so that there would be no fumbling when I was in trouble. Weapons were now an undisturbing part of us, they could not be noticed even by one of ourselves. Before I left home my brother's service Webley had been sent back from Greece. Then it had looked like a small piece of artillery. It was heavy, awkward, my hand shook when I tried to hold it steady, now it seemed to be as relative and as indispensable as a fountain pen.

Terence McSwiney's hunger strike in an English prison was coming to an end. The result was inevitable; we hoped he would not be released when his body was almost used up. Feeling at home seemed to have sent impulses abroad to the European Press. It seemed the most important event that had occurred in Ireland. In Washington women picketed the British Embassy, longshoremen walked off British boats. Ireland went into mourning when he died on the seventy-fourth day of his fast. He had become a symbol of part of a new nation; disciplined, hard, clear, unsentimental, uncompromising, a conscious using of vigour to build up strength.

Kevin Barry, a young medical student, was court-martialled in Dublin. He had taken part in an attack on a military lorry. A young English soldier had been killed. After dawn on the morning of the hanging crowds walked along the streets to Mountjoy under a cold November sky. Outside the jail gate armoured cars moved through the kneeling people who said the Rosary aloud. Tin-hatted Tommies with fixed bayonets stood in rows on the sides of armoured lorries. A quiet crowd, tense with emotion, hardly speaking to each other. "The poor boy, the poor boy," a woman cried, "God help us all." Tears came as she swayed on her knees, both hands held up; those near her began to cry, some could not stop, gulping noises continued

for a long time. A girl kept saying aloud : " Mother of
Perpetual Succour, help us; Mother of Perpetual Succour,
help us." Aeroplanes circled ; with a metallic beat the
noise crashed above the rise and fall of Hail Marys. " Bad
luck to ye, wouldn't less than that do ye," shouted a man
who straightened a fist at the sky. Kevin Barry was a
symbol of the enthusiasm of youth; resolute in giving, he,
for the people, was the nation, which, however warped,
futile and misdirected, had youth, life and a spirit of sacrifice.

It had been intended to rescue him by blowing in part
of the gaol wall. Rory O Connor was to be in charge
of the demolition party, but the British, alarmed at the
gathering crowds, had strongly reinforced the gaol garrison.

Our Headquarter's Staff had become more organized.
Throughout the city were their offices and duplicate
offices, and those of government departments of Dáil
Éireann, houses where ministers and staff officers could be
met; others in which they ate and slept. They carried
on their work as if they controlled the city. Dublin for
over seven hundred years had been held by the British.
It was their sea-opening to the plains and their principal
base; for the past hundred years it had been the centre of
separatist Ireland. Hidden meshes of either government
stretched in tenuous nets below the everyday life, but the
enemy web was now nearer to the surface. Dublin Castle,
the great symbol of misgovernment in the people's minds,
was again a fortress which higher officials seldom left
openly. Towns built around a King John's keep or a
Tudor castle were again garrisons ; their influence varying
between their armed strength and the people's resistance.
The gap between the two was becoming more impenetrable ;
it was deepened by a steady withdrawal of the factors in
which a joint life once met.

I saw Mulcahy, the Chief of Staff, to discuss the situation
in Munster, talk of operations and read reports. He would
spread out a number of half-inch maps as he talked, and
point a pencil at barracks or battalion headquarters. He
said, " I see," at intervals when I answered questions about
relative strength of our men and the British.

In general, the Staff were too absorbed in routine to
dissect minor points in tactical evolution. Rory O Connor,
Director of Engineering, had not yet devised a simple

container for throwing petrol or inflammatory material under pressure from a distance; the blowing up of some men who had been experimenting with a Stokes' trench mortar had deprived us of a useful weapon against posts and barracks. We had no armour-piercing bullets. Munitions Department had few hand grenades, there were no rifle grenades, no explosives worth talking about. There was no standard land mine for dealing with armoured cars or steel-coated lorries on the roads. A man was lucky if he had two fills for his automatic or revolver; no brigade had more than forty or fifty rounds for each rifle; there was not much shot-gun stuff, and it was useful only when it had been refilled with buckshot pellets. It was hard to keep our weapons in repair, harder still to keep arms and stuff dry and clean. Police and military raids were becoming more thorough; they tapped walls, tore up floors, dug up backyards, measured heights and lengths of rooms to try to ferret out hiding places.

Headquarters staff officers were always spoken of by their initials: C.S., Chief of Staff; A.C.S., Assistant Chief; M.D., Minister of Defence; D.O., Director of Organization; D.I., Director of Intelligence; D.T., Director of Training; A.G., Adjutant-General. They signed their names in different ways. Mulcahy used a hieroglyph; some of the others used their ranks without names. Michael Collins in clear writing always signed his name in full. A hand grenade was now an "egg," an ambush was a "job" a "hit-up," or a "bush"; papers might be spoken of as "dope," and explosives made by our Director of Chemicals, Jim O Donovan, were "war flour" or "Irish cheddar."

O Connell, known as Ginger, was Assistant Director of Training. Ginger was willing to discuss Foch's principles or Henderson's essays, call down the weighty Clausewitz, or suddenly illustrate a point from a text book or from wide browsing. He quoted precedents from the guerilla tactics of the Boer War or Cuban fight. Von Lettow Vorbeck, he spoke of with admiration; we had read of his campaign in German East Africa, cut off for years from Germany and supplies, against the British. He could deal with training in a mildly scientific way though he smacked of the text book. It was always easy to talk to him. Owing to lack of arms, however, we could only dribble at fighting;

precedents gained in other countries as a result of hard fighting might be stimulating to talk about, or to be proved possible, but we could only muck around.   The other members of the staff knew little or nothing about training and operations, their strong points were organization and administration.   The training staff, as far as the country was concerned, dealt with training through short notes in the monthly issues of *An t-Óglach*, which was smuggled to all brigades.

Ginger was of medium height and portly. He had a rather heavy red moustache, was inclined to baldness, about which he laughed but with apprehension. He had a slow reflective manner of speech and when he talked he stroked his moustache and plucked his upper lip. He made puns ; in an evangelistic manner he laughed at his own jokes, an expectant chuckle, dry at the base. Energetic men were "thrusters" and "stout" fellows; there were others who " saw the other side of the hill." He savoured the detailed circumstances of the plugging of a detective or the bloody mess of a successful ambush. His knowledge of strategy and general line of thought in terms of our fight evidently made contribution to the C.S. who now referred to men " who saw the other side of the hill."

Staff officers and Dáil officials changed their offices to avoid suspicion. There was a constant movement, an unceasing watchfulness, but small sign of tension. Communications were carried by special messengers as telephones could not be used. The Post Office was used only for correspondence sent to people who were not associated with the movement, or suspect. They would then pass on the letters to our officers. This made for extra clerical work and paper records; or made meetings of individuals more necessary to relieve the load on, and the danger run by, dispatch carriers.

With Desmond Fitzgerald, Director of Publicity, I met foreign journalists and labour men who were getting angles from either side. It was a mild adventure for some, an exciting thrill for others, to talk to men of the hidden government, for whom castle officials, seen earlier in the day, were hunting. Mick Collins was busy as Minister of Finance and as D.I. His armed intelligence squad moved about looking for enemy officials, secret service men and detectives. Collins was often with Arthur Griffith, Vice-President of the Ministry. Griffith had seen the development of the military aspect with misgiving; since the German Plot arrests of 1918 the I.R.B. had gained more control in all organizations. Griffith had hoped to build up a constitutional movement, Sinn Féin, and through it slowly to absorb the power and control of the British. Some of us thought that he was not a separatist, and I did not like to see Collins become more friendly with him. My doubts voiced the pseudo-military mind of the I.R.A. and its fear of constitutional respectability.

One Saturday Collins said, " Mind yourself to-morrow, Earnán." No other explanation. Probably there was to be some kind of a general round-up. The last time he had told me to watch out had been on Armistice Day, 1919, when men from the Dublin Brigade had been mobilised to wipe out Lord French and his staff as they took the salute during the march past. Volunteers, who had lined the streets, and their concentration at the saluting base outside the Bank of Ireland, had been demobilised as they were ready to hit up the well-drilled lines of chest medals.

That night I went to a *céilidhe* run by a literary society, actually by a company of the Fourth. An excited captain from the University whispered to me in the dressing room: " My God, it's awful, a H.Q. job, damned awful." He cracked the joints of his fingers with loud snaps. He laughed with a nervous whinny as he pressed back his hair, then his hand pressed tightly and grasped the other till the tendons were white. At the college I had heard him talk of footling military details amongst girls and non-volunteers with pauses and chuckles as he covered his mouth with his hand. Once he had been a legend, now I thought him windy. He had been out in '16. I did not know what all this talk of his meant. Later I gathered tags from two others who talked as if I knew what was to happen. Next day British secret service officers, who had steadily improved their system until it now overshadowed ours, were to be shot in Dublin. " The other battalions are on the job," said a law student, " all attacks are to be timed, but I have my doubts. Won't you come with my bunch? It will be tough. Maybe it's a no-come-back job."

I went home to Sears' house in Terenure. He was a
member of the Dáil and thought it too risky to sleep at
home as he was well known. I had not many houses I
could change about to; I was unattached to a unit and
made my own arrangements. I lay awake for a long time.
I found it hard to sleep, thinking of what would happen;
how many people besides myself knew about it, who should
not? I tried to read bits about headstrong Bhima and the
hero Arjuna in the Mahabharata, but sleeping officers and
Volunteers overhauling guns jumped into the pages.
Dublin would no longer be a picnic.

Next day a stop press: thirteen officers scattered through
the city and suburbs had been shot dead, three had been
wounded, others had escaped. Some had been killed in
their beds beside their wives. Dublin was jumpy, passersby
were nervous; they spoke less as they walked, and groups
at street corners took on a new significance. Something
would happen, but what? The British would not take that
lying down. The city had been safe enough so far. City
people had not experienced the desolate remoteness of the
country during the raids of threatening soldiers, drunken
Tans and fiercely arrogant Auxies. Dublin had not felt the
loneliness and awed night of a country town or small city
controlled by its garrison.

Soldiers held up men walking in threes or fours. Crossley tenders nosed up and down as if the Auxiliaries did not
know what to do next. Heavy lorries stopped outside
flats and private houses; soldiers hurriedly helped to move
the belongings of other intelligence officers, and those who
might be open to attack, to the Castle or to an hotel which
was heavily guarded. In the afternoon the crowd at a
Gaelic football match in Croke Park had been surrounded
by soldiers, police and Auxiliaries: twelve killed, eleven
seriously wounded, fifty slightly wounded by machine
guns and rifles. I had heard the distant rattling.

Steel plated Lancias and armoured cars with swinging
turrets dashed through the streets; they curved in towards
the footpaths, people scurried. The troops had blood in
their eyes. Streets were suddenly held up by soldiers and
men in plain clothes; at the top of Dawson Street I saw
two lorries spill out Auxies who snapped on bayonets as
they ran to cut off a part of the street. They hit men with

the butts of their rifles. I was told at McGilligans in Leeson Street where I often slept that it would not be safe for me to stay the night. Kathleen McGilligan was worried: "Seán MacBride will find you a place and, get there as soon as you can; what's that?" A sound of shooting. Seán MacBride was the son of Major John MacBride who had been executed after Easter Week. We voiced our fears as we walked.

It was seven o'clock. Soldiers and Auxiliaries were firing over the heads of the moving people shouting " Go home, you bastards, go home." Curfew should begin at twelve o'clock. Seán MacBride brought me to the flat of an Abbey Theatre dramatist. It was on the top floor of a four-storey house. " I have two guns and an egg," I said. " I'll fight if there's a raid."

" I'll take one." But he did not know how to work a Parabellum. Sitting on the stairs I showed him the action, the use of the safety catch and how to clear a jam. We were welcomed. I was introduced to Lennox Robinson, whom I had often seen at the Abbey and to Thomas McGreevy. They did not object to us remaining there the night. It was risky to be outside now. Robinson played Beethoven on a pianola; McGreevy took his turn to press on the wide wooden pedals. The instrument coughed and wheezed when the movement of the feet was irregular, or the music came in pauses. Robinson pedalled furiously, his long body bent itself as the notes jerked out. " Should I tell him we'll fight?" I whispered.

" No, better not," said Seán, " there's not much chance of a raid anyhow." I got drawn into the music and I felt still inside, but squeaking wood or a cluster of shots would enter as a motif. He was trying to take his mind away from the brooding horror of the day and the outside street.

Our attempts to talk had been short meaningless sentences. McGreevy clicked the switch. " It's better to put it out; nearly all the other houses are without light." Robinson closed the pianola. We sat in front of the fire. McGreevy talked. He had been a gunner officer in France. He had a sensitive face; he must have suffered in the hell of the World War. I ate hazel nuts out of a red bowl. The others said " Good-night," and went into the next room. We, watching the twisting yellow of the flames, sat on the

floor.   " It will go hard with any prisoners taken to-night,"
I said.

There was a feeling of uncertainty as if something was
going to happen. We talked in whispers as if afraid of the
sound of our own voices ; outside in the street the noise
of heavy cars and sharp commands. Later, as we looked
out a window, we saw an armoured car stop below close
to the curb under an arc lamp Men with dark bonnets
jumped down ; they were joined by others from a tender
which pulled in. There were few people on the street.
Three men walking on the footpath were held up They
were backed against a shop window. They held their hands
over their heads. I saw an Auxiliary hit one of the men in
the face with his fist. The three were searched, something
was brought over to the lamp post, the armed men crowded
around whilst it was being looked at. I heard a voice shout :
" Run for it." The three ran towards the corner of Clare
Street, spreading out. A tearing smash of rifle fire, the
metal snap of bolts throwing out cartridges. One man
twisted and sprawled forward out of sight. The rifles flared
again.

We went away from the window thinking we might be
seen. We ate nuts. In the darkness the crash of the nut
shells boomed up and down the room. Heavy cars,
armoured evidently, from the vibration, rattled; soft
gliding noises of tenders, revolver shots in the dull distance,
close by the jerky beat of a Vicker's gun. From the next
room came low voices whenever a loud burst of shooting
woke us up. The others could not sleep. " Do you think
we have their beds? " I asked.

*   *   *   *

Troops drove through the street at a more rapid rate.
Shops were raided at all hours of the day, and streets held
up ; in the dark, houses were searched, often half a street
at a time. At night I could see soldiers moving quietly on
rubber soles as patrols, or in extended order, followed,
perhaps, by the cobbled bumps of a steel-plated Lancia, or
I watched the shafts from a movable search light turned on
houses. A wreck of a car might noise along, followed at a
short distance by a strong smooth engine without lights.
That was a night trap for those who might attempt to tackle
the first one, or who would be off their guard when it passed.

One night the house opposite to me was raided. I saw figures outside my gate as I laid out automatic magazines on a chair. A search light swept on to the fronts of the nearby houses and picked out a swarm of soldiers, trailing rifles as they left the house without prisoners. A week after " Bloody Sunday " sixteen cadets were killed in an ambush by the West Corkmen in the mountainy pass of Kilmichael. They had killed some of the men who went out to take their surrender, and the column men wiped out the rest of them.

In two recent raids the British had found papers of Mulcahy, Chief of Staff, whom they had nearly captured. That captured information seemed to be the most reliable insight their Secret Service could get of the movement. Amongst the papers were plans for a systematic destruction of docks, warehouses and technical plant in England. Touts, spies, and secret servicemen were thick in Dublin, but they worked too much in the dark of faulty psychology.

I was given a message by word. The C.S. wished to see me urgently that night in Ranelagh on the south side. I met him with Ginger and Emmet Dalton. Ginger was now D.T. Dick McKee, who had been brigadier of Dublin and Director of Training, had been murdered at the Castle with his Vice-Com., Peadar Clancy, on the morning after " Bloody Sunday."

Mulcahy had a thick fair moustache, although his hair was dark. It looked out of place in relation to the moustache, but I suppressed my smile. He was more than usually serious. On the table was a large scale map of the South of Ireland. " We intend to give you command of the Martial Law area," he said. " You can move around selecting your staff as you go through the brigades." The Martial Law area comprised five counties. " I would suggest Liam Lynch," I said, " he is a good officer ; he has his command well organized ; he could use that as a basis from which to work outwards."

" You know Limerick, Tipperary and part of Cork," Mulcahy said. " You will soon become familiar with the remainder of Cork and with County Kerry." We discussed likely staff officers for the new command. Organizing and training an area was one thing, I thought; taking command of a province with twelve brigades was a big responsibility.

Would I meet with hostility? How would the other brigades take the appointment? Cork County had no great love for G.H.Q. officers. Its brigades had developed of themselves; within the past three months the concentration of British had intensified. In their new development they might not be willing to be dictated to. I was younger than any of the officers. They would probably like someone with the weight of years and gravity. Of course, I could grow a moustache, but many of them knew me. Aloud I said, " All right, sir. I will do my best."

" Before you go to the South there is an operation the Staff would like you to undertake. What do you think of the Auxiliaries? "

" They are a fine body of men and a tough problem."

" We must tackle them at once. The adjoining Cork Brigades will co-operate in taking Macroom Castle where there's an Auxiliary Company. I want you to capture Inistiogue, the headquarters of the Auxiliaries in County Kilkenny."

" Kilkenny County has done little fighting."

" You will have help from the Waterford men."

" Waterford hasn't done much either and I don't know any of the officers in Kilkenny."

" You can summon a Brigade Staff meeting and meet them."

" Are there any flying columns in Kilkenny? "

" No, I don't think so," said Mulcahy. " Are you prepared to undertake the job? "

I hesitated. Operating with men whom I did not know in an area that I had never previously visited, and which had not seen much fighting did not appeal to me. Besides I had been directly ordered to capture a post which our best command would not undertake.

" This is your last independent operation. When it is over you will command the Martial Law area."

" Yes, sir," I said, " I'll take Inistiogue."

It was easy to say, " I'll take Inistiogue." That night I thought over the problem. I had no information about the strength of the Auxiliaries or of the British in the County, or even of our men there. It was hard enough to capture a small police barracks. Why didn't the Staff supply us with small artillery, trench mortars, Stokes guns, machine guns, or rifle grenades, even with decent land mines? We had not anything like a good supply of ammunition for our rifles. Why didn't the Staff pay attention to pure Staff work, leaving the political field to the others? The Chief of Staff was a member of Dáil Éireann, the Director of Intelligence was a Minister of Finance, the Director of Organization was a Secretary to the Dáil, the Director of Engineering was the Secretary of the Local Government Board.

Next day I met Mulcahy in Parnell Square, in Banba Hall.

" Have you any plan of action to outline? "

" We might attack a barracks near their headquarters and wait for their reinforcements, then Inistiogue might be tackled while its garrison was weakened."

" Well, you'll see the situation for yourself when you reach Kilkenny." We shook hands. " Good luck now, Earnán." I saluted and was walking out the door when he called me back.

" Is there any activity down town? " he asked. " I'm going to Brunswick Street Technical Schools."

" No, I've just come across the Liffey and through O'Connell Street; no hold-ups and not much activity. I'll scout the way for you."

" And what about yourself? "

" I'm armed."

" No, you could not be replaced either," he said, smiling slowly as he gripped my arm. " Don't you know that? Take care of yourself and good luck."

That was the first sign of personal regard I had received from him. I was happy as I walked across town, whistling.

* * * *

Lloyd George yet had faith in unofficial reprisals: burning of creameries, factories, shops, town halls, private houses, went on. Towns showed jagged stumps of broken teeth where fire had spread; raiding parties smashed property and looted. Perhaps the Premier thought the destruction of the economic life would cow the people and turn them against the Dáil and the I.R.A.; but it irritated neutrals and made our friends more bitterly staunch. The American elections would soon be due; if reprisals wore out weak links in the separatist chain, martial law, which admitted serious trouble, would not be necessary.

Rory O Connor, D.E., went to England on a tour

of inspection.   He was responsible for operations there.
Irishmen and men of Irish descent in the cities had been
organized in units on the lines of the Irish Volunteers.
They could destroy power plants, warehouses and supplies,
and burn the houses of Tans, Auxiliaries and officers. The
counter demonstration would throw light on the destruction
in Ireland and possibly slow it down.   At the end of
November fires burst out in English warehouses and docks.

*   *   *   *

I left my papers in a concealed cupboard. There was
no sense in risking my notes and papers in a county like
Kilkenny.   I left my two guns in another dump.   I
felt I had a tough job before me, and I knew nothing
about the type of men there.   A friendly checker brought
me through a side door at the Kingsbridge station, which
was carefully watched by enemy intelligence.   Seated in a
carriage, I waited impatiently for the train to pull out.

Passersby scanned the windows in a casual way or glanced
sharply with well-trained eyes. I tried to read a magazine ;
but always behind the page was a sense of being cornered
in a carriage, open to a stray memoried snapshot.   At a
junction police and Tans came on board, but they did not
search. The engine driver walked off the train ; he would
not drive armed police.   The Tans threatened him.   Two
pulled guns and one said, tapping his ribs with a Webley :
" Do you know what this is? " An hour later a new driver
who was willing to drive armed police was found ; but
they remained behind on the platform when the train
started.   The new driver had been threatened by railway
workers as to what would happen to him when he came back.

I passed by the police on the platform on Kilkenny
station, outwardly calm, but confused enough in my mind
on the difficulties I sensed would lie before me.

THE BOLD BLACK AND TAN

The town of Balbriggan they burnt to the ground
The bullets like hail were all whizzing around.
Lloyd George said to Greenwood, " Now this is our plan,
We'll conquer Ireland with the bold Black and Tan."

From Cork on to Limerick, Clare and Mayo.
Lies a trail of destruction wherever they go.
We'll shoulder our rifles, we'll fight to a man
And we'll humble the pride of the bold Black and Tan.

CHAPTER SIXTEEN

DECEMBER, 1920

*

COUN Y KILKENNY was slack.   It was difficult to meet officers, dispatches took a long time to travel.   A brigade council met in the city to elect a brigade staff.   Poor material, I thought, no direction from above and no drive. Answers to questions showed that none of them had tried to solve the problem of their commands; very different from Cork meetings where men spoke their minds somewhat and intelligence flared up.   Quietly, somewhat dully, they sat around the table in awe.   They would talk when the meeting was over, now whilst they voted a staff there was mute acceptance.   The new brigadier did not impress me by any show of energy or resolution.   He was more of a steady business man, stout, easy spoken, the Mayor of the city; he did not refuse to accept responsibility.   The attempted capture of the Auxiliary headquarters would be outside of his life.   In an area that had not seen fighting the elective system was not satisfactory; men would sit and vote for a man whom they knew was not fitted for a position; who lacked alertness and was not young enough in mind.

There had been no staff work.   None of them were accustomed to questions.   The Inistiogue Commandant had little information to give about the Auxiliaries who lived two miles from his house.   Through questions, I found a little about their discipline, drinking habits, relationship with the people and movements of patrols, but he knew nothing about the defence of the building, sentries and outlying defences.   At the end of my probing I learned that Woodstock, their headquarters, was a large, old, well-built house on rising ground, surrounded by a wooded demesne and enclosed by a high stone wall.   The grounds were well patrolled.   On one side was the deep, swift running Nore; there were no fords, but it could be crossed by a weir.   Men were to be sent from each battalion to form a flying column; each area was to plan simple operations at once.

I set off with O'Hanrahan, the Inistiogue commandant, and a young boy, Holland, in a pony and trap. Holland was to work with me; he was on the run. I had been lent a .32 Browning for which I had no respect, and two percussion eggs. They were clumsy for use on the road and hard to handle in a confined space; they would explode on impact, and if they struck anything whilst they were in my hand it was good-bye. O'Hanrahan was tall, swarthy, and hairy, loose-limbed with large heavy hands sprawling about and a rather heavy face. He was elderly; his moustache curved out like a waterfall. He worked hard on the land. The Auxies he spoke of as "them Tans."

Recently Auxiliaries had captured two boys as they jumped over a hedge on to the road. One of the boys had a rifle on his back. The Auxiliaries took his rifle, shot him against the hedge and brought his dead body and his live companion back with them to their headquarters. Auxiliaries had raided and evidently terrorized the county. One day searching for " rebels " they had stopped to question an old lady of eighty. " Seen any rebels around here, mother? " one of them queried. " Yes," said she, reminiscently and wearily, " there was Stephens and Smith O'Brien, and John O'Leary and———"

" Where are they? " shouted one of the Auxiliaries, excitedly. " Where are they? "

" Oh," said she, " that was over fifty years ago." And they disappeared in dust, swearing.

In the darkness we reached O'Hanrahan's house on a by-road. I studied a bundle of half-inch maps of the country, then sat over the Inistioge district until I had a good idea of the lay of the land. O'Hanrahan's large fingers prodded helplessly at the map as he followed me along the roads and across hills, adding local information. Before we went to bed, we decided that I should visit the estate next day as one anxious to buy timber. I would then have an idea of outpost positions, the buildings and the best lines of approach.

Next morning I worked over the maps, then left them down and took up *Mr. Britling Sees It Through*. I had read two chapters by half-past ten when I heard the distant blurring of words; people were talking to the woman of the house. A few moments afterwards, the door was opened and an Auxiliary with a bonnet perched on his head came into the room. There was a rifle slung on his shoulder, the black butt of a Webley stuck out of his holster. I felt myself rising; but I sat down hard on my chair. I gripped the table with my hands. His movements were too casual for one on a special raid. I wondered if my eyes looked startled or frightened. He was as unexpected as death.

"What's your name?" he asked.

"Stewart."

He was a small man, he spoke with a Cockney accent. "And you," turning to my companion.

"Holland."

"What are you doing here?"

"Visiting my aunt," I said. I looked at *Mr. Britling*, trying to think; there was no one outside the window, but my table was in the centre of the room. My maps were on the window, my note-book was open on the table. I closed and pushed it to one side. The window could not be opened. I would have to smash it. He walked about opening drawers, peering into a cupboard. Stick him up, I thought, gag him if he does not shout, and get through the window, if he does not put up his hands, shoot—take his rifle and gun and rush through for the outside door. I must take my note-book. I had my hand on it when he said, turning towards me.

"This is a rotten job, I'm sick of it; wish it was over."

I nodded. "You must have a hard life of it." Just then the door was pushed open and an officer, followed by a number of men, burst into the room.

"What is your name?" he barked.

"Stewart."

"Your Christian name?"

"Bernard."

"What are you doing here?"

"Visiting my aunt."

"Did you search him?" he said, turning to the first intruder.

"No, sir."

I sprang from the chair, made a bound towards the door, pulling out my automatic, but it had caught in the lining of my inside pocket. He sprang at me, revolver in hand, and clasped his arm around me whilst the other searched my pockets and found my gun.

" I'm sorry I did not shoot you, you dirty swine," remarked the officer. " Take him out, blindfold him, and stick him up against a wall." The others began to search Holland. They brought me outside the house, bandaged my eyes and put me up against the wall, whilst a group stood around calling me foul names.

I was in for it now, I thought. At last I had been trapped. That damn little automatic. If I had had my own guns they would have been on the outside of my coat attached to my Sam Brown, and it would have meant a quick draw when the door was opened. If I could only see, maybe I could make a dash for it, or look at what they were going to do to me. The woman of the house came out. " For God's sake don't shoot him, he's young, God help him. Do what you like to the place, but don't shoot the lad."

" Get in, you old bitch, quick," roared a voice, " you'll get what's coming to you, too."

The bandage was taken off my eyes as an officer approached. He was dressed in naval uniform and spoke with authority. He snapped : " Who are you? "

" I am a member of the Irish Republican Army."

" What rank? "

" Volunteer."

" What is your Company?" No reply.

" Who is your Captain? " No reply.

" So you're not going to talk, you bastard," he said. " Well, we'll make you." Then he went away.

One of my guards cocked the hammer of his Webley, and told me to put up my hands, he kept the revolver pointed at my heart.

" I know something better than that," he said suddenly, as he whipped off his bayonet and placed it on his rifle, and got into the " Ready " position a few feet from me. I knew from his face that he would like to twist it in my guts. At the end of about ten minutes I was blindfolded, handcuffed, kicked down the lane and into a motor car and driven away. When they took off my bandage I was in the hall of a large building. Inistiogue, evidently, so I had arrived at last, but not as I had expected. " Take off his

boots," said the naval officer, " and bring him below stairs."
Whilst they were taking off my boots Holland was brought
in, similarly bandaged and handcuffed. They took off his
boots and walked us down stairs to the vaults. They shoved
us into a darkened room and searched us. They took my
watch, fountain pen, my pocket-book containing £18 in
notes. " Ha! " said one, " He was well paid for his
murders." Said another, " This is as good as pay day."
They continued the search, they took my beads and a small
Jeanne d'Arc medal which had been sewn on the back of
the lapel of my coat.

The cellar was dark and the flags were cold; it was a
December day. They pulled my hands behind my back and
handcuffed me, then they tied with ropes my hands at the
wrists, below the elbows and above the elbows; my legs
above my knees and at my ankles. They tied Holland,
but not in so many places. Before they left, one of the
Auxiliaries put my beads back in my pocket. "You will
need these to-night," he said. They had left me standing
against a post.

" Where are you? " I called.

" Here, over here," said Holland. I dropped to the
ground and rolled over until I was beside him. We sat
close and whispered in each other's ears. " Now, don't
forget, I'm Stewart. You met me in O'Hanrahan's last
night and you know nothing else about me."

" I'll do that," he said. " Do you think they'll shoot us?"

The ropes were tight and cut into my flesh as I moved
away from Holland. About an hour later light flashed and
a man was kicked into the cell whilst the Auxiliaries spewed
out a stream of curses, some of which were diverted to us.
He was placed near me. He began to talk, asked me what
was my name; why I had been arrested. I said for carrying
a gun. He asked what I thought would happen and I
replied that I thought we would be shot. The conversation
languished. I managed by moving my forehead to work the
bandage off my eyes so that after a time I could see a form
seated near me. I said, " Do your ropes hurt you? "
" Yes," he replied. " Have they tied you on top of the
handcuffs? " " They have, and my wrists hurt like the
devil." I rolled over, sat up and touched his arms with my
fingers. He had no handcuffs and his arms were loosely

tied. "What kind of a hole is this?" I asked. "I am blindfolded and cannot see." "So am I." Then I talked to him, told him extravagantly simple tales of my not being in much sympathy with the Irish Republican Army and of my being tired of it all.

An hour later some Auxiliaries entered and told the prisoner to sit up. As they hustled him out one said, "You'll get what is coming to you." Ten minutes later they returned and shone an electric torch on my face; one of them pulled down my handkerchief a little, kicked me repeatedly, and hard, then said: "Oh, you're a cunning bastard. Wait till to-night." Another said "And when we've finished with you, you . . . " He shook both fists at me to express himself. They left Holland alone. Later I heard them shouting outside the door. I was from Macroom, they said, where the big ambush of cadets had taken place. They threatened the sentries. "Let's get at the red-headed bastard."

"It looks as if they don't like me," I said to Holland, and we laughed.

Time passed slowly in the cold darkness. We did not talk. Each was thinking his own thoughts. Had they found the percussion grenades, what had they done to the O'Hanrahans and their house? I felt sure that if they found out who I was then it meant a lingering or a quick death, or both. But they wanted to shoot me; they had been told by their officers that I had been in the Macroom ambush which had taken place two weeks ago. The British official report stated that the sixteen dead Auxiliaries had been "Chopped with Hatchets." Shooting would be much better than torture: I did not know if I could stand it; even a toothache made a wreck of me.

It must have been midnight when an Auxiliary came in, loosed the ropes on my ankles and legs and said: "Come on." My feet were cold, the ropes had made them numb and swollen. It was hard to walk. I went down a narrow passage, the guard kicked me hard from behind every few steps. Once I cried, "Ow." He gripped me by the neck with long pincer fingers: "you're a queer soldier." Evidently a soldierly quality is the silent endurance of kicks.

I was shoved into a large room. There were officers seated behind a table, one in the centre wore a regulation military cap. Auxiliaries in the sombre bottle green of the Royal Irish with blue green bonnets stood around. It made them look very stern. Many of them had sergeants' gold V's on their sleeves and war ribbons on their tunics. They looked smart, neat and impressive. This was a ceremony of some sort. The light was not good, the dark walls were gloomy in the shadows, reflected light shone on the hard set faces. The officer in the regulation cap began the questions:

" What is your name? "

" Bernard Stewart."

" Your address? "

" Kilkenny City."

" Are you in the I.R.A.? "

" Yes."

" What rank? "

" I'm a Volunteer."

" What rank? "

" No rank."

" What is the name of your Company? "

" 'C' Company."

" Tell me the names of your officers." I did not answer.

" H'm; who gave you the automatic? " No reply.

" So, you won't talk, eh? "

An Auxiliary standing at my side clenched his fist and swung to jab. " No don't," said the officer in naval uniform. " Untie his arms," said regulation cap.

" Where did you get the cardigan? " " I bought it."

" Where? " I did not reply. At O'Shaughnessy's in Cahir, I remembered.

" Don't you know it's a military jacket? "

" No, I bought it."

" Where? " I did not answer.

" Where did you get the officer's trench coat: at Macroom? Stole it from a dead man, of course? "

" I bought it."

" Where? "

" In a shop."

An officer leant across the table and said, " You're the man who stole the plans. I saw you in Grafton Street." He continued to stare very knowingly and fixedly at me. What did he mean, what plans, and why Grafton Street?

They wanted to connect me with Dublin. I looked him in the face, his eyes had streaks of blood on the whites; we eyed each other.

" Where's his pistol? " demanded regulation cap. " Here it is, sir," said a sergeant. " It's loaded."

" What do you carry it for? "

" For protection."

" No, but for shooting down our men from behind a hedge. Shooting them in the back."

The sergeant turned the Browning in his hand. " Put that damned thing away. It might go off. Now, see here, I'm going to give you one more chance to answer. Who gave you that pistol? " I remained silent. " If you don't answer by the time I count three, we'll blow your God damned brains out."

" I am ready to die," I said.

" Now," said regulation cap. " if he doesn't answer when I count three, fire." The sergeant pushed me back. He drew his Webley and shoved the cold muzzle hard against my forehead. The skin contracted slowly; it seemed to draw my eyebrows upwards, a cold spinal shiver ran down from the back of my neck. I suppressed it. " Stand back from behind him." A space was left between me and the wall. I brought my stockinged heels together.

" Will you answer? " " One." " No." " Two." I shook my head. " Three." I shook my head.

" Were you ever in the army, Stewart? " " Yes."

" What regiment were you in? "

" We have no regiments in the Irish Republican Army."

" Stewart, you will be shot at dawn to-morrow. Take him away."

They brought me through a long passage and seated me on a wooden form. They tied my hands and legs as before. I felt trussed; they put a cloth across my eyes. I heard the voices of men singing and the tinkle of glass. I must have been near the canteen. Men stopped to threaten me, some said : " We'll put you through it for Macroom." A few walked in their heavy boots on my stockinged feet. My toes were crushed ; some stamped hard with the full weight of their legs on instep and toes. They lifted their boots again and came down on the same place ; I tensed my body to stop myself from moaning. Two guards jabbed me a few times with their bayonets below my ribs on the abdominal muscles. Blood dribbled down my buttocks and legs. Other prisoners were brought in; they were kicked and beaten; some of them shouted in pain.

I could not walk when I was told to move on. The guard lifted me, carried me along and flung me into a room. My head struck the stone floor and I was dazed. My bandage was removed. Beside me on the floor was Holland; he smiled. On benches opposite were about twelve or fourteen prisoners. I sat up and spoke to Holland, my voice was weak. Auxiliaries came in and gave food to the others. We could have bread and water they said. " Do you want anything? " one asked. " No," I said. Later some Auxiliaries came in and went through all my pockets. They opened all the buttons on my shirt, coat and trousers. One took off my tie; " It's a good one," he said, as he put it in his pocket. Another tried to take off my shirt, but he had to stop; he would have to untie my ropes. It was very cold lying there unbuttoned. It must have been freezing hard. The prisoners looked at me with a kind of dumb pity. " May they be cursed to their seed, breed and generation," said one.

Later the guards came in. " Do you want your bread and water? " " No," I said, and Holland shook his head. " Hunger striker," one jeered. " You'll shoot me at dawn, I might as well go fasting." During the night men came to look at us.

" Were you in the army, Stewart? " asked one.

" Yes, I was."

" What regiment? "

" No regiment."

" But how," and he stopped. " In the Irish Republican Army." " Damn you anyway," he said, as he went out.

I said to Holland: " Don't ask for food and stick it out; they'll shoot me at dawn." My arms were burning with the cold and numbness, my legs and arms tingled. They seemed to weigh down on my body, and I felt that they were many times too big. My crushed feet and the bayonet wounds hurt me. My mind was a jumble with pain, cold, and criss-cross thought, but at the back of all was a strength that I knew would help me to face my end calmly, although the racing thought in front of it swirled and eddied me into a whirl.

" You're a brave man," sneered an Auxiliary.

" Leave him alone, can't you? " said his companion.

" It's getting on to dawn," said one of the guards, " do you want a priest? "

" No, I'll take my chance."

Later there was a clatter of heavy boots. " Carry him up," someone said. I was brought upstairs. My boots were pulled on with trouble; my feet were swollen. Some one said in an authoritative voice : " Bring him outside." The bandage which had just been put on was taken off. " This is your last look at the sky," said an Auxiliary who leant on the muzzle of his rifle. I was stood against the door post. Lorries were being warmed up ; men were putting on ammunition slings outside of heavy coats. Cold looking clouds held back the rays of the sun, trees slowly changed from outlines to stronger forms, backed by a grey shivering sky and a bird's clear notes came slowly out of the mist. Lights on tenders showed up parts of the building and the men who walked out of the shadows. I was placed in an open tender, the bandage was put on my eyes and the convoy moved off.

" There's the house you were caught in," said one ; " not much left of it." I was sorry for the trouble I had brought on the O'Hanrahans. The convoy halted. " This is good enough," I heard, " quite a nice shooting spot," and the reply, " Quite." My lips were dry; they were of rough leather. I had been trying to say some prayers, but could not. My thoughts ran on ahead crossed and recrossed. I was not afraid of death now. Faces I knew came up, my brother Frank's, Seán Tracey's ; then I felt at peace. It was hard to pin anything down, to think I was going to die on the roadside. I would tell them that they were fools, that they could not win ; dead men would help to beat them in the end.

" I don't understand all this," said a pleasant voice, on my right. " Are you cold? " " No." " Yes, you are," and he wrapped a warm rug around my legs and slung a coat behind my shoulders. " Thank you," I said.

" Did they feed you? "

" They offered me bread and water, but I refused."

" I thought our people fed their prisoners well," he said. " Why do you do it? "

" You would not understand."

" Well, I wish it was all over. I'm fed up with it."

I heard the men who had been talking some distance away get back into their tenders; we moved off. I felt more kindly and my heart glowed.

We halted again. I was carried upstairs. I was placed on the ground. " We're handing you over to the police." The police, that meant the Royal Irish and the Tans. My heart sank, the Black and Tans. " Here you are," said a voice. " Two dangerous birds, but watch this murderer here," he emphasized with a kick in my back. My bandage was taken off; beside me was Holland. A soldier, a purple-red beefy faced man with a spiky moustache who smiled, bent over me and untied my ropes. My hands and wrists were blue and puffy. The ropes had broken through the flesh. My trousers and shirt stuck to my skin with blood. My feet felt as if they had been through a mangle.

I was put in a cell with Holland, there were two men in it. The beefy man, they said, was the bombardier in charge of prisoners, and we were in the detention cells of Kilkenny military barracks. " Are you hungry?" asked the bombardier. " Yes," we said. Soon he came back with bowls of tea and a large plate of bread and sausages. Sausages were divine, tea had never seemed such a delicious drink. The bombardier warmed us with his smile.

The cell was a dirty grey which had once been white, the floor was black and greasy. In a corner was a pile of torn brown army blankets. I did not know the two men. They were from Thomastown, near Inistioge. The Tans had arrested the whole countryside, they said ; mad with rage they were half murdering anyone they took. Evidently we had disturbed their little Auxiliary Eden. They played Twenty-one and Banker with Holland most of the day, and chatted the rest of it. They told tales of Johnstown and Thomastown; in the shadowy cell the stories grew as they searched darkly in the minds of the townsmen. Fathers slept with their daughters and girls scattered babies almost at will ; their talk built phantoms, but as I did not show any particular surprise they had to search out further facts to impress me.

On the walls were sketches, remarks, pointed, unpointed, rich and obscene, with ballads and rebel songs. The cells had held British soldiers and our men. Sergeant-majors, marines and military police seemed to be the chief aversions to men of good will. Their ill fame decorated a large portion of the cell.

I walked up and down, five strides up and down; swift strides and sharp twisting turns. I thought of the tigers in the zoo, their flowing sinewy thrust forward, the lithe tenseness of contracted paws as they prowled around the cages, brushing their heads on the bars. "Take it easy," said one of the men who sat wrapped up in a blanket, "take it easy." For days I walked the cell then sat up against the wall thinking of escape. I tried to think out how they could prove who I was. I was not known to the police by sight except in Offaly, Roscommon and Westmeath, and that was some years ago. I was known to them by name in some counties, by my numerous false names in others. This was a halting place; where would I be sent to next?

We listened to the sentries in the passage outside our door. They sang ballads about the sergeant's wife. Some one must have had to rack his thoughts to put marines and soldiers in unexpected physical relationship to the Gargantuan body of the sergeant's wife. Often they were dirty without being funny. They told us what would happen to us here and hereafter. They had a special down on me. I wagged my finger at them and threatened to tell the parson, I corrected their mistakes in pronunciation. I was to be 'unged. I was a . . . . murderer, I would then roast in 'ell, 'strewth. In return we sang our songs whilst they howled at us to shut up.

> Drunk and uproarious,
> Punk and notorious
> God damn the king.

> Gather all the socks you meet for the English Tommies' feet
> Whilst they're running from the Germans far away.

> From the G.P.O. to Boland's Mill
> We made poor England weep his fill,
> But old Britannia, loves us still,
> Whack fol the diddle, diddle di do day.
> Soon we will all be civilized,
> Neat and clean and well advised.
> Oh! Won't mother England be surprised,
> Whack for the diddle, diddle di do day.

We laid bets as to how often they used the adjective known as the soldiers' word. Sometimes it was mentioned every five words, then again a group might use it every four.

I was called outside my cell and brought into a room where were six men in civilian clothes, smartly dressed, keen looking, a few like hounds, as eager to get on the scent. " So you're Stewart," one said. They looked at my full face and profile carefully. They walked around me as if I had been a horse which they wanted to buy ; they asked me to walk across the room. It was more like a fair than ever, soon they will ask me to trot, I thought.

" Well Stewart, were you ever in Dublin? " asked one, with a heavy strong chin thrust forward.

"Yes." My trench coat bore the name of a Dublin shop.

" How long since? "

" About a year ago."

" Were you in Dublin recently? "

"No." They wanted to connect me with Bloody Sunday.

" Where did you stay? "

" I won't answer that."

"You won't answer?" His chin dug forward spading the words ; " No, I won't." He turned to the others. " He won't answer." There were heavy nods. " So." Evidently that was considered important. Their foreheads wrinkled with intensity, searching for clues, perhaps.

" What is your home address? "

" I won't say."

" What county do you live in? "

I shook my head. " Mayo? " " No."

" Kilkenny? " " No." " Carlow? " No. " Louth? " " No." County after county, I continued to shake my head. I was losing my temper. My answers had become crisp and jerky ; then, I thought, that's foolish, tell them to go to hell or answer quietly. I would be put through it anyhow, here now, or later.

" Where did you get the trench coat? "

" I bought it."

" Where? "

" In a shop. "

" What shop? "   No reply.

" Who gave you the pistol? "

" I won't tell you."

" You won't tell me? "

" No." Heavy nods, the situation had become serious again. " If you tell me the name of the man who gave you the pistol you will be released."

"I'm not an informer."

" Very good, Stewart. So you won't talk. Well, you'll be made to talk: *Do you hear?* "

The questions meant that they knew nothing about me, but were anxious to link me up with Dublin. I wondered what was next to come. I talked of escape with Holland, but he could not give much information about the barracks. The latrine was outside the cells, a soldier without weapons went with us as an escort; there was an armed sentry in sight. I might get to the barracks wall and climb it, but I would then be under fire and would not know how to get cover till I was out of sight.

The bombardier announced an officer. He had a revolver in his hand. He called my name, stuck the Webley at the back of my head, told me not to attempt to escape and walked me out amongst the barrack buildings. He steered me round a corner with an arm grip. There I saw a photographer who simultaneously clicked. My photograph had been taken. I felt myself forestalled and walked back in bad humour. Besides, ever since I was a child I disliked my first photograph. I had been told to look at the birdy, and there had been no birdy, just a likeness of my brother, sister and I gazing in expectant wonder.

Next day the officer, whom the Bombardier had assured me in the meantime was decent and kind, came into the cell. " I'll be straight with you, the photo was a failure. Now we want to take you."

" I refuse, you ask because you failed."

He said grimly: " Well, we'll see." He brought me outside. A man came up with a tripod and began to set up a camera. When he was ready, I moved my body. " Stop that," ordered the officer. I ceased the movement, but screwed up my face. The officer got red in the face, " I'll soon stop that." He ordered two soldiers who were standing by with rifles to fix bayonets. They snapped the steel on to the boss. "*On Guard.*" They got into position on either side of me, their bayonets pointing at my chest. I continued to make faces. "If you don't stop, I'll give them the order to jab." I did not stop. He told the privates to stand aside. "We'll hand you over to some people who will be less polite than we were. Then you'll change your mind." The bombardier was worried : "Why couldn't you let them take you?"

CHAPTER SEVENTEEN

DECEMBER, 1920

★

" PACK UP, Holland and Stewart, pack up," was shouted in the early morning. We rolled out of our blankets as the cell door slammed back with a crash. Six Auxiliaries walked with us to the large square of the barracks. Others with rifle butts on their shoulders or with rifles swung from straps ran up and down, stamping feet, blowing on their hands. " Get up," said one. We swung ourselves into an open Crossley tender. " Sit down." It was cold, there was wet straw on the boards. We both shivered.

An Auxie hung around the lorry jeering; his companion ground his teeth, but did not say anything. A sergeant-major very neat and trim, stood in deferential closeness; a black cane tight under his arm. "We'll take you to see some gentlemen who know how to make you talk," said the first, who had a small moustache, " and then you'll hang, you bastard."

" We can die only once," I said, and we laughed at him. The eyes of the sergeant-major twinkled.

The escort lined up; there were more than thirteen tenders. We were handcuffed wrist to wrist. In front near the driver was a guard of two Auxiliaries in plain clothes ; they had given evidence at my trial in Woodstock House. A tall officer halted our tender. " If there's any shooting on the road, you're the first for it," turning to me. "Do you understand?" I did not speak. " You're the first—*Do you hear?*" I looked at him but I did not answer.

The convoy moved slowly. It was very cold. About noon by the sun a man in front with a fair moustache asked if we were cold. We shook our heads. Holland and I decided that we would not complain of cold or hunger. Later they stopped in a town for something to eat. " Prisoners," someone shouted. Soon the tender was surrounded by women and girls.

" Where are you from? What were you taken for? "

" Don't answer," ordered the fair moustache.

" We're from Kilkenny, going to Dublin," I said. The cadets drove the people away, but they came back. Soon, girls brought up cups of tea, steaming in the cold air.

" Here you are," said a lithe, blackhaired girl, reaching out a cup.

" Get away," said one of our guards, he who had clashed his teeth, " or . . . " He pulled a Webley thirty-eight from his pocket. The girl did not move. She still held out the cup of tea. "Back, you bitch." The girl stepped back then walked forward until she was close to the Webley. She threw her head back, colour petalled high on her cheeks.

" And you," she said, " what are you? "

" Oh, all right, they can drink," said the fair moustache. Later he asked, " Do you want anything to eat? "

" No," I replied. He walked away. When he came back he handed me a bag. " Biscuits," he said. We thanked him ; they tasted very good.

Toward dusk on the Dublin road we heard a scream. The convoy halted ; one of the heavy lorries had run over a civilian. He died with gurgling rattles on the roadside. The men on the tender did not stop their conversation. The fair moustached one told us to run up and down as we were cramped ; he did not come with us. We increased the length of our runs till we were in front of the first armoured lorry. " I think I can wriggle my hand loose if you're game to make a dash," I said to Holland.

" We haven't much of a chance," he said, " besides we don't know the country " I was nearly sure I could squeeze my hand out of the steel clasp, but I did not want to try unless he was willing. They would probably shoot him even if he did not run away with me.

We drove through the lighted streets of Dublin. I thought of all those people walking about as if nothing had happened whilst for me, who looked out at them, the whole current of life had changed utterly. I could not

realize that I had been in those streets only two weeks
ago. We passed the Castle and Trinity College and went
to Beggars' Bush barracks. Inside, Auxiliary officers and
men crowded about our tender. I was told to get down ;
all suddenly stood to attention. The head lights of a car
were turned on me. " This is Stewart, sir." A figure
looked at me from beyond the light, evidently someone of
importance. We drove back to the Castle, as we went
through the entrance gate I plucked the fair Auxiliary by
the sleeve : " Thanks for being so kind," I said. He
patted my shoulder, " That's all right, son."

In the Guardroom I signed my name: Bernard Stewart;
occupation: farmer, Inistiogue, County Kilkenny. I used
a backhand scrawl which I had practised in the detention
barracks. There were eight or ten prisoners seated on
wooden boards or blankets along one wall, talking quietly.
The room was large. In front were two windows ; one
of them looked on to a narrow passage that led by the side
of the City Hall towards Dame Street. Around a warm fire
opposite the windows a guard of four Auxiliaries in police
uniform sat. One of them, a section commander, stood up
and stretched his legs apart in front of the hearth. " Don't
let any of you people try to escape. See that," pointing
to white splotches on the light green wall, " that's what
happened to two birds not so long ago." Impressively:
only dead men can escape from " F " Company. So it was
in this room that Peadar Clancy and Dick McKee had been
murdered. Men clattered through the door carrying rifles,
ammunition slings, and holsters strapped low on their
knees. Some stopped to chat with the guard.

" Where are you from? What are you in for? Why
were you pinched? " was asked of us. I knew one of the
men who questioned me. I had first met him during the
attack on Drangan barracks in Tipperary ; then as a commandant at the brigade council in Kilkenny. " Let's sit
together," he whispered, as he gave me a grey blanket.
He spoke slowly. There had been a world of arrests. De
Loughrey the Brigadier was taken around with them on all
their raids; he was a hostage; they said if they were fired on
they would blow his head off, and O'Hanrahan was to be
tried for harbouring rebels. They said they'd shoot him
for it. These boyhoes are a bad crowd. "What do you

think will happen; why am I here?" His face was nervous, his hand gripped my arm.

" I don't know," I said. " Let's not talk too much and try not to let them know you're worried. You know we're not sure of the other prisoners."

" Turn in," shouted the Section Commander. " Show the new prisoners how to make down their beds." The stout Kilkenny commandant placed two thin pieces of board together on two wooden trestles, one lower at the foot; on top he put three lemon brown, hard padded squares, known as army biscuits, then blankets. Most of the men knelt down to say their prayers. The guard looked at them, then turned away speaking in whispers. The commandant got into bed beside me. " You're a lucky devil," he whispered, "it was General Wood who stopped them from shooting ye at Inistiogue : most of the company wanted to shoot ye. What'll they do to us? We're not safe with them hangmen." The lights were kept on. I closed my eyes but I did not sleep.

The guard talked of "F" Company, of raids and arrests of women and the I.R.A. " I don't understand them," said one. There was a coming and going from the door leading to quarters through the guardroom. " Who are they? " asked a guard as three men in mufti passed through. " S.S." said another. Later two men came to where we lay.

" Where's the Macroom fellow? " asked one.

" Don't know," was the reply. Macroom : that meant me. Inistiogue cadets had evidently spread the good word that I was from Macroom. They stopped beside each bed. " Are you from Macroom? " they asked, shaking each sleeper till he awoke. One shook me twice, repeating, " Are you from Macroom? " I moved as if awakening slowly, my heart thudded hard, " No," I said.

We ate at the table when the guard had finished. We got the same food as they did. We had a knife and fork between four of us, a piece of bread or our hands served instead. Some of the men always tried to wolf another man's share. Prisoners were mixed; some Volunteers, others arrested on suspicion, possibly a few pigeons to get information. Every night fresh prisoners came in; they had been out after Curfew or had been taken by raiding parties. I answered questions in an oblique way, studied their faces and actions, watched the guard and all passing through the Guardroom. Auxiliaries often rushed through from their quarters buttoning tunics and adjusting holsters; that meant a special raid or a round-up. We were allowed to exercise two at a time for less than an hour in an alley turning toward the entrance to the lower Castle Yard. We could see lorries going out or waiting by, and all the bustle and movement of a fortress seat of government.

At night I pretended to sleep, whilst I listened to the guard; if I heard anything worth while I might be able to send it out with a Curfew prisoner. Once an officer rushed in, tapped me on the back and said, " Quick, what's your name? "

" Stewart," I murmured, sleepily.

" Your Christian name? "

" Bernard." Then he left. The simplest question would probably conceal a trap. I answered possible questions in my mind, trying to put myself in their place.

Another time I felt men were standing over me as I slept, " It is." " No, it's not." Through one eyelash I saw two police look at a photograph and at a printed sheet. Suddenly, I thought, they take me for Jack Ryan, the Master, and that paper is the *Hue and Cry*. He had shot a peeler the morning we had set off from Glenough to attack the police barracks at Hollyford in County Tipperary. " Look he has no big freckles." My guess was right for Jack's face was a snipe's egg from freckle splashes.

Once in the evening time an Auxiliary sitting by the fire, reading, said: " You can't beat old Villon." He read aloud :

> " Finablement, en escripvant
> Ce sor seulct, estant en bonne
> Dictant ces laiz et descripvant
> J'ois la cloche de Serbonne
> Qui tousjours à neuf heures sonne."

Another with his feet on the mantelpiece said, Good, let's have this one:

> " Dictes moy où, ne'en quel pays
> Est Flora, la belle Rommaine."

The Section Commander said sourly : " For Christ's sake can't you speak English? "

I was supposed to be a farmer from Kilkenny, my speech was thick, my hair unruly and unkempt. I did not wear a collar, had had no change of clothes since my arrest and I felt dirty. My skin was beginning to itch. I had caught the common complaint. I watched the Kilkenny man, how he used his lips and the way he walked. The skin on his shave-red face hung loose; there were more lines under his eyes, his lips would twitch. He had a wife and family, he told me. He could not sleep much. Beside me he would whisper: "What are they going to do to us? When do you think we'll get out of here?" He would clutch me at night; and I talked to him in whispers and tried to calm him. If I awoke suddenly I found him watching the guards. In the daytime he talked about torture and asked questions of other men about doings in the Intelligence Room and in this guardroom. It was easier for me to take my situation more calmly. Mentally I had often faced death. I expected it if ever I was captured and I had been close enough to it in Kilkenny. I had no ties outside of the movement which claimed all my energy. Here for the first time, perhaps, he realized that anything could happen to him. A drunken Auxiliary would point a gun at us and threaten to shoot, or describe what he would do if he had his way.

A man with kidney and stomach trouble came amongst us. The guard would not allow him to see a doctor. His face was blue grey with pain. At night after Curfew drunks were brought in, some became sober when they realized they were in the Castle and with the Auxiliaries. A member of Dáil Éireann, Frank Lawless, and his son joined the prisoners. Lawless was struck in the face by an Auxiliary because he would not answer questions. I knew both of them; I had stayed in their house less than eight months ago when I had been organizing North County Dublin, but neither of them recognized me. I was pleased. That meant my assumed part had some reality.

There was nothing worth reading. I tried to capture barracks in the brigade areas I knew, rebuilt details of the nature of counties I had cycled through, or tried to reconstruct the work of painters who had meant most to me, but mainly I thought of escape. There was a row of closets at the back, behind the kitchen; they were separated from the houses in Dame Street by barbed wire. It would not be hard to get through the wire, none of the guards came with us when we left the Guardroom, but I could not find out if the houses in front were held by troops. The men in "F" Company were primarily soldiers, they were in no sense warders; that would make them less observant. Guard duty was routine, even if there had been no prisoners men from the company would take their turns in the Guardroom.

A working party made a sand-bagged position for a Lewis gun behind the window that looked on to the passage that led by the City Hall. The gun could traverse. The guard of three men and a section commander was changed daily now, each fresh group brought a Lewis gun. The company was made up of soldiers of fortune: men of private means, clerks, journalists and a few from universities. Many had probably been drawn by the good pay and the swaggering efficiency of an elastic discipline. They were all officers, therefore, gentlemen. They elected their own officers. The men had been specially selected as they were a guard company for part of the Castle. They had permission to carry out raids in areas beyond that one which they nominally controlled. They had seen service in France, Mesopotamia, India, Russia, Gallipoli, and held rank from Major down. Some were boys, the majority were mature. A few had greying hairs. There was a sense of individual assurance; lusty animals, conscious of their strength after hard fighting; they had been tested in command, their *morale* was good. In an emergency they would stand out, but they might be worn down by lack of the organized warfare that suited them. Few might be elastic enough for guerilla fighting. When they sat at the fire I could see brooding bitterness in many faces. The World war had left its mark; behind organized efficiency and a sense of comradeship was a glum, swarthy melancholy.

In the day time they did not talk much; sometimes they would watch us as if to resolve their impressions as to what kind of strange animals we might be, but we were an unknown quantity, save judged in the pattern of their hereditary contempt and the current interpretation of the papers they read.

" Why do you shinners all wear long hair? " an Auxiliary asked me. " Strong man, Greenwood, strong man," they would say impressively, when they read the paper or the

Weekly Summary. They jerked their heads knowingly. They spoke of arrests and raids, about their own and other Auxiliary companies, made up ballads about the I.R.A., and sang the song of the R.I.C.

During the day time there was a constant movement; men would stop to talk, order a drink or sit down at the fire with the guard. Their manner to the new prisoners was always aggressive and harsh, questions were asked in loud overbearing tones. I knew their faces; when different groups returned for duty they would welcome or curse me according to mood and disposition; a few would talk to me in jerky sentences. I was handed the *Weekly Summary* twice. I chuckled as I read their bellicose threats and lofty assurance of police methods to save the country from cowardly gangs of well-paid murderers. I could not associate these men with much of a missionary spirit. " Funny, eh? " I smiled. The man who had given me the paper laughed. The others looked at me as if I had broken a taboo. There was a weighty solemnity about these men as if they were playing a very important game with undue emphasis on the details. There was a sense of ritual about their actions. The military groove canalised thought. I watched them as they grouped six feet away from me. Here were the enemy whom we saw through hereditary contempt, distrust, suspicion and hatred. We had been memoried to expect certain traits in them and they in us. To-morrow if I escaped I would be trying to kill them, and they would do their best to get me. Yet here we sat not far away from each other with some kind of human contact between us. These men believed their own propaganda; they saw us as types. We saw them as part of their government machine that wished through them to produce a certain effect.

In the night they talked more. They sighed for the good shows of London; not a decent show in Dublin. They missed their women; it was so damned hard to click here now. They felt the hostility of the people. A tall whip-like officer told of his erotic experiences in Cairo and Salonika. The others fidgeted on their chairs. Questioned about an exotic thrill he said, " It's much too overrated. Really." Some drank hard. One was young. His forehead had pink blotches amongst the grooves in the puckers.

He borrowed money from the others to look for women. He told of his amours in the back lanes and tried to get money from the prisoners. An old major with a partly bald head that shone like an egg and a blooded face from good living, often spoke to me. His kindly face was a contrast to the taciturn looks of others. " How are you to-day my boy? You'll soon be out of this. There's some mistake—you'll be released."

The Kilkenny man was getting more nervous. " Why do they keep us here? There's some reason, the bloody hangmen, they'll murder us yet."

" I don't know," I'd say, " they can shoot us only once. We can't stop them."

" But if they torture me? " There was no answer to that. I thought of it often, then tried to bury the thought before it would grip me too hard.

During exercise we were often brought across the Castle yard to walk beyond the Chapel Royal. I recognized the steps up which I had once walked in uniform to get a revolver permit in the Provost's office. The Birmingham Tower brought memories of escapes : Red Hugh O'Donnell and young O'Neill in Elizabeth's time. Stray snatches from Carew and other manuscripts came into my mind. Maybe it was over that gate Fiach MacHugh O'Byrne's wife was caged naked until she died. Two tenders with Auxiliaries, seated on boards, were always drawn up inside the gates awaiting emergency calls. Double and single-turreted armoured cars moved up and down the yard with a prowling, gentle purr ; lorries of tin hats drove up.

Five of us were told to go over to the Intelligence Room, we were lined up outside a window whilst eyes peered out at us. I had heard tales of this Intelligence Room. . . .

Again I was paraded with three men in front of the room. A man of about fifty with a heavy coat and quick blue eyes walked up and down in front of us. He was portly and moved slowly on large feet; his eyes looked as if they had been trained to detail. He would give a sharp glance then turn his eyes away. His face was red and flabby with bluish tinges as if his heart was bad ; he needed exercise. He studied our backs and watched us walk. He was one of the few members of the original detective force extant; now he lived in the Castle for protection.

Two Auxiliaries called my name; they walked me over to Ship Street Barracks, which was inside another Castle gate. I was handed over to the military. A military policeman, over six foot three, walking loosely on stilted legs as if they were a special addition to his body, led me down a dark passage. He carried a huge key in his leather belt. When he spoke there was a deep cavernous, weighty rumble. He fitted the key in a heavy lock which resisted with a sliding metallic sound. He threw open the door "Here's a visitor," he boomed. Seated at a table near the fire was a man in the brown habit of the Capuchins, on his head a small round black skull cap. He had a long, light dark brown beard which he stroked, it had a silky look. " I'm Dominic," he said.

"My name is Stewart." We shook hands. I had read of his arrest; he had written a letter about " Bloody Sunday." I bent towards his ear and said," Beware of dictaphones." I wrote on a piece of paper which I handed him: " There is some strange reason for us being put together, let us talk of everything except Ireland." He burnt the slip when he had read it.

The cell was large, there were two beds, the ceiling was a ribbed, barrelled vault, the walls were old. There was a large window opening on to a basement, but the light was bad. Outside I could see two soldiers from the Lancashire regiment with bayonets fixed. At times they pressed their noses against the glass and shaded their eyes with their hands. The window sill was very thick and the door opening was deep. I thought we were being watched. I searched the cell slowly each day, but I could not find a hole or a slit; the vault would probably carry our voices more. The policeman and the journey to the latrine in a long narrow passage gave me a subterranean feeling. He was firmly polite, his movements were slow and important, he took the key with ponderous deliberation from his belt, he fitted it in with precision. Every movement counted. When he spoke the words had significance; they filled the darkness of the passage, they hit against the sound of my feet on the flags and both went away carrying the roll further along. Belt, large key, flags, grinding lock, ribbed vault, the age of the walls and his voice turned the cell into a dungeon. We were not let out for exercise, and there was no change or contrast to the atmosphere of our cell. Down the passage might be thumb screws or a Star Chamber, through a chink eyes might watch. Why had I been put in with Father Dominic? Was it so that I could confess in a loud voice that I had shot police and Intelligence Officers, or to allow us to boast at leisure of our part in the movement or to talk of men we might know? Why was I removed from the hands of the Auxiliaries to those of the military, and what did this isolated cell mean? We whispered our doubts and guesses in each other's ears.

We talked of foreign countries. Dominic had been a chaplain in Serbia and I knew the country. Frank, since dead, had told me living stories of the fighting and of the pell-mell retreat when their friends plundered them. I found it hard to associate Dominic with a soldier's life. He had soft full lips, colour came and went in his cheeks when he was excited or said something that presupposed a doubt in my mind. He stroked his beard, he was proud of it. He had been Terry MacSwiney's chaplain when he was Lord Mayor of Cork, and he had followed him to England and remained through the hunger strike. It did not seem human that a man could endure such slow agony or that will could fight to the end.

We were fed from the officers' mess. The food was good; I enjoyed it. Dominic would say: "They must think we're important; why do they feed us like this?" The better the food the more depressed he became. "What do they mean to do with us? They are feeding us too well." He saw a significance in the good food; it was like the fattening of a turkey in December. I was not worried by the food. Many things could happen; they could do us in quietly, or torture us, or keep us in suspense. I had not expected anything but death to end my part in the struggle; we had seen the grey face of death too often not to be able to know his shadow as we wandered. We did not expect to live through the war; there were too many risks to be taken, but we did feel that our cause would win. However mean and petty our individual lives and thoughts were, there was something in us now, bigger than ourselves, and that could make up for a certain futility when we looked too closely into our thoughts.

One day Dominic said, "You know, it was in this room that Dick McKee and Peadar were murdered; the Auxiliaries fought like mad dogs to see who would first get at them." Less than a month ago I had met Dick McKee to talk about training schemes. We had exchanged our notes on tactical tours and staff rides, and had discussed military work in general and books in particular. He had liked a long memo. which I had written on the organization, training and operations of flying columns. At one time he had set up and printed *An t-Óglach* by hand. He was tall, dark, quiet, but a strict disciplinarian, respected by his officers and men. "We'll have a good long talk the next time you come back from the country," he said, in his pleasant drawl. Peadar Clancy I had first seen in County Tyrone during the election. I had marched three companies from Coal Island to a meeting near Loch Neagh. I met him at a cross roads marching at the head of his party. He gave me a firm hand grip; as he swung out in front of me I watched the way in which he tilted up his chin. Was the same bunch going to plug us : was that why we had been brought together? Dominic would say : "They are going to murder us." In bed I often woke up at a slight noise. I could imagine a crowd shouting outside, then the rush into the cell as we huddled in terror in a vaulted corner. Dominic showed his nervousness. A priest, I thought, should be more ready to meet them than myself.

*   *   *   *

The following six pages (247–252) were deleted from the edition published by Rich and Cowan of London in 1936. They were included in the Four Square edition published in London in 1961.

An Auxiliary walked into the guardroom. "Stewart, Bernard Stewart. Major Y wants to see him in the Intelligence Room."

There were two men in the room; one was in civilians, the other in khaki. The man in the uniform of the Connaught Rangers was medium-sized and slight in build. He walked with a limp. His face was pale, the pupils of his eyes were large and black, around them was a thin rim of blue. He worked his lower lip. The other man was over six feet; well built, with an air of command, the lines on his forehead were drawn together when he spoke. He was Major Y; the other Captain X.

"What's your name? " asked the Major.

" Stewart."

" Your Christian name? "

" Bernard."

" What are you? "

" A farmer."

" Where do you live? "

" In Inistiogue, County Kilkenny."

" But you don't live there."

" No."

" Where do you live? "

No reply.

" Take off your coat," he ordered.

I took off my coat. He saw the cardigan jacket.

" Where did you steal that military cardigan? "

" I bought it."

He came over, clenched his fist and struck me over the heart.

" Where did you steal the cardigan? "

" I bought it."

He struck me in the face with the full weight of his body. I fell to my knees.

" Get up. Who gave you the gun? "

No reply.

" Are you going to answer? "

" No."

He struck me again in the face and blood began to flow into my mouth and to drop onto the floor.

The Captain said, " Where do you live? "

" I will not answer."

" Why? "

" Because if I did, you would burn my mother's home. I am her only son."

" But we would not burn it."

" Well, houses have been burned, and I am ready to suffer rather than have her suffer."

" So you are ready to suffer," said the Major.

He struck rights and lefts to my face and body. I wiped the blood from my face with the back of my hand.

" Place your coat in front of you," he said. " We don't

want the floor all blood."

I did so.

" Turn round," said the Captain.

I turned round.

" Do you see those photographs? "

" Yes," I said, looking at the wall.

" Well, some of them refused to give information and they are dead now."

" Will you answer me? " said the Major. " Where do you live? "

I did not answer and he hit me again and knocked me against the wall.

When I stood up again he said, " Will you fight me? "

" No."

" Afraid? " sneeringly.

I knew that he could knock me out in ten minutes, if not in one, but I did not want to let him have the satisfaction of thinking he had fought clean and beaten me in fair fight. If he wanted to abuse his manhood, he could do so, but he would have no excuse for it.

Said the Captain, " Do you know that your mother is supposed to have your name up on the back of her door and if she has not got it there she will get into trouble? "

I nodded.

" If you just give us the name of the man who gave you the automatic you can go free, nobody will know, and you can go back home and save your mother from trouble."

" I cannot give information."

" Yes, you can," said the Major, hitting me again.

The Captain came over near me. " I can issue orders to have your house saved. I am the Commander-in-Chief and I will sign the form now if you will give us your address."

" I won't give my address, for fear the house might be burned by parties of police or auxiliaries."

" Are you a farmer? " he asked.

" Yes."

" Nice small hands for a farmer; you're a nice bloody farmer. What county are you from? "

I did not reply.

" What is your mother's name? "

" O'Brien."

" Oh, I know where the O'Briens come from. You're from Clare."

I shook my head.

" From Ennis? "

" No."

" Galway? "

" No."

" Tipperary? "

" No."

" Limerick? "

" No."

" Kilkenny? "

" No."

" Kerry? "

" . . . No." I paused purposely before saying " No." I had never been in Kerry save on the border, so he could think I was from that county if he wished.

" Ha, Kerry! "

He asked me if I was from different towns which he named, and my " Noes " became monotonous.

" Were you ever in Dublin? " asked the Major.

" Yes."

" Where did you stay? "

" With my uncle."

" Where did he live? "

I did not reply.

" I saw you in Dublin once," he said. " You were on a tramcar."

" I often went on tramcars," I replied.

" You passed up Harcourt Street and turned Kelly's Corner."

" I don't know Kelly's Corner."

" You went on across a bridge."

" Over a river," I interjected.

" No, over the Canal, and you went along Rathmines Road past Portobello Barracks; that's where I live," he added.

" I remember seeing a building."

" On the right? "

" I'm not sure."

" Yes," said he, " it was on the right. Then you came to the Town Hall; what did you do then? "

" I got off the tram."

" Oh, you went up Leinster Road, I suppose," said the Captain, "or perhaps you walked on straight."

" What did you do? " the Major asked.

" I went to the pictures."

They looked at each other, as much as to say, " He's too damned ignorant."

The Captain consulted some notes. " Oh, a nice little plan about the Kilkenny patrol," he said. " You wanted another murder."

" Stop," said the Major, and the Captain shut my black notebook.

He referred to my notes of the strength of the armed party that went daily from the military barracks in Kilkenny to the gaol to relieve guard.

" I have a little plan," the Captain said. He walked in front of me to a stove and picked up a poker from the floor. He dug the poker between the bars. He pulled it out, the point was a soft crimson; he shoved it back. The Major looked at me, then turned to the stove. I felt a hollow in my stomach. The Captain looked at the poker; it was bent, the crimson glow ran up close to the handle. " Now you'll talk." He held the poker in front of my face. I moved back from the heat. " By God, you'll talk." He held one of my arms tight, then angled the point forward as if to dig it into my eyes. He swung it horizontally until it was on a level with my eyes. My eyebrows were singed; the heat made my eyes burn. He brought the poker nearer, I tried to move back, the smell made me cough dryly. My eyelashes curled up; the lids smarted. I tried to keep my eyes open. They were hurting me. My God, I thought, my eyes, if he touches them I'll jump for his throat and tear it. " Will you answer? " I shook my head. He raised the poker as if he was going to hit me. He put it back between the bars of the stove.

" Do you think you are going to beat us? " said the Major; " you're going to answer questions, do you hear? " he shouted. " Where do you live? " He hit me hard in a passion, smash after smash.

I got up from the floor. My cheeks were cut, blood ran from my forehead into my eyes. My eyes were swollen, it was hard to keep up the lids. As I swayed on my feet, I could see their faces jump forward and back like land seen under hot sun or through thin smoke. The blood in my eyes made the room a distorted jumble of reds and blues. A hot, salty taste of warm blood flowed down my throat, and through my lips when I took breath. My tongue seemed to loosen my teeth, which were now as big as fingers when it pressed on them. My nose was pushed aslant; I snorted when I exhaled. I felt myself trying to sing. I heard the words plainly, but I did not know if the sound was coming from my voice.

> I know my love by his way of walking,
> I know my love by his way of talking,
> I know my love by his eyes of blue.

" Damn you, you swine," the Captain shouted, his voice skidded to a shrill note. He gripped my throat with one hand, he pressed hard over my heart with the flat of the other. He squeezed my neck with both hands, shoving his thumbs well in. He turned to the Major, eagerly.

" Will we do him in? "

" No, not yet."

I dropped to the ground when he took his hands away, I gulped for breath.

" Get up," the Major ordered.

It was hard to get on my feet, the calves of my legs trembled as I knelt on one knee.

" Will you answer questions? " he asked.

" No, I won't, but I'll fight you."

" Oh, no, you won't fight him," said the Captain; " you're not going to have the satisfaction of hitting a gentleman." He walked to a desk near the window, took a Webley forty-five Service revolver from a drawer.

" Do you know what this is? "

I nodded.

" Now watch." He broke the action and spun round the cylinder on either side, showing me the lead points and the base of the cartridges. " You see, it's loaded." I watched the six cartridges. " Get up against the wall." I backed until I was touching the wall.

" I am going to give you three chances; if after the third you don't answer your brains will be on that wall." He spoke slowly. " Who gave you the automatic? "

" One."

No answer.

" Two."

He slowly cocked the hammer. I looked along the bluish barrel, my legs twitched in shivers at the thighs. I brought my heels together with a snap.

" Three."

I stood stiff. He pressed the trigger; there was a bang. He

had used a blank cartridge.

Two men came into the room, one small, undersized, furtive; the other had a khaki bonnet, a greatcoat covered the uniform. He had a long thin face, mobile lips; little lines ran from the edge of his nose to the corners of his mouth. He looked a lawyer. He spoke with a quiet, pleasant, educated accent.

" Do you want to be hanged? "

" No."

" Well, you're going to be hanged for the Macroom ambush."

" But I was not there."

" We have witnesses to prove you were there and you'll hang. Are you afraid of hanging? "

" No."

" You'll hang unless you tell us your address and where you got the pistol. We'll give you money and see you all right. Are you fond of your mother?"

" Yes."

" Don't you know you are bringing her trouble, and if you are hanged she will be disgraced."

" With us, hanging is no disgrace."

" Look here, my boy, you are young; don't be a fool. No harm will come to you, you will be saved. Can't you give us your address? "

" No."

" Then you'll hang for Macroom."

" Wipe your face," said the Major.

I used my hands and coat but the blood still came.

" I'll see you again, Stewart, remember."

As I crossed the yard, a tall Auxiliary with a bandage round his head stopped me. " What's wrong? " he asked.

" They tried to make me give information over there." I pointed to the Intelligence Room.

" Did they do that to you? "

" Yes."

" Oh, damn," he said as he walked away.

The guards looked at me, but did not speak. After a while one said. " Try some boracic acid."

" I'm all right."

Two Irishmen from the company came in. They looked at me. " It's a shame to muck up a kid like that," I heard one of them say as they walked out.

Two girls walked towards me as I exercised with another prisoner in the passage leading toward the main gate. I knew one of them, Aunia Malone. She did not recognize me. "We are prisoners," I said. I asked my companion to drop behind.

"Aunia, don't you know me?" I asked.

She stopped. "No."

"Look again."

"My God, Earnán. Is it you? I did not know you. Oh! who did that to you?"

. . . .

"This is Dick McKee's sister." We shook hands. "We got a permit to come here. We want to look for clothes and things belonging to Dick and Peadar."

"Aunia, my name is Stewart, Bernard Stewart; I was taken in Inistioge, County Kilkenny. Don't tell any of the boys or you know what will happen to me. Get word to the C.S. or to Mick at once. They are going to hang me for Macroom."

"Do you want anything, Earnán?"

"Yes, a shirt and some hanks; I have no clothes and I can't write to anyone."

"Anything else? How about sweets?"

I smiled, she knew I liked sweets. "*Beannacht Dé*, for the present." She walked away with Dick McKee's sister.

Later, Aunia crossed to where I sat in the Guardroom; she handed me a box of sweets and a parcel of clothes. "What are you doing here?" asked an Auxiliary, who came over to us.

"Talking," said Aunia; she did not turn her head.

"Show that parcel." As he stretched out his hand it touched her arm. She drew back with the quickness of disgust. "Take your dirty hands off me, you Tan."

"Get out of here; you have no right to enter the Guardroom."

Aunia tossed her head. "*Beannacht Dé leat*." She walked out quickly.

"Let's have a look," said the Auxiliary. He opened the parcel. He had always talked to me in a friendly way when on duty. "All right, you can keep them."

Captain King came into the room, he looked at a list as he called prisoners' names. He came to Coughlan.

" Coughlan? "

A young boy with a dark, fiery head stood up. " Yes."

" Say, ' yes sir ' to me," ordered King.

" Answer the officer properly," said one of the guard.

" Coughlan? "

" Yes."

" Yes, what? "

" Yes."

King looked around at the prisoners. · His eyes went up to my blood-stained overcoat hanging on a nail.

" Whose coat is that? "

" Mine," I said. I spoke in a low voice; suddenly I was terrified. I had been expecting him to come in again.

" All right, Stewart. I'll see you again, soon."

The lawyer who had been in the Intelligence Room walked over to me : " Have you changed your mind yet? "

" No, I have not."

" You'll hang for Macroom, then, Oh, you're a fanatic."

My injured eyes now hurt me a good deal. I found it difficult to read, and the pupils seemed to enlarge quickly as if under strain. I would spend more of the day now watching the Auxiliaries and studying their individual expression, characteristics and speech.

The cook was a friend of mine. He stopped to talk to me as I went through to the closets. Often he gave me apples or oranges. " You'll be soon released," he'd say, " don't worry." He walked with the quick decided emphasis of a man who had served a long time, " old soldier," he'd say, " we know the ropes ; old soldiers never die—they simply fade away." He had tangled eyebrows and a jet black moustache, his face was shiny from heat.

Christmas was coming, there were now three prisoners, the Kilkenny commandant and a boy who said he was from the Dublin Brigade. The old major came in one day.

" How are you, my boy? " The smile went up to the gleam of his bald head.

" All right, thanks."

" You'll have a good dinner to-morrow. We'll see that you get whatever is going," he patted my shoulder.

On Christmas Eve the cook walked over to where I sat on an army biscuit. " Come on and I'll cut your hair and shave you, then you'll look well to-morrow." He talked

as he snipped. " I'd never pull a gun on an unarmed man.
I don't hold with that sort of thing." He brought me
upstairs to the rooms where the Company slept. By the
side of each bed was a rifle with bayonet fixed. Some of the
men were lying down. " Always ready," he said.

We sat at a table beside the guard on Christmas day,
four Auxiliaries and three prisoners. It was a good dinner ;
we did not talk much. I was thinking of other Christmas
dinners. Last year with Countess Plunkett; we had a
good time at table, and the year before with Miss Ward at
Killybegs, after a long ride through Donegal mud. When
we had eaten the Christmas pudding the section commander turned to the Kilkenny man : " Do you drink? "
He filled his glass and that of the Dublin boy with port.
" And you? "

" I don't drink," I said.

" Fill your glass with water."

The guard stood up. " Stand up," said one. We stood
up. " Gentlemen, *The King!* " said the Section Commander.
He shouted the old toast as if his loyalty had been questioned. It rang tensely like a confession of faith. The
prisoners drank with the guard. I sat down. The four
kicked aside their chairs and came over to me. One of them
swung me round by the shoulder as he drew his gun, the
others had guns in their hands They were cursing.

"Why didn't you drink the king's health you bastard?"
shouted the Section Commander. " Why? "

" He's not my king."

" That doesn't matter, these two drank it and, by God,
you're going to. Here, take it." He shoved the glass of
water into my hand ; the water splashed on the floor. He
stuck his gun high up on my back.

" That's the stuff," said the swarthy Auxie who had
previously been pointed out to me as a bad egg. He was
leaning against the mantelpiece. "Put the swine through
it."

A tall officer with a Sam Brown strap slanted across his
greenish black uniform strode in.

" What's the row ; I heard you shouting outside? "

" That swine won't drink the king's health, sir," said
one. He turned to me: " Is that true? "

" It is."

" Why did you refuse? "

" I am a soldier of the Irish Republican Army, and I owe no allegiance to your king."

He looked at me. He held out his hand. " Shake hands," he said. We gripped each others' hands firmly. He turned to the guard; the anger was going out of their faces. " You heard your orders, didn't you, that prisoners were to be well treated on Christmas Day? My name is Captain —— " (I forget the name now). He said to me : " If there's any more trouble send for me. Now, remember." He turned to the guard. The four came over to me, we shook hands one after the other.

" I'm sorry," said the section commander, he put his hand on my shoulder.

" That's all right," I said. " I'll drink your health." We raised glasses and drank together.

" I know what I'd do with him," said the swarthy one.

The other prisoners were brought out of the room by Auxiliaries. My friend, the Major, came in : " Why don't you come on up, come on to the mess room and have a drink."

" There was nearly dirty work here over a toast," I said. " I don't want any more of it."

" No one will say anything, I'll be with you. Come along to the mess room."

Auxiliaries were talking and singing in a large room upstairs, some were trying to dance. Bottles of wine, liquor, whisky and champagne were on the table.

" Will you drink with me? "

" I'm sorry, but I don't drink now."

" Oh well, your health and mine in a little bubbly." He poured out two large glasses of champagne, we clinked glasses and drank. We joined hands around the tables and sang : " For the Sake of Auld Lang Syne." We roared the chorus, swinging our hands to the words. They cheered when the song was over. With one knee on a chair we drank " Good Luck." "Prisoner's speech," shouted the company. The others spoke. My turn came: I did not like to speak. I said that I was glad that we who fought each other could be human for a while. The Major linked my arm as we went down stairs.

I sat by the fire. One of the guard ordered the other prisoners to sweep the floor. " It's good enough for them," he said to me. " They haven't much principle." They offered me cigars and stuffed them in my pockets.

Auxiliaries came in; they sat down to talk. " It's a rotten job, this," said a man with a Scotch accent. " But what can we do ? I was out of work." There was a difference in their tone of voice; they dropped the official soldier manner. I had a glimpse of men who did not believe in what they were doing, but who would carry out their work thoroughly ; they forgot that they were talking to a shinner and a murderer. They asked me to sign Christmas cards ; I wrote in my large backhand scrawl. " Won't you sign your names? " I asked. They wrote their names on a card for me.

" It's funny, you know," one said as he signed. A young boy led me over towards the window; we leant against the Lewis gun. " Could you let me have your name and real rank as a souvenir, I'll keep it."

" I have no rank," I said, " it's dangerous these times."

" All right, as you wish. You spoke like a varsity man above stairs, better look out; but I don't think they noticed. Grace is my name, I'm from Trinity." We talked on.

" You must admit that the R.I.C. have guts to stick it out."

" They certainly have ; but we can't admire Irishmen who fight for foreigners against us."

He laughed. " That's one for me, too. I wonder when it will all be over, then I'd like to meet you and have dinner together."

" Two years from now when the Irish Republic is recognized we'll meet on Christmas Day and dine."

" Remember, that's a bargain," he said, as we shook hands.

CHAPTER EIGHTEEN

JANUARY, 1921

★

AN OFFICER of the regulars came into the Guardroom. " Stewart, pack up. Hurry now." It was evening time and dark. I had become used to the movement and life of the room. I felt lonely; what was I in for now? I was ordered into an armoured car. The officer sat beside me; two privates in the darkness talked in deep, low tones. I tried to follow the windings of the car, but after a while I could not make out where we were going. " Come on." I followed the officer, he had a revolver in each hand. He put one muzzle against the nape of my neck; the other tipped my side. " None of your bloody monkey tricks. Move on." " Good night," I said to the soldiers. There was a pause, then " good-night " in echoing rumbles. Was an armoured car crew picked because of their voices, or did the gloom and steel make them sound so funereal?

I was in a gaol, which one, I did not know. Cold thick shadows and ugly walls; my boot crashed off the flags. A clerk in uniform asked questions; an officer stood by and looked at me. He spoke in a cold, thinly contemptuous voice. I disliked him thoroughly. " Come to attention when the officer speaks to you," said the clerk. I did not move my feet or hands. " Am I to be treated as a soldier?" I asked. There was no reply. A soldier walked in front of me with a Webley in his hand, down a gloomy looking passage. He opened the iron door of a cell, the door clanged.

The gas came through a weak jet which spluttered and gasped, lighting up slightly, now dimming the outlines of the bare walls; shadows jumped up, fell and climbed again. I sat on a few dirty, brown army blankets in a corner. I felt a sense of desolation sitting there all alone. The hard voice of the soldier who had brought me through the tall narrow passage up the clanging stairway kept coming back. " There's your blankets." The word " blankets " rolled in again and again as if it had untold significance. He had not answered my " Good-night."

I was part of an automaton which spoke a regulation voice and was dehumanized. It could not attempt to assimilate so it would destroy. Outside we had laughed at the British, here it was different. I felt them now as a machine; their officers could be replaced by others, a spare part efficient for a specific function would always be found. We ourselves had to depend, not on organized strength so much as on personality, understanding and intimate or intuitive knowledge.

There was always something ponderous about the British in the outward effect of their organized efficiency, parade solemnity and purpose. They were important; they took themselves seriously. The inherited class hatred of their officer type, which helped to maintain the isolation of a caste system, filtered through to the lower ranks of the army. Behind the mask of assurance and arrogance was another appearance; it could be seen in the uncertainty and insecurity that a movement of the people produced. Facing men of their own stamp and mentality the mask was a skin and did not change much, facing a people whom they had exploited, walked on, or laughed at, the skin became a mask. I had seen it lift. Under it was what we feel when we view aspects of our own futility in a clearly dispassionate way, aspects hidden by the outward mask which others think to be wholly strength, poise or arrogance. Fear of the unknown quantity, a spirit, uneasiness at a strength which they could not paperise in an organized rooster way or hit at with organized force, and the repercussions from their own propaganda which, to show their achievements, had given us a stature in terms of their own. Their unreal summing-up of the situation cancered them and traditional bureaucracy infected them with traditional fears.

I found a but in my pocket which I smoked slowly. I held it with a pin to make it last. The lock rattled, I was given a bowl of tea and a piece of hard dry bread; the tea was cold, it tasted like weak soup mixed with tea leaves. The soldier sniffed: " No smoking here," he said. I slept between blankets on the floor.

Next day I was brought to another part of Kilmainham Gaol. I was put in a cell at the corner of a passage. I had a point of view at any rate. On the left of the passage was the gaol wall, on my right a row of cells. I was brought out for exercise with a number of other prisoners, they looked at me curiously. Even with them I felt alone, they seemed to know each other. We were not allowed to talk, but went around in file in a half-circle.

The officer who had been in the clerk's room stood at the door and watched us coldly. Whenever I came round I stared back at him. He had a thin face, his skin was sallow, he had a slightly cynical expression, thinking, I expect, of us swine whom he had to keep prisoners. I did not know any of the other prisoners, but I answered their questions in spite of the frequent command "no talking." Some of the men seemed to be able to talk without moving their lips. The small yard was closed in by grey walls, and buildings ribbed with tiny barred windows. The wall was thick on top and a gallery ran through it.

In the morning, by fours, we washed in the basement in rusty enamel basins. We talked, splashing in the numb cold whilst a soldier roared " Stop talking. *Stop your* . . . . . *talk.*" Then a banging at doors, opened one by one, a prisoner orderly shouting, " Burgoo up, burgoo." He rattled on the cell doors with a tin mug. The stirabout was thin, but good, soupish tea and a hunk of bread. The jacks was at the end of my passage. I could see it from the round peep hole in my door and could too often smell it. It seldom flushed. Urine overflowed into the stone passage, its acrid smell spiralled about, backed by sickly overtones of faeces making the air taste. A military policeman from a Welsh regiment led us to it when we banged on our doors. He kept his hand on his Webley.

The gaol wall was over six feet thick, the cell window narrowed like a loophole. It was clogged with dust and high up. I could reach the ledge with my finger tips by springing, but they slipped off before I could get a good grip.

Murky light made reading difficult, the books lent to me were detective stories or tripish novels. The cell walls were crusty with age, dirt and misery. The passage was damp, the walls oozy and smelly, boots beat out a noise that hit back off the walls, cell doors opened and shut in iron strength with a nerve-jumping tear. Gaol was at first a half-world of bone-cold, smells, muddy light and crushing walls. I would stand up to yell with a high sustained note or sing songs. It was hard to throw myself mentally outside of the walls and to think what the martial law area was doing, or of what change winter was bringing to the land. Rain would pelt off the walls and wind swirl and scream; both were cheerful sounds now. The itch spread, when I rubbed my skin small swellings came; it was impossible to prevent myself from scratching.

"Do you stand to attention for the officer?" I asked, at exercise the first day. "Yes," said a boy behind me. "Have we an O.C.?" "No, there's no gaol organization." The sallow officer came to my cell every morning. Expecting him I sat on the floor.

"Get up," he jerked. I stood up.

"Stand to attention for the officer," said the orderly. I angled my heels, the officer looked at a list.

"Bernard Stewart?"

"Yes."

"Say sir." I kept silent.

"Bernard Stewart?"

"Yes . . . sir." Later, an orderly officer would come in, give a quick glance around. That meant that exercise time was near.

"Any complaints?" "Why complaints?" or "no."

We scrubbed out the flagged floors of our cells, in turn we helped to wash the passage. We dipped the dirty rags in cold water then swabbed dirt from the flags, and rinsed them again until our wrists were blue and numb. Grit, dirt, and urine floated in the heavy, zinc basins, clung to our hands, and shrivelled them to a corrugated redness. But we could talk, a cigarette would be slipped into my pocket, a candle and some matches. At night, wide smelly buckets were clattered on the cell floors; we could not go to the jacks after lights out.

Papers were not allowed. One night a paper was pushed under my door. I read it beneath the fizzling gas jet. There had been a raid on Eileen McGrane's flat in Dawson Street, raiders took away piles of papers; she was brought to an unknown destination. Mick Collins had an office there and a large press stacked with papers and files. He had been using the room for over a year. My maps, note-books, military library and clothes were in another room. Who had shoved the paper under my door? It came as a warning. My maps bore a geometrical pattern as a sign of ownership. I had conventional signs of my own which I inserted in coloured inks on my maps. The note-book contained abbreviations in code, especially where ranks of men or enemy strengths were mentioned. They would correspond with the maps and note-book captured by the Auxiliaries in Inistiogue. In the Intelligence Room at the Castle now they might be reading some of the captured papers, and I had seen my note-book with Captain Hardy in the Castle. My handwriting was distinctive in its illegibility. They would connect up the two sets of information. Captain King, who commanded "F" Company, had been in charge of the raid, I afterwards found.

In the guardroom I had felt that Eileen's flat would be raided. When Aunia Malone came back with the sweets I had begun: " I'm sure there's a raid coming. Tell Eileen . . . " then Aunia had snapped at the Auxiliary. " Eileen McGrane," I added as she left the room, but I did not know if she had heard me. I sat with my back to the wall. It was very cold, but I did not wrap a blanket around me. Soon I would know. I would not have much of a chance this time ; they had the drop on me. They would have fun pretending they did not know anything about me as they asked innocent questions. My notes would prove I belonged to Headquarters, my note-books on counties would show parts of the country I had been through. I did not know much, but now I felt I knew too much. Offices of departments of the Dáil and of G.H.Q., arms dumps, a grenade factory, names and ranks of officers and random threads connecting up the movement. I was due for a hearty manhandling and I was afraid of myself. I knew I had got by very lightly in the Castle ; now I remembered stories of deliberate torture practised thoroughly.

For hours I sensed my extreme isolation in this hostile world of jailers and possible extractors of information. I seemed to shrink in size before their approaching shadows. I could not draw courage from any outward source or memory; often enough I had handed on my own small share to tune up men, and I would get it back in increase through the corporate strength of our union. One plan I had. I would rush one of their guns, and grab one, or make them shoot me. Later a reserve of courage began to work its way slowly until I felt more confidence and an assurance that I would have enough desperation to meet what would come my way, but courage went suddenly when I felt the disparity between thought and action.

A cold fog of fear came in around the cell. I was now facing a situation in my mind, answering another's possible line of thought or action, but the interrelation of events in actuality had too often no relation to my mental process. The rough scratchy blankets had a friendly feel under my hands as I stroked them. Tired, trying to see into a future that I could not avoid, I folded the hairy blankets about me. The gaoler officer came next morning. No slithery smile of triumph on his face. That was well. He suited his work. A measly-faced Cockney guard came with him.

Life had to be adjusted to fit this vacuum, and dimensions had to be changed. My sense of time and space did not exist now, cell volume might close in like a hat box or draw out to an infinity of blurring shapes. Air, light and darkness were different, but passing days brought an acceptance of conditions and an adjustment. With a stump of a pencil I worked out tactical problems on the cell walls and out-manoeuvred the enemy to my satisfaction. The new world had to be faced and penetrated slowly or by sudden flashes.

Slowly I studied the prisoners. Diagonally across from my corner was MacNamara. Mac was on trial in connection with " Bloody Sunday." " They call this the Murder Wing," he said, " we're all bloody murderers." He sang loudly, I answered alternate verses; down the passage would come a chorus bursting with discord or a wild whoop, then an angry shout: " *Shut up! You* —— " When the police rushed at a noising cell they met a silence, further down the words would be continued, or a shrill yelp would take them in the rear : " I'm here, Mary Ellen, I'm here." Mac had a gay air, he swung his shoulders when he walked and his smile flamed up from white teeth to his brown red hair. He had a way with the police.

Paddy Moran was in the second cell down the passage towards the jacks. He was due for trial for the supposed shooting of Intelligence officers. Of stocky build, but

sinewy ; fuzzy thick hair, showing two moons on his broad
forehead. He had a strong, pleasant face. He knew Collins
and Mulcahy, and he spoke of himself as "the old gunner ";
he was captain of a Dublin company and had been, I was
told, second in command of the G.P.O. during Easter
Week. He had lived in Keadue near Loch Meelagh in
the county Roscommon. It was easy to begin an acquain-
tance when I could talk of a country I had liked. The men
carried their home places in their minds ; it was pleasant
to take them out of themselves by building up the skeleton
of what they had known well; their memories would supply
details, and people the new country of their minds. When
you knew a man's district well and could talk about its
personal geography, you became, for a time, closer than a
blood relation. He knew the lonely shores of Loch
Allen, the bare recession of hills towards Leitrim and the
smells of ferny undergrowth of woods near the lakes of
Skean and Meelagh. He was happy to talk of Crossna
and of the people he liked.

Thinking back we could leave out clashes that then
seemed of most annoying importance ; we could laugh at
the mellow richness of what had furred our tongues. To
test his memory, and to take him out of gaol, I would ask
him to walk down the right bank of the Shannon from
Loch Allen to Carrick and come back on the opposite side.
Next day we would add further details. At exercise now he
walked behind me. " Do you remember the colour of the
Curlews after rain? " After another round of the drab
yard, I'd say " and the reeds near the shore in the early
morning. Wouldn't it be fine to stand on the Rock of
Courage in Loch Key and look across at the Rock of Doon?"

An orderly who served up stirabout always kept an
extra plate for himself leaving someone else short; he
cut bits off our over-boiled meat ration. Red-haired, very
thin, with a sly face and a shuffling back-throat Dublin
accent ; we wondered where he put the food. "He should
have a belly like a poisoned pup," said a Cavan man, " but
it's more like a frying pan." "Maybe he has worms,"
suggested one. " O man dear, have sense ; its serpents
more likely." An elderly Wicklow man, a firm believer
in the Redmondite Parliamentary Party, was almost a
curiosity. He was a great believer in the power of speech.

To draw him, the boys would shout: "Up Redmond" or "Where's the poor old Party now? why don't they ask a question about you in the House?"

Some would appear to be sympathetic, let him talk of meetings he had attended, then lead him on slowly till a laugh showed their purpose. Often enough the taunt " and what about Parnell?" would end the chaff by a fiery outburst of admiration from the others. A wrinkled knob of a man with bent shoulders and long thin bony wrists, hanging from short coat sleeves, spattering grey moustache and an indulgent nose, which he often wiped with his sleeve. There was good feeling in the banter; we were all prisoners.

One day an egg was shoved through the hole in the door of my cell. " Break that in your tea," said Moran's voice. The yolk was too viscid and I did not like the raw taste; I was told to beat it up first, then pour in the tea on top. It made the tea taste as if I had cream in it. Father Dominic, I was told, had sent me the eggs; he continued to send them daily. He raised his hand in greeting when we saw each other in the yard. When in front of me, he talked back of Cork and about the boys there, but I did not say that I knew any of them. Once, he said, " The Auxiliaries burned the centre of Cork City the other day."

Prison discipline changed. The police did not handle their guns; they did not keep themselves in a fearful tenseness as if some one was always ready to grip them by the windpipe. They had been told that we were murderers. That meant an image from a Sunday paper; twitching hands and a furtive walk, or sullen hardness. They heard us laugh and sing, rag and annoy each other, joke and refuse to take prison regulation seriously. Even their officers were not respected. Gradually they learned to talk to us, to laugh, to enter into the interior life of our wing. They joked about arrests and hangings.

We stopped to talk at cell doors on the way back or to the lavatory; we slipped out to meet each other when cell doors were opened at meal time. There were long delays downstairs when we washed in the morning, we began to eat in one another's cell and the smell of cigarette smoke would delight the passage air. The police asked for rosary beads and medals; they were safe now, they said, against ambushes. None of them were Catholics. They

sat in our cells to enjoy our forbidden cigarettes and
they smuggled in half-pints to a few. Cell doors were
left open save when officers were expected. They played
tunes on a mouth-organ; an enthusiast with a melodeon
taught them the steps of country sets; we held concerts
and dances in our cells. They taught us some of their
songs and bits of regimental tradition. We taught them
our songs and ballads. We parodied their words, they
returned the compliment. Some of the stricter police
cursed violently when the words of some of their songs
were changed.

"*All prisoners out.*" We were herded in the small
exercise yard. "What's up now?" "Is it a move?"
was asked. Military police looked at lists of names. Two
prisoners were taken away. "What does it mean?" a man
beside me asked; his lower jaw jerked nervously. "Identification parade," said Moran. Two more prisoners were
led off. "No," said Mac, when six had passed out through
a small gate, "we're going to have our photos took, the
policeman told me; any of you criminals a comb?" No
one would refuse to have his photo taken, I found. Two
Auxiliaries stood near a tripod in a far away yard. "Here,
hold up your face," said one, "don't be afraid; what happened to it? Oh, I remember, the Castle, eh?" said a tall
streak of a man as he pushed my profile into position.
"Christmas-day we had a good time. Here you are."
He handed me a packet of Abdullas.

Other prisoners got parcels from home; the food helped
them to avoid the monotony of gaol cooking. I did not
like the food and I ate little. I crumbled the bread up into
pellets; that made it last a long time and I bit lumps of
candle. I did not care to tell any of my neighbours that
I was hungry. Moran must have guessed that there was
nobody to whom I could write; he asked me down to his
cell one morning and I had a good feed. When I was
leaving the cell he gave me a parcel of food. I did not want
to take it, but he showed me a box of groceries to prove
that he had plenty. A long drink of good tea in his cell
was something to think about before and after.

He used to talk behind me at exercise. One day when
we were walking around, the officer brought a new prisoner
amongst us. "I don't like that fellow's face," said Moran,

" he looks like a quitter." The new prisoner had stooped shoulders, a sallow complexion, though his face was white as if he'had been long confined. We met him when we went back to our cells. He was acting Intelligence Officer in the Fourth Battalion, Dublin Brigade. I knew that two friends of mine had been promoted recently, one was commandant and the other company captain in that battalion. Both I had known in the University, and I was anxious to talk about them, but I did not speak, I knew not why. Moran and I did not seek his company. He was nervous, his eyes strayed when one talked, that and his stooped shoulders gave him the appearance of being broken-spirited or of being fearful of identification.

We dismissed him from our thoughts; one often met men in gaol whose spirit had been broken, who were afraid of being tried by court martial, who felt they were fighting an Empire whose resources were practically inexhaustible. One day the newcomer was called out by sallow face and returned after an hour. There was a rumour that an officer of the "Q" branch at the Castle had been to see him, but as he showed no signs of ill-treatment we did not query the visit. It had been rumoured that he had been "beaten up" at the Castle, but such cases were of common occurrence. A few days later he was removed and that night one of the police,—the one who used to laugh when he said he belonged to the Welsh-Irish Republican Army—told us that on his way to the Castle he had jumped from the lorry, although handcuffed, and had disappeared in the darkness. We hoped he would not be recaptured.

Later a broad shouldered man with a bandaged head was put in a cell. He was said to be the Dublin assistant-brigade Intelligence Officer. He had come from the Castle. "What happened?" he was asked. "Oh, I was bashed in the Intelligence Room." There had been raids in the City; some of our ammunition dumps had been seized.

At exercise time I saw Rory O Connor, Director of Engineering, in the next yard hidden by the angle of the gate. I did not know he had been arrested. He waited until the soldier was not looking, then slipped through, and worked up till he was beside me. His sunken eyes smiled out of their dark blue hollows:

" Where did you get that sweet face? "

" From noble hearts in the Castle."

"We didn't think you'd come through it; the C.S. was sure they'd do you in. Only a few knew you were pinched."

" How are things outside? "

" Slow enough. They'll begin to move soon and it's about time. The Brigade will bomb lorries on the streets and give them general hell. Now, I'll have to buzz ; see you at Mass on Sunday."

As we quickened our steps to keep warm I heard a voice : "O Malley." I did not turn round. I wondered if my face or shoulders showed any signs of the name being mine. I had prepared myself mentally for that; it might be sprung upon me if they heard I had been arrested and were not sure of my description. The sallow officer stood in the door way, slapping his trousers' side with a malacca cane.

" Eh ! O Malley !"

Later a half glance showed a boy waving at me. I dropped back, man by man, until I came to him. He was from my old Dublin " F " Company. " Don't howl," I said, " and forget that you know me. My name is Stewart. I'll talk to you upstairs." He had been captured with three others in an ambush. " They're going to hang the bunch of us," he said.

I brushed against a newly arrived prisoner from Mayo. I smelt the tang of turf-smoke on his homespuns. That brought back a memory of firesides and their associations and the whole sweep of the country in every nature and mood and season. For a whole day the thought of escape did not come to me.

A boy named Teeling had been sentenced to be hanged. Mac, Moran, Whelan and another prisoner were still on trial. The bearing of the sentenced men and of those waiting for trial by court-martial varied. Teeling was gay-hearted and easy-going. He had been captured on the morning of " Bloody Sunday," whilst on guard at the back gate of a house in which officers had been killed; he had been wounded. He was the only prisoner who had actually been taken that morning. For him there was no escape, and his whole manner and expression, the way he held his head, his laugh, his talk, rugged and direct, showed that he was not afraid to face death, that it was all in the day's work. He walked with a slight limp and did not often come down to the yard with us.

Whelan's features were finer and more delicate; smooth-faced, quiet and brown eyed with wavy hair; he smiled quietly and steadily. His voice was soft and when he laughed with others one knew that the fibre was not as hard and that there was a shade of wistfulness about him. Moran was stolid and serious. There was a roll in his walk. Daily, food was brought up to the gate for him, a thermos of tea and often an apple cake. He showed me his girl's photo. " That's a great girl," he'd say, shaking his head with a remembering smile which made his face softer and more gentle. " She brings the grub and the apple cake. I wish . . . " but he never spoke his wish.

There was another boy whose name I forget. He looked broken, and his eyes were sad and bewildered, something was happening that he could not explain to himself, and death was going to dangle him for no reason he knew of. He was not connected with the army, the burden of in-security and uncertainty weighed him down. It was pathetic to watch him and compare him with the others. Looking at him, one felt what a terrible fate hanging was; studying the others, one forgot the noose; there was a young courage which death would hand on to the generation which was going to see this struggle through.

I read *The Brothers Karamazov*. Several times outside I had tried the book, but I was not able to read far. I began *Crime and Punishment*. I was so excited that I could not sleep well. The mental excitement of Dostoyevsky came over to me, it put my mind in a whirl of delight and warmth and overstimulation. I re-read the books. They changed the cell.

Hostages from amongst the prisoners, including T.D.s, were being used by the British. The prisoner had his hands stretched over his head; they were then tied to a steel bar that ran from front to rear of the lorry. " Bomb now," was painted on a card near the prisoner. The enemy thought that their use would slow down or prevent the daily bombing of lorries in the streets. To us this practice meant that the British were being hard hit. The Dublin men continued to throw eggs.

A hostage from our wing was taken out one day. His

lorry had been bombed as it passed through that part of Camden Street known as the Dardanelles, on account of the narrowing of the houses and the number of ambushes that took place there. Two bombs had been hurled at the lorry; they had rolled off the sides before they burst. The Tommies had the wind up proper, he said, they yelled and threw themselves down and the officer could not make them get up for a long time.

New prisoners told us what was happening outside. We cursed in the silence of our cells. It was rotten to be shut up when everyone was wanted outside. The fight was getting hotter; that was some satisfaction. I tramped up and down my cell, banging my nailed boots hard, kicking the walls, wild that I could not take a part, thinking always of escape. Military police told us of the raids they had been on : " Get Collins and Mulcahy dead or alive, that's what the officers told us; but 'strewth it's hard, them blokes are well armed."

Moran and I often talked of escape. Teeling, who was now closely watched, came into us one day on his way back from the jacks. The police liked and admired Teeling, they told us what a fine fellow he was ; most of them would be sorry to have him hanged. " Mac told me one of the police is friendly" Moran said, " you'd better talk to him." I met the soldier in my cell. He seemed sincere; that evening I gave him a note for the Chief of Staff, and told him where to leave it. I got a reply, then I sent a sketch of our wing and outlined our plan. Moran and I had gone through the nearby yards in the mornings when we went downstairs to wash. There was a heavy gate in a far away yard ; its two parts were backed by a heavy steel bar which was kept in position by a huge padlock. I asked for bolt cutters and a gun ; Moran and I were ready, I said, to take any chance so that Teeling should escape ; we would need men from the local company to guide him through the streets after Curfew. The C.S. wrote that any plan decided on must include Teeling and me.

I had been out on several identification parades ; one of the men called them " indentification." Seven or eight prisoners were walked out and drawn up in line in front of two zinc boxes. There were slits near the top, and through them we could catch the flash from a pair of eyes as we were slowly scrutinized. A few of the men shuffled their feet and jerked their bodies uneasily. Sometimes we were examined in silence; one of us would be made stand in front longer than the others. An officer standing to one side of the line would say: " Hold up your head. Turn round. Walk this way." We looked at the man turning, walking, showing his full face or profile. Once I held the hand of a man beside me. He was shivering.

" To hell with them," I said.

" I can't help it," he whispered, then the shivers stopped.

A ticket checker in uniform had been arrested in connection with a raid by the Dublin men on the Kingsbridge Station; two waggons of stores and ammunition had been captured and the military guard disarmed. He was very nervous, it would be easy to pick out a man in uniform.

The parades were probably in connection with " Bloody Sunday." The British could not admit that their detectives, Secret Service, and large police force were somewhat powerless. They could always quote in the House of Commons or in newspapers the number of arrests and suspects held. In England, an arrest would read as an implication of guilt; to us arrests meant that the British had to do something to justify their armed men and to bolster up their frequent statements that " they had murder by the throat." There was no doubt in my mind but that the bombing of troops in the city would mean the identification of some groups of us for another offence.

Sixty of us were drawn up in ranks in another yard, numbers were hung around our necks on a piece of cardboard; we were moved up slowly in ranks of seven till we were opposite to a row of six zinc boxes. There were long intervals between ranks. Men stood at ease, slouched or laughed; faces looked peaked and drawn. Some tried to talk to prisoners from other wings. The long wait became tension. Nothing to look at but drab grey, thick walls, small prying windows with dirty rusted bars, soldiers herding us and officers watching carefully. I might be picked out for Macroom or for something else; if I knew what I was up against I could face it, I felt, but the uncertainty was hard. We had no idea who might be behind the slits. This was a big day and there was a ceremonious feeling about it. We're like the burghers of Calais, I thought, as I looked down at the piece of string about my neck; was it the thin shadow of a rope? Our rank halted in front of the slits, I heard a foot scraping against zinc; an officer to one side of a box whispered to someone inside. " Right turn." In file we passed the row of boxes slowly; two men had to stand longer than the rest of us. Afterwards, we talked about it; what did it mean, why were so many prisoners brought out; what was going to happen next? A boy said there had been a woman present. " How did you know? " he was asked.

" I just knew and I winked back at her. It's a long time since I gave one of them the eye."

I was in the exercise yard. "Stewart!" shouted sallow-face, with his thin precise lips. " Come this way." My notes to the C.S. must have been caught; maybe I was going to be interrogated, or they might have found out who I was. I followed him into another yard. I saw twenty police in uniform; they had rifles. They looked swarthy and forbidding; all of them had dark hair. My mouth became dry, I began to swallow in my throat; my hands were cold at the tips and clammy when I closed them. " Put him up against the wall," ordered their officer, a District Inspector of Police. I was frightened—this I had not expected. Would they shoot me? Anything seemed possible. The police stood about fifteen feet away, some leant on their carbines with both elbows, a few had the long-barrelled Lee-Enfield. They looked at me. Some began to walk about the yard, others got further back and talked. I saw an old sergeant with thick gold V's on his arm shake his head. I heard some of their voices; they had Connacht accents. Suddenly I thought that they suspected I was Liam Mellows. He had escaped from the west coast after he had led out the Galway men in Easter Week. He had tried to get to Germany; recently he had come back from the United States.

At exercise we now walked in twos, getting into file when the police told us the sallow-one was coming. Paddy Moran stepped up beside me. " You'll get a parcel this evening; it must be the bolt-cutters." We laughed aloud. At tea time our soldier walked into my cell. He closed the door. He opened the buttons on his tunic and took out a long package. It was heavy. " And here's something you'll like." He drew a revolver from his pocket. His cap was slanted on the back of his head, he wiped his forehead. " Christ, that was heavy. Your sister said she'd send you some books to read. I met her to-day." Eileen McGilligan, whom he thought was my sister, probably brought my notes from him to Headquarters and gave him the replies.

The bolt-cutter had two long detachable, three-foot handles. I wrapped it up in a shirt. The revolver was a six-chambered Smith and Wessen '38, and was loaded. I put it in my trousers pocket. I tried to work a hole under one of the flags with a nail, but I would have to take up one completely to hide the gun, and two to get rid of the cutters. I gave up the idea of hiding them under the flags. That night I practised quick draws and got my hand used to the grip.

I was moved down the passage to the cell beside Paddy Moran. It was good to be near him, but I would have to pass two guards to get to Teeling in the night. At exercise time I fitted the handles in the cutters and tied them from my shoulders, under my shirt. I padded them with strips of flannel underclothes to prevent them from rattling. I carried the gun in my pocket. Cells might be searched while we were out in the yard and the least suspicious place seemed to be myself.

At night we listened for the movements of sentries; in the day time Teeling, Moran and I talked of what we had observed. There were two lots of night guards; one of four or five men in the second cell from mine, and four in a cell close to Teeling, around the corner from my passage. I would have to pass the guards to get to him. Then if I could unlock his door we could reach the iron stairs, go down two flights through a door to our exercise yard, across another yard to the bulky gate. The bolt-cutters would easily get through the steel bar, Moran said.

Our soldier, when not on duty, unlocked the padlock of my cell and fixed the shackle so that it seemed to be fastened. My hand was small, I could put it through the peephole, unfasten the shackle, attach it to a ring in the bolt, raise up the bolt and slide it back. I worked at the bolt, slowly sliding it backward and forward in the day time, opening and closing the door without noise, whilst Moran kept watch on the passage. Teeling's cell could not be left unlocked at night; it had no padlock, but its lock could be opened by pressing against the jamb with the handle of a spoon. I practised opening it while Moran and I talked, with our backs to Teeling's door.

My door cramped my hand, but I was able to work it. One night I opened my door and listened. I was in my stockings; I carried my boots around my neck and the cutters inside my coat. Small stirs made me nervously ready to dash back. It was one thing to listen from my cell, another to be out in the passage. I got to the first guard cell. I looked through the crack made by the swinging in of the door. The light was on, and the soldiers were lying down; their rifles slanted against the wall or across their knees and they seemed to be asleep. The door hinge was on my side of the opening; I had to close the door in case I should have to return in a hurry; a sleepy soldier could notice a figure passing in the light from the cell gas. I pressed hard on the angle of the door; the metal moved slowly. My fingers were stiff, I had to rest. I pressed again; there were squeaks. I heard a noise from Teeling's passage. Someone was coming towards me. I moved back quietly to my cell, closed the door, shoved back the bolt, attached the padlock and rolled my blankets around me. A soldier passsed my cell. I tried again when all was still. My door squeaked, my wrist was cramped. When I reached the guard cell I lay flat and looked through. A soldier was sitting up, smoking.

For five successive nights I tried to get through to Teeling; on two nights I closed the doors of the two guard cells and reached him. We whispered and I scraped back the lock; the first time it took a long time to move back. "Have you got it yet? hurry up . . . no, take it easy." Up the iron stairs from the lower landing came the clang of boots. I shut the door. I ran to the angle of the passage and watched. Two soldiers came to the head of the landing; they looked in through a peephole and halted. Outside Teeling's cell they talked; one looked in, he beckoned to his pal and he peeped. Teeling was a curiosity; he was to be 'unged. As they walked toward me I scudded past the other guard cell, jerked back the bolt, and got inside the blankets.

Another night I was working on his lock when I heard movement in the guard cell nearby. I ran back past the door, the bolt-cutters swung with my rush and clanged together. As I took the corner I heard the door open. My door closed quickly with a groan of metal; I had not time to fix the bolt. Two soldiers passed and came back after a long while.

The guards slept uneasily, some held on to their rifles. I could never be sure if they were even half asleep. Sometimes the noise made by the slight movement of their door made some more alert. I was becoming nervous, unimportant sounds made me glide back, but my fingers were now more hardened to the swinging backward pressure.

During the daytime I could sleep a little, but not much. We could not be sure of the other prisoners, some were pigeons, or might have been set to watch certain men; others, although they were sound, would talk if they noticed anything strange, or might unconsciously give it away by secretive expression. Outside, in the night, men from the Fourth Battalion waited for us, ready to guide us and to fight. They might attract attention. Every evening when darkness came lorries and tenders were bombed, more civilians were killed than soldiers. The military police told us how nervous the soldiers were passing through the streets. Teeling's hanging might be hurried up if an unusually heavy ambush were brought off.

At Mass on Sunday, guards tried to prevent us mixing with men from other wings, but someone always talked. That meant more news from the outside. I knelt behind Rory O Connor, he sat back in his seat.

" What luck? "

" Rotten so far, to-morrow we'll try after tea. Maybe you can get to the yard; we can't time it, but if we get through, the gate will be open."

" Go ahead, don't mind me. I think they're getting ready to move some of us, and things will be easier to work in the camps."

" How about the bolt-cutters, are you sure they'll work? "

" It's a gift; they'll go through it like cheese."

I sent out a note to say that we would try again, this time after tea or before Curfew; the men outside should bring a rope ladder in case the cutters failed.

Dusk came slowly that evening. I had tea in Moran's cell, but I could not eat. We waited until Teeling's corridor was clear of guards. Moran followed me, then Teeling. I gave the cutters to Moran and knocked at the heavy gate, voices whispered. Men from the Fourth Battalion were outside. I stood back in the corner of the wall near a gate in the partition wall with the .38 in my hand. Heavy walls bulked higher than ever in the dim light; night made them thick and desperate looking. This was their strongest prison. I could hear heavy breathing from the big gate. "Oh God," in a groan came from the darkness; from cells on top came the words of a song:

"It's fifty long years since I saw the moon beamin',
On brave manly forms and on hearts with hope gleamin',
I see them again in all my day dreaming."

From the stairway by which we had reached the ground floor came the clatter of boots. " Ssh," I whispered. Small noises at the big gate stopped. The sound of boots went into distance. "All right, go ahead," I said.

Moran was leaning against the gate feeling his hands. Teeling was pressing hard on the handles, groaning. " I can't—the bloody things won't work. You try." I pressed slowly on the handles, I increased the force, my arms became taut and my body trembled with the effort, but nothing happened. Teeling took one handle, I used the other; sweat gathered on my eyebrows and dripped over my eyelids, my shirt became sticky. "I'll try again," said Moran. I could hear his short, grunty breaths.

I rapped on the door. " Cutters won't work. Throw over rope."

" All right," came through the gate. It was cold, but my face was in a glow from excitement. It would be harder on the last man to climb as there would be no one below on our side to hold the ladder strands taut, and he would have to jump from the top of the wall. I was going to be last. If Teeling got away Moran and I would be content even if we were interrupted from inside. I was going to shoot it out, but Moran had no gun. We could hear light noises against the wall. There came sharp, snapping rattling crashes; they seemed to continue when I could not hear them with my ears. The terrible silence that followed was even worse. " For God's sake, what's that? " whispered Moran.

I shivered with the cold. Something had rolled on the sloping corrugated roof of a shed which jutted out from the wall. Groping in the dark I came upon a length of twine; it was weighted with lead. I pulled on the cord. It would not move. It was caught on the top of the wall. I sent Moran back to the gate to tell the men to jerk up the string. I tried to move it at an angle, but there was no give. " I'll have to pull," I said to Teeling. He caught my left hand and pressed it hard. He laughed. " All right, heave ho!" I pulled, the twine became taut; I pulled again. It snapped. I had a piece of twine and a lead weight in my hand.

Through the gate I said, " we're going, good-bye." All I could hear was " better luck."

" Hurry up," said Moran, anxiously, " they must have missed us."

I hid the cutters under a pile of lumber in the shed. Up-stairs we ran, springing quicker when we heard the sound of marching feet on the second corridor; the night guard was coming on duty.

We had no faith in the cutters, but we meant to try again. If the weight was padded and luminous; if the ladder had extra cords attached, an accident might be avoided. " If the next attempt fails we'll have to fight it out," I said, " my nerves may crash." Moran agreed. Day guards carried Webleys; they had rifles; night guards had rifles in their cells. If we disarmed them we could rush the main guard at the front gate with bayonets fixed. If we failed or were beaten back we could fight it out in the yard, or fall back on the unused part of the building.

" Teeling is game," Moran said; " if we fail the next time we might be able to pick up two other men to fight to a finish." That would make five. Simon Donnelly, whom I had last met handling men at the election in East Tyrone, had been brought in that morning; he would make six. Our soldier came into Moran's cell, always he cheered us up with his dancing laugh. His tunic was unbuttoned, he rubbed his hair and perched his cap. " Strewth its . . . . hard; what will Micky Collins say? " A week ago he said he had met Michael Collins. " In a public he was, an' he said your name will go down in the history of Ireland."

ON ANOTHER MAN'S WOUND

"Teeling is not going to be hanged," I said, "we'll fight." I told him we were going to seize the rifles. "We are sure of three men—Moran, Teeling and myself."

"Yes," said Moran, "and its going to be a fight to a finish."

"You have four," said the soldier.

"What four?" asked Moran, "we're dead sure of three."

"Four," said the soldier, "I'm your fourth, Ga blimey." We smiled into each other's serious eyes. There was a pause, then we shook hands and linked our arms on each other's shoulders. I felt a rich, happy glow; we knew what we were going to do. Our soldier would find out the strength of the guards, their hours of relief and general alertness, and the quickest and best way to the main gate.

The unorganized condition of the prisoners in the Murder Wing helped us to plan an escape. There was nothing tangible for the enemy to thrust at; we had slowly won over most of the day guards by adjusting them to ourselves. Our morale, through increasing control of our part of the gaol, was good. The police were slack; they were soldiers first, and soldiers make bad gaolers. Sallowface alone, of the officers, was more watchful; his face and manner made a warden of him. The real danger would come from anyone amongst the prisoners who might be watching Moran or Teeling, from a slip made by our soldier, who was as intense as we now were, or from the betrayal of our purpose through our close-knit comradeship. I had no intention of being hanged. I was going to escape, dead or alive.

A small bottle of drugged whisky was sent in. If we could give it mixed with more drink to the night guards I could get quicker to Teeling's cell, but how to get on proper terms with them was a problem. Some of them would ask for cigarettes after lights out; I often pushed some through the peep hole. I would hear "Thank ye, mate," and an awkward silence as the man continued to stand against the door.

A man in plain clothes came into my cell. He looked like a pleasant official from the R.I.C. depot; there was an air of protective humanity when he spoke.

"Bernard," he began "I'm your friend, now don't forget that. They have made up their minds to hang you for the Macroom ambush."

"But I wasn't at Macroom, and they know it right well."

"They will hang you unless you give your mother's address. Think of what she is suffering, she doesn't even know where you are. I can tell her you're safe, can't I?"

"But they will burn her house, that's what I'm afraid of."

"Bernard," he said, soothingly, "don't be afraid, remember I'm your friend, I don't approve of what some of them do."

"I know that."

"Well, Bernard, think it over. I'll be back again in a few days, and that will be your last chance, and they'll hang you for Macroom if you don't give your mother's address." He placed his hand on my shoulder, "It's not much to ask. Remember, Bernard, I'm your friend."

"I know you are, thanks very much."

He had kept me back from another identification parade. As I hurried down the identification yard I wondered if there was any connection between his visit and my possible selection through the slits.

That evening Teeling came into my cell after tea; his eyes were beating up and down with light. He grabbed my arms.

"Come on, quick. It's all right, the bolt's cut." He rubbed his hands.

"When? You don't . . . "

"Just now, the soldier and I. Like this," he snapped his teeth. We held our hands crossways and gripped hard. We both laughed.

"We'll get Paddy and take Doyle and the boys from the First Battalion," I said.

Paddy Moran was writing a letter. "Come on, Paddy, Teeling's cut the bolt." He stood up. "God, that's great, but . . . I'm not going."

"You must. You're with us, you were willing enough the other night."

"No, I'm not going. I won't let down the witnesses who gave evidence for me."

"To hell with the witnesses," I said, "come on."

"O, come on, Paddy," said Teeling, "come on." Moran shook his head slowly, smiling.

" I'm your senior in rank, but what's the sense in giving an order. You talk to him, Teeling, I'll get Doyle and the others." The First Battalion boys were not in their cells. That morning they had told sallow face what they thought of him; he had sent them to punishment cells on a lower landing. I could not find our soldier; there was no chance of getting a key. I went to Simon Donnelly's cell.

" Hop it, Simon, we're escaping—now."

He smiled. " Is that all? "

" I'm serious, Simon, come on. You know the neighbourhood."

" Good," he said, as he followed me.

Teeling's face was strained. "It's no use, he won't come."

" Someone has to die for this, Paddy," I said. " Maybe Teeling or myself, but they'll hang you for certain if we get through."

" God keep you now," said Paddy Moran, as he held our shoulders. " I'll start a concert to keep the police busy, you'll not be missed until lock up."

We were sad as we left the cell. On the passage towards the stairs I went into Desmond Fitzgerald's cell. He had been Director of Publicity.

" Any atrocities, Desmond? "

" No, but I saw Mabel to-day; she was asking for you."

" Desmond, could you please lend me sixpence for tram fare? "

He smiled. " I can give you five shillings."

" No. Sixpence will do. I'm tired of this place."

He laughed at my joke as he handed me the silver. " For tram fare, young shaver."

We opened one half of the gate, it was heavy to move; then we closed it. I was first with the .38 in my hand. I saw figures in the darkness close to the wall; one had a peaked cap, but they had not heard me. I touched Teeling with my hand: " Soldiers, there's something wrong; an outside patrol, I think. I'll stick them up and if I have to shoot, you two make a dash for it." They halted whilst I went forward. A soldier was holding a woman tight in his arms. I went back to tell the others. We moved on under the wall passing other soldiers and girls locked together.

The wind was cold, it blew clean and sweet in our faces. Gas lamps beamed out of the blackness; front porches shone on to small evergreen shrubs in tiny gardens and the stars winked at us in a friendly way. " You'd better hide the gun somewhere," said Simon, " you're never sure of a hold-up in the streets." It was fine on top of a tram. We felt inclined to sing and shout; instead we pinched each other with delight. There was so much colour, dun brick shining, people walking along the South Circular, and talk coming up from the street. We held our faces into the wind. Simon got off near Camden Street, we went on to Malone's in Heytesbury Street. Aunia opened the door. " Hello, we've paid a call," I said.

" Oh, oh, oh," she said, pulling us in by the hands. " This is Teeling."

In the kitchen we were hugged and kissed by Mrs. Malone, Aunia and Bridge. Mrs. Malone wept and smiled by turns; she ran her hands over my face. " They hurt you," she said. " But it's all right now; if only poor Peadar and Seán Tracey were here to see this day." Aunia put on her coat. " I'm off to the Brigade. This house isn't safe now, we think it's watched." Later she linked our arms as we walked along the Canal bank to Dr. R.'s house near Mount Street bridge.

CHAPTER NINETEEN

FEBRUARY, 1921

★

TEELING'S ESCAPE itched Dublin Castle. The only prisoner against whom there was definite evidence in connection with " Bloody Sunday " had escaped from their strongest gaol. Dr. R.'s mother knew who we were. She went in the evenings to play a game of bridge with her Unionist friends. They had discussed the escape. " They're afraid now of other escapes, and the Unionists don't know what to think," she said. She chuckled as she thought of her talks at the club, when her house held the escaped men.

Seán Russell, our Director of Munitions, walked away with Teeling, who wore dungarees and carried a set of plumber's tools. Tom Cullen, Assistant Quartermaster-General, brought me to the south side, to the house of two elderly ladies, school teachers. My name was now O'Brien.

They waited anxiously when I was out close to Curfew, which now shut us up at 10 o'clock. They hovered near me at meals. "I'm sure you don't like that; it's not properly cooked," one would say when I had eaten what I thought was a large amount of the disparaged dish or dainty. They said I had no appetite. They went to Mass and Holy Communion every morning. Their confessor had told them that the men in charge of our movement had been appointed by God to make Ireland free.

"Ireland will soon be free, thank God," they said, "and the boys can go back to their homes and work for her in another way." They talked eagerly of the escape. Teeling had left Dublin, they said; but Stewart was still walking about the city. Wasn't it dangerous for him?

At night I slept on a sofa. Near my head was a holy water font; an oleograph of the Sacred Heart and a picture of our Lady of Perpetual Succour had been pinned above my bed. In case of a raid, I was to hide in a small triangular space underneath the stairs and I would be quite safe there. One morning I left one of my guns under the pillow. When I came back the pillow had been neatly patted into shape. They did not talk about the revolver, nor did they again mention the retreat under the stairs. They chatted and talked eagerly to me. They leant on the table and looked at me when I used maps or wrote. They were very kind and staunchly timorous.

On the North side of the city troops had begun the round-up of a district which was beleaguered for five days. A house to house search went on, all traffic within the area was stopped and permits were given to those who moved about. Machine gun posts on the roofs, barbed wire, sandbags and sentries on the streets backed by armoured cars and tanks, made the occupation impressive. The combing gave some prisoners and an ammunition dump. At an hotel away from the encircled district I met Mick Collins who had cycled to keep the appointment. He shook my hands a long time. "Well, Earnán, you're born to be shot, you can't be hanged. Why didn't Paddy Moran come with you?"

"I don't know. He thought there was no case against him."

His face became grave. "They'll hang him as a reprisal now. His trial is still going on."

" What do you think of the Auxiliaries? "

" A tough bunch, they look good soldiers."

" Yes, a bloody fine crowd." He nodded his head with force. Perhaps he had met some of them, I thought.

" I think the Castle could be attacked through " F " Company quarters," I said.

He placed his elbows on the table, he leant his chin on his right hand. " You think so? "

I drew a plan of the lower Castle on a sheet of paper, and marked in the buildings and defences as I had seen them. Our men could get through the houses in Dame Street to the latrine, hold up the guardroom, block the sleeping quarters and deal with the landings in turn. " I'd like to guide an attacking party."

He looked at my sketch, asked questions and took notes. " It might be done," he said. " I'll see about it."

I was nervous at first in the streets, then I became surer of myself. I saw Auxiliaries whom I knew from " F " Company swirl by. They would be sure to recognize me, I thought; and I had often to stop myself from trying to run. Troops spilled out suddenly from armoured lorries, which were now wire-netted to protect them from grenades, and from armoured cars ; both ends and byways of a street would be blocked simultaneously by soldiers and Auxiliaries. All between their converging bayonets were searched by patrols and intelligence officers, for papers and arms.

Through the streets in file, well strung out, passed the squads of Igoe's Gang, consisting of police from the county, in civilian clothes. They were on the look out for men whom they knew. They could hold up quickly and their formation would protect them against attack. They lived in the R.I.C. depôt. They changed their assumed names frequently, and were known by numbers even when giving evidence in secret. Patrols from " F " Company Auxiliaries, in mufti, moved out on foot from the Castle on special work. Our armed H.Q. Intelligence Squad moved around looking for intelligence officers and detectives; they watched suspects or waited for members of the Castle murder gangs. The A.S.U. of fifty men from the Dublin Brigade were also on the prowl.

At times I heard the quick loud crash as one of our eggs burst and the answering fire from rifles and machine guns.

There was a sense of tension in Dublin. The quietness of an evening could become strain that might only be eased when it was fearfully broken without warning.

Outside Stephen's Green I saw men attack a netted lorry and an armoured Lancia of troops. Eggs shattered in a tearing smash, one burst above the Lancia; automatics shot quickly, rifle reply came more slowly then the rifles merged with the swaying thresh of a machine gun. The passersby ran or threw themselves on the pavement. I lay down, watching. A man flattened on his blood in the cobbled street, two soldiers lay loosely against each other in a corner of the Lancia; up the street men tried to stop the red stains on a woman's white blouse. Women beside me were moaning and praying: "O Sacred Heart of Jesus, help us." I ran for a lane beside the College of Surgeons and was soon in York Street.

At dusk on almost deserted streets duels took place between bombing squads of our men from the five Dublin battalions and armoured lorries. In the night time, after Curfew, patrols of troops moved on rubber soles, and enemy intelligence officers went about on raiding parties or rushed a house. Night was their prowling time. The underground meshes could open to send out their agents in security. Circulars offering money for information, and telling what information to give, were slipped under doors.

I changed from house to house. Three men from the Fourth Battalion took me in one evening; they were well armed. During the night I heard screams. " Oh my God, save me. Quick, save me." I rushed towards the noise with my gun, thinking that a raiding gang had got quietly into the house and were going to shoot their prisoners. One of the boys sat up in bed screaming; his companion was hidden under the bed, his body twitched and his hands swayed like an autumn leaf. Their nerves had gone suddenly. We sat up with them till dawn. In Ranelagh I slept with two boys whom I had known in the University. I was shaken out of my sleep one night; " A raid," said one. "Get your gun." I pulled on my trousers, slung my boots by the laces around my neck. Lorries had halted outside. We saw men in civies and tin hats get down. We heard footsteps further down the street and in the cinder lane at the back of the house. One would hold the back

ON ANOTHER MAN'S WOUND

door, two of us would open fire as we drew back the front
door, then dash out the backway. We heard the heavy
thud of a knocker being swung violently and a shout:
" Open the door ! Quick !" The raid was taking place
next door.

I met the Commandant of the Fourth whose men had
waited for us outside the walls of Kilmainham. " It's
well you escaped," he said, " our men were fed up waiting
for you night after night ; we had to arrest three Tommies
and four girls whom we found near the gaol walls, and we
kept them prisoners until the escape came off. We thought
you'd never be able to escape. Some of our men had to be
near the gaol in the early morning and two of them used
Corporation brushes to sweep the roadway in front of the
main guard room so as not to attract attention."

I told him about the broken-looking man who had
escaped from his escort going to the Castle. "Fouvargue's
his name. He was our Assistant Battalion I.O. and that
escape of his was faked. The British let him go. It's
said that he broke under torture in the Castle, and that he
gave information. Yet judging by results he mustn't have
for he had plenty of information to give."

A month later the body of a man was found on an English
golf links ; pinned to his chest was a card : " Spies and
Traitors Beware ! " It was Fouvargue. Under the name of
Somers he had tried to join our groups in England who were
burning the homes of Tans and destroying communications,
but he had been tracked down. I often thought of what Paddy
Moran had said : " I don't like his face, he's a quitter."

Later on I was told that he had been taken out, rushed
four times on raiding parties when in the Castle, and had
then been sent to Kilmainham as a stool-pigeon. Perhaps
terrified by ill-treatment he was trying to deceive the
British, and yet he must have known that even if he didn't
give away important information his life was forfeited.

Frank Gallagher was busy in the preparation of the *Irish
Bulletin*, which was daily forwarded to the foreign press
and to members of the English House of Commons.
Somehow, the *Bulletin* always got through the cordon.
" It's time for you to acknowledge the I.R.A. at last, Frank,"
I said. Previously we had been referred to as a suffering
people who in desperation were attacking their oppressors.

We went to a house which we had often visited before my arrest. Honor and Sheila Murphy worked for our publicity. Mrs. Murphy's son had been a naval officer; the house was safer than most on that account. Frank, to rag me, discussed the Kilmainham escape, and I listened to their pleased talk about it; previously I had been O'Brien to them, so they did not suspect his allusions. That night I slept with a naval sword on a chair at the foot of my bed to reinforce my other weapons.

*   *   *   *

I endeavoured to pick up the threads of the movement from random talks and conversations, by reading reports forwarded to our Headquarters from brigades and by meeting officers of the H.Q. Staff. A week after my arrest, Lord French, the Lord Lieutenant, had issued a Proclamation stating that the counties of Cork, Tipperary, Kerry and Limerick were subject to Martial Law. Four days later, General Macready, Commander-in-Chief of the Forces in Ireland, sent out another proclamation.

" After the 27th of December, 1920, any unauthorized person found in possession of arms, ammunition or explosives will be liable, on conviction of a Military Court, to suffer Death.

" Any unauthorized person wearing the uniform or equipment of His Majesty's Naval, Military, Air or Police Forces, or wearing clothing likely to deceive, will be liable on conviction to suffer death . . .

" Note well . . .

" That a state of armed insurrection exists; that any person taking part therein or harbouring any person who has taken part therein, or procuring, inviting, aiding or abetting any person to take part therein, is guilty of levying war against His Majesty the King, and is liable on conviction of a Military Court to suffer death.

" The Forces of the Crown in Ireland are hereby declared to be on active service."

Three weeks later, in January, the Martial Law area was extended to counties Clare, Waterford, Kilkenny and Wexford.

Major-General Strickland in the Martial Law area began to shower proclamations. People could be prosecuted for not reporting that others were in possession of arms. Motors were dismantled. Those still in use could not be used beyond a twenty-mile radius. He prohibited the use of motor cars, motor cycles and pedal bicycles between 8 p.m. and 6 a.m.

" It is forbidden to assist rebels in any way, or to provide them with food, clothing, vehicles, shelter. People are warned that they must not fail to report rebels or any movement of rebels, without delay. Anybody disobeying this order will render themselves liable to be prosecuted before a Military Court or dealt with summarily.

" No person must stand or loiter in the streets, except in pursuit of their lawful profession or calling. All meetings or assemblies in public places are forbidden and for the purposes of the order six adult persons will be considered a meeting.

" Anyone found defacing the proclamation will be rigorously dealt with. All occupiers of houses must keep affixed to the inner side of the outer door a list of the occupants, setting forth their names, age, sex, and occupation."

*   *   *   *

NOTICE IS HEREBY GIVEN that on account of the numerous attacks which have been made by rebel forces on motors and lorries conveying forces of the Crown, officers and leaders of the rebel force (commonly known as the Irish Republican Army) will in future be carried in Government motors and lorries.

*   *   *   *

In order to prevent outrages by strangers taking place in Dunmanway and district, it has been decided that six male inhabitants shall be held responsible for each week for informing the O.C. Auxiliary Police at the Workhouse, Dunmanway, of any suspicious stranger arriving in the Town, or of any occurrence or circumstance which points to contemplated outrage.

This plan is further intended to protect other inhabitants from intimidation and to render it possible for any *Loyalist* to give information without the rebels being able to trace its source.

The following individuals will be held responsible for providing information from and including 16th February, 1921, up to and including 22nd February, 1921 : . . . Should any outrage occur in Dunmanway, or within two miles of the Market Square, the whole of the above-mentioned will be placed under arrest.

Dunmanway.   *Lieut.-Col., 1st D.Q.*
                                    K Company, Aux. Div., R.I.C.

Removal of this notice will entail punishment for the entire District Council.

British generals and Irish chief secretaries since 1916 frequently assured Lloyd George that the Irish question would soon be settled. Macready, given a free hand in April of 1920, promised to settle Ireland before the opening of the autumn session of the British Parliament; the Tans and Auxiliaries were not enough. Orders in Council regulations were passed in September which gave him more power as Commander-in-Chief, civilian inquests on men killed by the British would not be allowed ; courts-martial replaced civil courts.

Lloyd George said there would be a solution by Christmas. Extra battalions came with tanks, aeroplanes, armoured car companies and martial law. Now, Strickland, Commander of the Sixth Division, promised to have the martial law area in hand by 1st April.

The Bishop of Perth, once chaplain to the Australian forces, had come over as an emissary. A truce was discussed and practically agreed to, until Lloyd George, backed by Wilson, again decided that arms would have to be first surrendered by the I.R.A.

" K " Company of Auxiliaries burnt the centre of Cork city in December, with the connivance of military curfew patrols, and the help of the R.I.C. The company was removed to Dunmanway where the cadets wore a piece of burnt cork as a cap badge.

Bishop Cohalan of Cork had pronounced sentence of excommunication on those in his diocese who carried out attacks on the British.

Barricades had been put up at the entrance to the British premier's house in Downing Street; detectives shadowed the British Cabinet and the House of Commons was strongly guarded. In England farm supplies and warehouses had been burned by our men operating to the plans of Rory O Connor.

As a result of the carrying of our T.D.s as hostages in lorries, it had been decided by our G.H.Q. to arrest about ten English Members of Parliament and keep them hidden in England. Then notice would be given to the British that if a T.D. was killed in an attack by the I.R.A. on a vehicle in which he was being carried, one of the prisoner Members of Parliament would be executed. As our men in England were ready to make the simultaneous arrests the operation was called off.

The English Labour Party appointed a Commission which visited Ireland and published a report. The English-women's International League and the British Society of Friends published reports.

The American Committee for Relief in Ireland, organized in New York, in December, 1920, sent a delegation who reported: "Material damage to Irish shop-buildings, creameries and private dwellinghouses inflicted by the British forces during the past twelve months amounts approximately to $20,000,000 . . . the cost of replacing the buildings will be approximately $25,000,000. We found there are 25,000 families in pitiful need of instant help . . . from the crippling of the co-operative creameries 15,000 farmers are suffering severe loss."

The American Commission on Conditions in Ireland was elected from a committee of representative Americans summoned by the New York *Nation*; it interviewed witnesses from Ireland and published the evidence.

January 7th, 1921: Official report after an attack on a police patrol at Midleton, Co. Cork.

"Although it had not yet been possible to identify any of the persons who were actually engaged in these attacks, the Military Governor was of the opinion that the pre-parations could not have been carried out without the knowledge of many of the local residents, who were there-fore held to be guilty, at least to the extent of having failed to give information to the military or police authorities. It was accordingly decided as a punitive measure and as a deterrent example to other districts to destroy certain houses in the vicinity of the outrage, which were definitely known to be occupied by the militant section of the Sinn Féin movement."

Irish Independent, 15th January, 1921: "An extra-ordinary scene was witnessed at Ballina yesterday when Crown Forces arrested Messrs. P. Beirn, John and M. Moylett, D. Molloy, D.C., and M. Corcoran, V.C., and compelled them to parade the streets carrying Union Jacks. One of the men was forced to trail the Republican flag on the street. The procession was headed by an itinerant musician playing a banjo, while a motor load of armed forces brought up the rear. Before being released the men were compelled to kneel on the ground and kiss the Union Jack, the Republican flag being at the same time burned. All the men were prominent merchants."

Irish Independent, 17th January, 1921. " We have received the following message from our Ballina correspondent : I am requested by the Commander of the Auxiliary Forces to contradict the statement that the merchants passed here on Friday evening with Union Jacks were compelled to join in the parade, or that they were temporarily arrested. He states that they were merely asked to come to the auxiliary headquarters, and that when desired to carry the Union Jacks through the town they did not object. He also states that the street musicians joined in the procession voluntarily."

Irish Times, 26th January, 1921. " Royal Irish Constabulary rounded up prominent residents of Fermoy, marched them to the bridge in the centre of the town where they were compelled to paint on the walls such inscriptions as

" God Save the King."
" God Bless The Black and Tans."

January 27th : " Any person who save in the due necessary exercise or pursuit of his lawful trade, calling or profession should stand, or loiter in any public place," is liable to arrest and prosecution.

All Dublin hospitals were required to furnish daily to the military authorities a list of patients suffering from wounds caused by bullets, gunfire or other explosives.

February, 1921. A.E. wrote : " On behalf of the Irish co-operative movement I demand the setting-up of an impartial tribunal to investigate the illegal destruction of co-operative property by the armed forces of the crown . . . actual injury is estimated by experts to be between £250 and £300,000, while the annual trade disturbed is almost £1,000,000."

Strickland, Commander of the Sixth Division, with headquarters at Cork, had sent a report to London about the burning of Cork City. Lloyd George promised to publish the Strickland report, but changed his mind.

March 6th. An English paper remarked on my notes, which had been captured by Auxiliaries whilst I was in a cell in Kilmainham : " The diary of this particular organizer is of great importance as showing the ' I.R.A.' depends entirely for its continued existence on such organizers, who going from place to place, paint the virtues of the Republic, and keep the show going. They are the Liaison officers that keep the various seditious societies in touch with each other, and with the civil population, and although isolated ambushes would still be possible without them, concerted action would be impossible. . . .

"The writer of the diary seems to have been an important itinerant 'I.R.A.' organizer whose travels extended into the four provinces."

Some English papers would have us sporadic gangs and would eliminate the mass feeling behind a simple operation. The *Manchester Guardian*, *Daily News*, *Westminster Gazette* and *The Times* wrote up incidents of the campaign in Ireland, and made discord in the general chorus of newspapers which made the most of gunmen shooting troops in the back.

My friends in Kilmainham were hanged on different dates: Paddy Moran and Whelan; and together the boys from the First Battalion whom I had been unable to reach: Bernard Ryan, Patrick Doyle, Thomas Byrne, Frank Flood. In Cork, prisoners had been shot by firing squads in Victoria Barracks.

I wanted to get away to the country again, but the Chief of Staff told me not to move until my health was better. I saw an oculist and I had to wear spectacles, which I hated, but as they changed my appearance I became more reconciled.

The movement was now becoming respectable, success had drawn in many who had not even a half belief. I saw a new paid bureaucracy being built up in Dublin, and I heard the comments of some, who looked down on the fighting men and others who were bearing their share of the dirty work.

I met Ginger O'Connell in McGilligan's of Leeson Street. He was now Deputy Chief of Staff. Ginger looked as easy-going as ever, yet he had changed. He was applying his organized thought in a more practical way. He was the only man on the H.Q. Staff whom one could discuss military problems with, now that Dick McKee had gone. In Dublin it was proposed, he said, to train a number of officers and send them out as organizers. " It's about time, Ginger : Dublin has an idea that drill instructors can direct the country at this stage. You know well what duds were sent out."

" Like yourself!" and he laughed. "Would you be willing to undertake training? "

" No, I would prefer to go back to the martial law area. I can be of more use there. I don't like the idea of being a paper officer."

He told me that Headquarters intended to start a military College in Dublin where officers from different areas would receive training courses.

" It will be hard to keep it going."

Ginger smiled. " We'll manage it all right. The C.S. wants you to meet the President to-morrow. He'll be there with the D.I. You'd better take extra precautions." Ginger left the house.

An hour afterwards, Mabel Fitzgerald, wife of Desmond, Director of our Publicity, whom I had left in Kilmainham Gaol, knocked at the door. " There's a hold up," she said, " the street is being surrounded, you'd better go to another house up the street." I remained at the head of the stairs leading to the garden. It was too late to move now. I heard banging at doors down the street and then loud knocks at our front door.

Listening out in the garden I heard footsteps in the lane beyond the garden wall. The night was dark and cold. I heard loud voices from the house, flashlights flared around rooms, men leant out of windows and prodded the blackness with light. They walked on the roof. I climbed to the next garden and lay on the ground. They might search the gardens, I thought. I climbed the back wall; at the end of the lane figures stood out against the light of a street lamp. I crossed the lane, climbed the opposite wall and worked my way across gardens towards the street, but soldiers were in the furthest gardens. If I open fire, I thought, they will take cover and search where the shots came from, then I can cross the lane and get back to McGilligan's garden. I fired with my Parabellum automatic. The range was about seventy-five yards. I heard soldiers shouting; rifle shots spread out then clumped together towards my last shots. Firing continued for a while. I got back to McGilligan's garden, waited, then slept in their house.

Mick Collins opened the door of a house near the sea. The house had a front garden. In a long front room with bay windows, screened a little by trees in front, were Eamon de Valera and Dick Mulcahy. The C.S. smiled slowly, the muscles of his mouth only moved when he smiled. " It's hard to kill a bad thing," he said. De Valera shook hands with me. He was tall, his lean stringy build overemphasized his height. His face was drawn and pale as if he had had little exercise or was recovering from illness. The lines running to his mouth edges made furrows; ridges stood out in relief. He looked worn. He smiled with his eyes. The lines on his face broke as if ice had cracked. His voice rumbled from the depths with a hard but not a harsh dryness. Dev. the Long Fellow, or the Chief, had come back from the United States two months ago. He had helped to float the foreign loan of $5,000,000, and had aided the Irish vote, influenced by Article 10, that kept the States out of the League of Nations. At home he was looked up to with awe. There was a sense of sternness about him, dignity, a definite honesty, and a friendly way of making one feel at ease. He had lost personal contact during the year and a half he had been away.

We sat around a table. " They tell me that you know most of the actual situation in the South," he said. The C.S. laid out a large map of Ireland on the table.

" Things have changed since I have been in gaol, sir, and my information is three months old."

He pointed to Tipperary. " Tell us about the county. What are the military and police strengths? our strengths?"

I pointed out posts and barracks, outlined our battalion areas, gave, as far as I could remember, our armament and told him the support the people gave us. He had not the human qualities of Collins, the Big Fellow. Dev. was more reserved, a scholarly type. He was cold and controlled. Collins might solve a problem boisterously, by improvisation, solve it by its own development. De Valera would find the solution mathematically, clearly, with logic.

He questioned me about Clare, Limerick, Cork, Kilkenny. He did not know the names of our senior officers. His questions showed that he did not understand the situation in the South. The main strategical strengths of the enemy he knew, but things had changed since he had been in Ireland. They had changed since I had been in gaol.

Mulcahy and Collins asked me questions to bring out points which the President had overlooked.

"We are forming divisional areas," Mulcahy said. "The Deputy Chief has already discussed the matter with you."

I nodded.

"You are to command the Second Southern Division; two brigades in Limerick, two in Tipperary, Kilkenny County, and perhaps Waterford. We will talk over the other divisional areas in detail during the week."

I always felt that the C.S. could not be flurried or rushed. He had a quiet strength that was impressive He had thought over each area in his mind. He could summarize a brigade quickly. The talk lasted for over three hours.

"What time is it?" asked de Valera. "There's a Cabinet meeting this evening. I must get my papers ready for it." He shook hands. "Take care of yourself now, *a chara dhíl, agus beannacht Dé leat.*"

I sat in a smaller room with Mulcahy and Collins. "What did you think of the interview?" asked Collins.

"He did not know much about the army in the South," I said. Both laughed as if amused. Collins mentioned some of the questions the President had asked; they laughed again. I felt uncomfortable. Dev. was the President. After all, I thought, how could he be expected to know the military situation thoroughly. Cathal Brugha, the Minister of Defence, did not know the senior officers well. He worked as a traveller whilst his deputy was paid his salary. That desire to work without pay was understandable, but his position as M.D. needed all his energies. Many members of the G.H.Q. Staff did not know the country. They depended for information upon reports which were forwarded by some areas only, and then never in detail, and on the spasmodic visits of officers to Dublin. They could add to their knowledge by talking with T.D.'s, but few of them knew the tides of our military effort. H.Q. Staff had ceased to inspect the country; only by inspection and by actual touch with men on their own ground could a complete idea of the senior officers, their difficulties and drawbacks be properly appreciated. I resented their jokes at the expense of the Long Fellow.

I moved into the city to Fitzwilliam Place. It was strange for me to come at night to a friendly house, whose

people were not much mixed up with our movement. I
listened to piano pieces and songs, after-dinner talk, and
chatter. I would have liked to read or write, to work over
my maps of the South. I carried a revolver, an automatic
and a hand grenade. They would not show as I sat on a
sofa, but I was awkward in such a place. Should I tell them
I meant to fight? As a matter of course a guest was shown
the roof and how to get to it; and the back yard. I met
Frank Gallagher. Fitzwilliam Place was very comfortable, I told him, but I would like to have somebody I
knew with me; then it would feel more real. He laughed.
" I can imagine you seated like a Sphinx trying hard to
adjust yourself. I'll tell you what I'll do. I'll speak to
Major Childers; he's now our Director of Publicity. He
wants to talk to you, anyhow."

" But, I carry two guns, Frank. I don't want to yank
anyone else into trouble."

Later I got a note. Major Childers would be very
pleased to meet me, and he would be glad to borrow one
of my guns.

After dinner, Erskine Childers sat with me by the fire.
We talked easily. He wore a double-breasted coat which
fitted closely to his slight form. His hair was greying.
There were lines of thought and of worry on his face.
During a halt in conversation his face would become
reposed and take on an abstracted look. He was serious
and courteous with no mannerisms. I liked him very much
that night. I told him of the country and the people; we
laughed at our blunders and the sayings of our men and
of the people. I told him the story of my imprisonment, bit
by bit. We were not inclined to talk, but he drew me out
slowly.

" I would like if you would write that story as simply as
you told it," he said, " you give them credit when they were
kind."

I hesitated.

" It will be of use," he said. " We have not had many
first-hand reports of ill-treatment. People are afraid to
write and to sign their names."

" I'll write it for you to-night and I'll sign my name."
We chatted of books and men. He told me stories of the
Naval Reserve and of his work as an aeroplane observer

during the World War, and we talked of the sea and of ships. I found him an admirer of my friends Moby Dick, Arabia Deserta and Hakluyt.

On the way to bed we examined the skylight to the roof. I placed a few pieces of furniture to one side on a landing. They would serve to block the stairway if we had to rush for the roof. I lent him my automatic.

Next morning I showed him what I had written. He read it. " That's good, it will be of use. I'll have it typed at once. You can write." We spent another pleasant night together.

Two days later, one of our Publicity offices was raided. —— and —— from the Castle were in charge of the raid. I laughed when I thought of their reading my statement about themselves in the Intelligence Room. It would not be healthy for me if I should ever fall alive into their hands again.

Two divisions would be formed at once, Mulcahy told me, the First and Second Southern, then would come the Fourth Northern under Frank Aiken. Liam Lynch, Brigade Commandant of North Cork, was to command the First Southern. It would consist of West Limerick, Kerry, County Cork and Waterford. It would be the largest command. I was to get to North Cork, hold a meeting of brigade officers there, form the command, and appoint Liam Lynch Divisional Commandant.

The girls and women glorified the fighting. Often one of them said : " It must be great to be able to fight. The men are splendid." I felt inclined to say what I thought to their enthusiastic talk. Where was the glory in driving men, of mucking around in rain and slush, trying to plan operations which officers would use up their energies to avoid carrying out? Where was the pleasure in staff work, sending dispatch after dispatch for information? Some would say " I wish I could fight." One wished they could. Then they might see the other side of the medal. They would have to accept responsibility for the lives of those under them and for the people. The women were more bitter than the men. If one had enough work to do there was not time for spleen. Soon I could forget all that talk when I met the boys in the country. Then again I would rage at the war and our subjection to its tyranny.

Would I never again get the taste of blood out of my mouth or sit down in peace to read a book?

I was given a heavy rug as a present by Kathleen McGilligan, so that I could sleep out with some chance of warmth. I called at a few other houses to see my friends. I did not say good-bye. It would seem a chance visit to some of them, but by this they were used to my sudden disappearances. Now there would be more anxiety. The numerous proclamations, imposition of Martial Law, increased activity of our men in attacks, the shooting of prisoners in the South, their hanging in Dublin, had made our lives to our friends more uncertain than ever. They thought the Martial Law Area meant certain death for men who were active. And we had learned of death. We were very glad to know our friends were still alive and when we met them affection was not hidden. When we parted it was again an unfinished story which the fearful imaginations of those not actively engaged filled in apprehensively. The strange loneliness of meeting people you liked, and whom you would go away from soon, mirrowed the overwhelming transience of life and its precarious tenacity. It created a melancholy mood.

CHAPTER TWENTY

APRIL, 1921

★

POLICE PEERED into the carriage windows at stations on my way down to County Tipperary. The day before two trains had been held up and the passengers searched by military. I had an attaché case filled with maps, memos about the new divisions and my own notes. Police, Tans amongst them by accent, got on to the train at a station, but did not search the passengers. The people in my carriage were quiet, as if they were not sure of each other; but one man who had heard the Tans laugh and joke suddenly burst into talk. He had an ashplant between his knees. His sharp Northern speech had a restraint that matched the settled gravity of his long jaw. He had been in Carrickmacross during a raid on a yard where there was a mare waiting for the stallion.

There were eight stallions in loose boxes. The Tans drew their guns and made the groom serve the mare with the other seven. " They ruined the poor mare," he said, " the bad beasts." And he swore and damned their souls here and through eternity as strongly as he had then sworn inwardly. He saw the struggle through the sufferings of the mare.

The men by me were country men and they nodded in heavy sympathy. That aspect of the fight in terms of cause and effect summed up for them the situation. The unnecessary cruelty of it made them bitter about other extravagant visciousness that shook them more than the ordinary aspects of the scrap. Their mouths opened to stories; through the episodes I saw the nightmare of the noncombatants and felt the strength of their inertia.

There were no police at Goold's Cross where I got off. We had used the station for the past year. I waited until all the people had left the station; perhaps I might meet someone I knew. As I was walking out the station door I saw two lorries of soldiers pull up at the railway bridge. The soldiers got down. I put my hand through a slit in my overcoat till it gripped the handle of my .45.

" What are they doing there? " I asked a porter.

" Devil a one of them knows. They often search the passengers, but they're late to-day. Maybe the boys have trenched the roads."

After a long halt soldiers unfixed bayonets and climbed into their lorries. I walked across the bridge and into the hill country of Glenough.

" Glory be to God, but it's himself; my, but you're heartily welcome," Mrs. O'Keefe said, as I walked into the kitchen. " We thought we'd never set eyes on you again ; but it's you have the devil's own luck, and we wouldn't doubt you."

Soon Con O'Keefe and Ned Reilly from the Battalion Staff hurried up. It was good to hear Ned's slow, careful speech. Around the fire we talked of what had happened, since I had been last there. " Poor Seán Tracey; God rest him, it's a little we thought he'd be over at the moat of Kilfeackle the last time you were here together."

I looked at the back of the door. No names hung inside.

" What about the proclamation? " I asked.

"Devil a one of us bothers about it, the people don't put any heed on it, either."

The girls of the house stopped work to listen to the talk. The hill country was the same, Martial Law or not. I laughed suddenly. I thought of the Dublin people who were hoodwinked by the might of a paper threat; they thought that terror stalked through the South.

"Séamus had a tight shave this morning," said Ned Reilly —Séamus meant Séamus Robinson, the brigadier—"We were crossing the road below, five of us, when two lorries came around the bend. We fired and ran for cover. Their Lewis opened on us, but they hit no one. Séamus stuck the muzzle of his Colt Automatic into a bank when he was scrambling through. He couldn't get the mud out to fire and he was raging mad." I could see Séamus trying to clean the mud from the barrel.

"It's well you got a fright," I said, "those were the soldiers that might have tried to search me at Goold's Cross." I left my rug and attaché case behind. I went on to the Brigade Centre.

Mrs. Davin came from behind the corner of the house. She held me at arm's length. "Well, Ernie, you haven't changed much except for your grand clothes, but you'll soon get rid of them. The boys nearly went mad when they heard you'd escaped."

Her daughter went away to tell Séamus and his staff. I sat down by the fire. Mr. Davin came in; slightly bent, grey haired, dignified, an old pipe in his mouth. "A thousand welcomes," he said. "Many's the time we talked about you and we didn't expect to see you walk into the yard again." He was fond of talk and he could remember word for word, poems he had read or a political speech that he had glanced at years ago.

"They're fine now, the boys," said Mrs. Davin, "and very independent. They have their own houses." I looked surprised. "Dug-outs, but it's you are behind the times entirely. A whole world of things happened since we saw you last. The local lads helped to dig them with Kennedy: dug-ins they should be called says one of the boys after he had sweated with the shovel."

Séamus came with Con Moloney, the Vice-Com., and Seán Fitzpatrick. They shook my hands and slapped me on the back. We sat around the fire talking, watching pancakes brown on a pan. I saw them nudge each other. They looked at my boots and laughed. "Nice yaller boots and a crease in his trousers. The regular staff officer for you."

"God be with old times when his coat was full of holes and he cursed with the mud beyond his middle," said Kathleen Davin. They laughed and ragged me. It was good to be in South Tipperary again.

"Let's go down to 48," said Séamus.

"Why 48?"

"You remember 48 in Dublin. That's the name of the Brigade dug-out."

Séamus's girl lived at No. 48 in Dublin. In a field with a rise in it they halted and searched about in surprise. "Why! we've lost it," said Séamus.

"It must be the fairies," said Seán Fitzpatrick.

I could not see any trace of a dug-out. Seán Fitzpatrick put his hand on a long sod of green turf. He lifted it up. I could see an opening. The sod rested on a trap door.

"The grass is watered daily," said Seán.

We climbed down a ladder. We were in a long wooden room, railway sleepers and part of the pavilion from Cashel golf links had provided the wood. Bedding was rolled up on one side. There were typewriters, files of papers, wooden slits; small arms and rifles hung from wooden pegs, grenades and ammunition were stacked on shelves. It looked neat and business-like. Motor-car batteries gave light. The room was dry, clean and comfortable. The officers worked away at typewriters and maps whilst Séamus and I talked. A brigade officer could always be found there. They were very proud of the dug-out; picked men from Rosegreen company had built it. Late that night we rolled up in blankets. The air was stuffy when the trap door was shut for any length of time.

Up and out in the open in the morning I smelt spring. A hawk swooped to show his speed lines. Lambs played follow the leader, supple calves kicked what seemed like disassociated hind quarters in the air and long-legged awkward colts tried to nibble grass through wide gothic-angled legs. It was good to be able again to lift a hand in salute to a mountain.

I could see the external world in a new and, to me,

ON ANOTHER MAN'S WOUND

a fresher way now. Gaol had opened up a wider gap in
my mind and eyes, or had stripped both of a skin that had
interfered with a more essential kind of seeing and feeling.
Houses in the countryside had a new sense of form that I
had not before felt in any conscious way. I had noticed
how white or colour-washed walls were lifted out of a
mountain side by rain. That lifting gave them a dramatic
sense, but here in the lowlands I could see sturdy strength
and a definite grace in their building. The people had
taste. Again I had to learn from the country rather than
from the towns.

Across the dip in the ground was the Brigade centre.
Dispatch riders came there daily from the eight battalions
on bicycles, by horse and trap, on horseback and on foot.
Intelligence reports, replies to orders and administrative
correspondence were read and checked by the brigade
adjutant or his assistant. An urgent order could be forwarded to all companies in the Brigade before the late night.
This system had been working for over six months. There
had been no leakage in spite of the number of dispatch
riders who used to change weekly from each battalion.
Hedges of branches or improvised gates were dug in at
crosses where by-roads left the main road. Enemy would
probably think the gates were the entrances to avenues
leading to houses. Their lorries did not travel the hidden
by-roads. The people were staunch. Every house supported
the Republic. Daily the people fed dispatch riders and
visiting officers ; they supplied oats to the horses although
each dispatch rider was expected to carry his animals' feed.
The area was safe, " safe as the Rock of Cashel, " they said.
In a ring were police posts : Golden, New Inn, Cashel, Fethard,
Cahir, Clonmel—the last three held military garrisons;
" 71 " was a dug-out near the Centre. In it I found golf
clubs and balls from the Cashel links.

" I'd like a game of golf," I said, as I tested a club.
" So would we," said some of the boys. "But you'll
have to learn us."

We brought the clubs back to 48. Next day we would
play golf on our way to the Centre.

South Tipp. . had two· columns of men now, about
sixty in all. One was under the command of Denny Lacey;
John Joe Hogan was in charge of the other. Both columns

had wandered around the area, but they had done no fighting worth talking about. No posts had been attacked since Drangan.

I waited for my attaché case but it did not come on. Ned Reilly was careless enough. I would have to start for Cork without some maps I needed. Next morning we played cross-country golf on the way to the Centre. I told the men how to use the different clubs, but they whacked away as if they were using hurleys. We looked at each other and laughed. Some carried rifles, canvas slings of ammunition and golf bags; others wore Sam Brown belts, and revolvers or automatics were strapped on their legs.

" If lorries surrounded us suddenly from the main road," said Seán Fitzpatrick, " wouldn't it make a fine newspaper heading."

" I.R.A. Officers Surrounded Playing Golf."

" Deadly Struggle at the Third Hole."

" The dead men were armed with golf bags and rifles."

" That would create the proper effect," I said. " It would prove that we were people of leisure in good social standing."

As I drove up the avenue to Tincurry, dogs barked. Moss, my dog, jumped forward. He scampered about in joy; he tried to climb into the trap. I was hugged by Mrs. Tobin, Mae and Eva. " God be praised, and His Blessed Mother," said Mrs. Tobin. " The boys said you'd never get out alive. He'll be surely hanged they said, and Dinny Lacey used to tease Mae and Eva here about it, but I knew nothing 'd happen to you. I kept on praying to our Blessed Lady."

Apple-cheeked Johanna wiped her hands in her apron. " Begor, Master Ernie, it's yourself. God help you, but you must have suffered with them bad beasts."

I wandered through the garden amongst the glossy green of the rhododendron leaves. I sat near the blasted pine and under the pink and white buds on the twisted branches of the apple trees. Moss was still by my side. My clothes were speckled with mud where he had jumped up; but this was an unusual event; he could paw away. He rubbed his nose against my trousers and licked my boots. His sensitive amber eyes were full of affection. I leant across

the railing of the wooden bridge. I could hear the water
as it gurgled in liquid sound below on stones in the brook
to make ripples, eddies and splashings; from the continuous noise came water cadence and a water beat with a
motif that could be followed up until one became lulled
by the sound. It was hard to think when one looked
at water or listened for the recurrent sounds of water
poetry.

Many boys had passed over this bridge? Where were
they now? Some dead; others serving with columns or in
charge of areas. Up the stream we had built a dam to bathe
in; further up we had made improvised bridges when we
had practised field engineering. Across the roadway we
had tested the visibility of various colours and formations
at different ranges. We had measured the penetration of
rifle, revolver and automatic bullets. On that tree we had
made a range card near a position which we could hold if
attacked.

At the elm trunk on the water's edge we had planted
slips from the large tulip tree in the garden, Seán, Séamus
and I. It would bear flowers. Eva, a little girl, in a black
and white print frock, had cried; she was to look after the
slips. When we were killed they were to be placed on our
graves. There was only one other tulip tree in Ireland,
Mrs. Tobin had told us, but the shoots had died. Straight
ahead was the valley narrowing as the out-thrusts of the
mountain closed in towards the South-West. Threads of
bluish smoke rose slowly. On the right the slopes of the
Galtees with patches of sloping wooded ground. Galty
Mór stood by itself, mist rolling on top; through patches
of thickened cloud I could see a glimpse of deep blue
steepness; beyond would be The Glen, well-wooded. On
my left the full range of the Knockmealdowns rose out of
the far-away hedges. There were woods low down on the
slopes, but further up there was an empty red-brown
bareness which showed up the mountain strength. In the
front lawn the copper beech, my land mark, had changed;
its leafless branches rayed out. On the lower mountain
slopes the winter bareness was relieved by the warmth of
the evergreens and the green and grey-green of the grass.
I met Eva as I came back to the bridge.

" Do you remember our tulip slips, Eva? "

" Indeed I do, and I cried. Poor Seán has no tree over his grave now."

" You had best sleep up the hill to-night," Mrs. Tobin said, as we sat around the fire. " I feel that something is going to happen and I'm all nerves."

I walked up the mountain. I was welcomed with strange courtesy by an old man. We talked of life on the hillside. Sheep herders there knew their sheep grazers by their faces, he said, even in a flock of five hundred. He was bitter against foxes. They killed the lambs in the lambing season. That was a hard time. I had often given a hand to men searching with lanterns for lambs that had been dropped. " And would you believe it," he said, " once a cub was caught in a trap and somehow the mother cut its throat with her teeth. She wasn't going to have one of hers a prisoner. I often think of that when I see prisoners pass along the Mitchelstown road." He had a sense of big words and he used them with care except once when he spoke of water ' perpetrating ' through the soil.

Tincurry had been raided in the night time. Cahir military barracks was less than a mile and a half across the fields. Near to Ballyporeen I took the mountain road to Araglin which was in North Cork Brigade. Military from Fermoy had raided the village that morning. They had taken six prisoners. Boys scouted the steep road to the river Blackwater. Often troops lay in ambush near our crossing places. Two men with English accents were fishing near where our boat was kept. The scouts arrested and brought them down stream; they would keep them prisoners for two hours so that they could not get back to Fermoy.

A company on the far shore sent on cyclists' scouts. Cork always took good care of senior officers. Tipperary was lackadaisical; protection was left more to chance or insistence. As the road climbed I halted to look towards Fermoy. We were on a bluff. " Whist," said my driver, " Look." A mile away we could see horses moving, about ten of them. I looked through my prismatic glasses. They were cavalry and coming in our direction.

" Some of the battalion column are yonder," he said, pointing towards a clump of trees. I found three men there, one of whom had served in the column I had trained last October. I sent off word to the column commander telling him to hurry on with the rest of his men, to place his machine gun on our left. Nearly half a mile away was a small hillock. We lay down behind it to take breath and then spread out. I looked for the horsemen. There they were in twos spread out at intervals, but behind them was a large force of cavalry. That meant a round-up of some kind and the small column would be of no use. We ran back as quickly as we could. The rest of the column was straggling towards us from different directions.

On the bare slopes of Claragh Mountain, near Millstreet, I met Liam Lynch and some of his staff. The Kerry border was five miles away; the West Cork men could come through the passes or across the lonely stretches of the Derrynasogart Mountains; East Cork had the Boggeragh to climb.

"We have your Winchester for you," said Liam. "We kept it clean, and I had a hard job to prevent some of the boys from lifting it. And we have a lance and sword from Mallow that yet belongs to you. And here's a present for you."

He handed me a copy of the photograph taken by the Auxiliaries in Kilmainham. My hair was wild, my face was so battered that nobody could possibly identify me from the photo.

"It was sent out to the police," he said, "and I must say you look a murdering tough."

He talked of what had passed in North Cork since I had been there, and I told him of Kilkenny, Dublin and South Tipperary. The column I had trained had been broken up; officers had gone back to train a small active service unit in each battalion.

"Do you remember our Quartermaster Paddy McCarthy? He was killed in a fight with Tans in Millstreet. Paddy O'Brien was wounded by an ambush of Tans near his own place. He's now Brigade Quartermaster."

Paddy McCarthy was a loss. I thought of his unfailing good humour, his broad laugh and the lilt of song that would burst out at unexpected times. His quartermaster's magic sack would no longer open to disgorge ammunition, cigarettes or mine batteries.

Liam Lynch told me about the attempted round-up of

the old column. A new man, an ex-soldier, deserted one night when the column was in the mountains and made his way to the Buttevant Camp. His absence was not heeded. Before dawn next morning fifty lorries of troops attempted to converge from different directions. The column sentries opened fire on an advance party of soldiers who were rushing a house. Liam got out of his billet in his shirt and trousers but saved his papers. The column retreated up the mountains where another party of the British should have been, but trenches, broken roads and mud had delayed them. Three boys had been killed, two of them when prisoners. The ex-soldier had been traced to Bandon barracks in West Cork, but he never ventured outside. "What do you think he did it for?" asked Liam. I could not guess. Traitors ran too many risks now to make life pleasant for them.

"You'll be excommunicated, Liam," I said, "when you take Cork One into the division." He laughed. "Old Cohalan had dinner with Strickland I suppose, before he took the pen in his fist, but nobody minds him now."

Liam Deasy, Brigadier of West Cork, came over the mountains. Tall, finely built, quiet and deliberate in speech as it rose and fell in the singing Cork cadence. With him was Tom Barry who commanded the brigade column. His light bushy hair stood straight up like a wind-blown hedge. There were two guns on his belt; they touched almost when he stuck both hands in his trousers' pockets. He had a battered nose. Assertive, aggressive almost, spitting out his words directly; he was fearless and very much admired by West Cork. "Free" Murphy came west from the Kerry border hills. Loose of gait, with a Kerry brightness; he had been a school teacher. West Limerick, then Waterford came. We waited for the Brigadier from North Cork.

"There must be a round up somewhere," said Liam Lynch, "or he'd be here by this." Early next morning we saw a man coming down the hillside. He wore a light blue swallow-tail coat and trousers. The woollen coat was heavy. He wore a derby hat and carried a twisted stick under his arm.

"By the living God, it's Seán Hegarty," somebody said. He lifted his hat to our shouts. He had a beard

and mutton-chop side-whiskers. We stood around in a
ring laughing. It was a perfect disguise. He scratched
himself vigorously. We knew only too well what was
wrong—the itch. He had been delayed by a large round-
up on the far side. Now whole villages and part of a
countryside were ringed by soldiers and police; intelligence
officers questioned each man in turn.

I presided at the meeting; Seán Hegarty interrupted
often. He had a biting gnarled tongue that flayed. Remarks were evidently expected of him, everyone grinned,
but Liam was getting annoyed. He spoke of our Headquarters Staff and the ease with which memoranda could
be written, but it was another story to carry out their
fanciful instructions, that rigmarole about strategical neces-
sity was all right; but how about arms and why was the
pressure on the South not relieved? why didn't some other
part of the country begin to fight? And why doesn't H.Q.
organize or train the Midlands, the West or the East?
And why doesn't Dicky Mulcahy or Micky Collins
come down to inspect brigades in Tipperary, Cork and
Kerry? Then they could see how things were. Seán
Hegarty was the oldest there. He must have been over
thirty. Most of the others were under twenty-five. His
acrid spleen worked itself off; but he only voiced our
general discontent. I pointed out how hard it was for the
Q.M.G. to smuggle in arms, and how many trusted people
of ours in America or England had to handle them before
they would reach a brigade in safety.

A divisional staff was appointed by Liam Lynch;
brigadiers argued about his taking some of their best men,
but all realized that more co-ordination was necessary in
pitting strength. Officers discussed their several commands.
British columns of three platoons and larger ones of two
hundred men were moving through mountainy West Cork.
They slept by day and walked in the night, but they were so
absorbed in continuous protective work that they were not a
menace to us. Round-ups from cavalry and infantry directed
by aeroplanes were becoming more frequent. Larger areas
were being swept, but the results from the enemy point of view
were small. There was the difficulty of our wounded and
their treatment; we had not many stretchers and immediate
care had to be left to chance. Very few of our wounded died.

The men were hardy, they had lived clean, but British raiding parties would take them away and, to avoid them, wounded had to be moved often across country, on make-shift stretchers. Roads would have to be more thoroughly destroyed, railways were still intact. Many areas had made use of dug-outs. It looked as if they would help to solve the problem of sweeping or combing movements by enemy troops. We had used land mines with success on the roads against armoured cars and lorries, but there was a shortage of explosives and of grenades. The I.R.A. had complete control now of the hill districts and villages ; raiding troops did not move out at night, which was a relief. In many places the people made blowers by knocking the bottom out of a glass bottle. By blowing through the neck a booming horn sound was made which could travel a long distance. It meant enemy in sight. Our unarmed sentries on the further hill had some. Officers told of conditions in their areas; some spoke with a savage passionate bitterness; others talked directly as if they reported observed facts, and some with a sense of humour.

In West Cork townspeople slept out-of-doors in the night time or in each others' houses to avoid raiding parties. Funerals of men killed in action or murdered on the road were broken up by soldiers and police. Crowds of civilians with hands held high up stood there whilst their captors leisurely talked or searched. For long hours the people had to keep their hands up, sometimes they had to kneel or to sing " God Save the King." Tans or Auxiliaries had to teach them the words. People had been flogged with whips, belt-buckles and canes. During the funeral of an I.R.A. man or when one of their friends had been killed, people in towns went into mourning for the day, but police made them re-open their shops. If a British soldier or policeman was killed the shops were forced to put up shutters and houses had to pull down blinds.

There had not been many official execcutions by the British. Torture of prisoners by some of the Intelligence Staff of their 6th Division had gone on as usual. Kelly, one of their intelligence officers was badly wanted by the Cork men; they elaborated what they would do to him, but I had my doubts. I had seen how decent the men had been to police prisoners who had had a bad record. East Cork had shot many spies.

Hegarty had the name of not being very particular about evidence, but that might be talk. All information connected with an espionage case had first to be sent to Dublin and the sentence confirmed by our H.Q. before an execution took place.

The last subject for discussion made us all eager. Arms were to be run in somewhere in the South. The best landing place on the coast line from Waterford to the mouth of the river Shannon was discussed. That was over five hundred and eighty miles. Kerry, due to the slashes of its fiords, had three hundred and fifty miles of coast. Liam Lynch and I had worked out distances to points inland. We used a map showing the strength of enemy posts and the possible lines of distribution of the cargo. Now we filled in the arms each brigade had and the number of men serving with columns. The officers showed their minute knowledge of their areas. Finally West Cork was decided on. It had many bays and mountains to back it and difficult road access for the British. A Cork sea captain and some of our officers were in Italy bringing off a deal, twenty thousand rifles, two hundred rounds for each rifle and six hundred machine guns. My miscellaneous knowledge of weights of different types of weapons and ammunition was at last applied in a practical way. Our faces shone. It was too good to be true and almost like a fairy tale. Here were we who thought in terms of seventy or eighty rifles to a brigade and an odd machine gun talking of thousands of rifles and millions of rounds of ammunition.

" By God but we'll bate them into the sea when we land that stuff," said a Cork officer.

Between the two divisions there would be close on one thousand rifles—a rifle to about every one hundred and seventy men; but that number was small compared with the combined force of military, police and marines in the same area. The bulk of the cargo would be great, one hundred and fifty tons. During the landing, road communication in West Cork would have to be thoroughly destroyed, but wriggling through-routes would be kept open for transport. Columns would concentrate on the neighbourhood to hold the approaches, feint and actual attacks would be made through the Martial Law area to hold and divert garrisons. Some arms would be dumped in West Cork, the greater part would pass through our Division, the Second Southern, for Connacht, the Midlands and the North. Each officer had to work out how best to deal with the entire garrison of his area and contain them for at least forty-eight hours. The West Cork men showed the proposed landing place on their maps. They felt they could hold up the posts within striking distance. Looking across the table at some of the officers I had known previously, I could see our fight in the deeper lines of care and worry, in the general air of determination and in their pleasure at meeting again.

Towards evening we watched the officers start off on long journeys : some up the hills, others down the slopes towards level ground. Our last view of Seán Hegarty through glasses was a vigorous scratch as he crossed a fern-red crest.

Early next morning a scout rushed up to the house. He could hardly speak through excitement and want of breath. " Police coming hither across the fields. They're close by." We had heard no bottle boom from the sentry on the hill top. The scout could not tell me how many police there were. There was a hurried scramble for papers ; many were left behind. I packed mine into my haversack and with Paddy O'Brien, Brigade Quartermaster, followed the others. We two lay down behind a wall.

" I'm fed up," I said, " there are five or six of us and we can fight. I'm not going to frisk like a goat."

" I'll stay here," he said.

I had my Winchester. We could not see any police. We came back under cover to the house. It had not been raided. A patrol of ten Tans from Millstreet had come up from the road, passed within a field of the house and had gone back. They missed a good haul of papers. The sentry on top said his bottle had been shot out of his hand. He brought down a piece as evidence. We were sceptical. He had done what I had known many of our sentries to do—run or lie down when he saw the soldiers approach.

We moved to the foot of Musheramore. It was as naked as we were the day we were born. On the far side of the mountains in a valley were British troops on a small muddy road. " They're trying to make a round up, but they're

stuck in the mud now and can't move," the local commandant said. " More than ten lorries of them."

" Break all bridges in front and behind them," said Liam
Lynch, " and snipe them coming on evening time."

" Why not mobilize a few columns and let them have it
hard? " I said.

" Sniping will do," said Liam.

That night was wet. The troops who had encamped near
their lorries suffered from our snipers. Next day a convoy
with railway sleepers was sent from Cork to make roadways.
The long line moved back slowly towards their base. They
had to abandon lorries which were immediately burnt by
our men. The troops had no reason to love mountains or rain.

Up in cottages on the side of Museragh I heard the
story of O'Sullivan Beare's retreat from Dunboyne in the
middle of a harsh winter. A picked body of fighting men
guarded the women and children. They fought their way
through the mountains and the deep narrow passes. They
hewed through forests, squashed in bogs and starved till
they reached friends in the mountains of Leitrim. Here
the story was a living memory. It had happened in 1603.
I heard the names of the scouts who had guided O'Sullivan
Beare, and the Irish who had helped the Sasanach.

Near Millstreet and down towards Macroom the people
knew where he had camped ; the mountain sides he had
climbed. One could trace his path through the mountainy
Irish-speaking districts, where the foreigner, the Gall, had
never penetrated. Liam and I talked of this desperate,
hurried march. It was an epic. Sometime, when the
war was over, we two would start from the ruins of the
Castle of Dunboyne with a good Irish speaker and trace
our way through the tradition to Tír Conaill.

But the future was far away. Next day Liam and I with
three officers went in a motor car towards Mourne Abbey.
We wore trench coats and carried rifles. A volunteer
thought we were Tans. He hurried to report to his company
captain. Dispatch riders gathered the armed men of the
neighbourhood together. An ambush position was held,
the road trenched around a bend. They waited for the return
of the Tans.

Next day Liam showed me a report from Company
Intelligence to the Battalion Adjutant. " They're quicker

U

than you'd think sometimes," he said, laughing. " It's well for us we came back by another road."

The pupils of Liam's eyes blackened with rage as he read a dispatch. He handed it to me. Scattered houses had been blown up in North Cork as a reprisal for an ambush that had taken place near by. He stuttered : " I'll bloody well settle that ; six big houses and castles of their friends, the Imperialists, will go up for this. I don't know what G.H.Q. will do—but I don't give a damn." We selected six houses and castles from the half-inch map, then sent off the order.

Liam and I talked together of our areas. We wanted to issue a proclamation stating we would shoot any of the British captured in arms, but that would have to mean a steeling of our men in a determination to fight it out themselves when armed ; in the end we decided to shoot any armed officer captured. Soon all motor car traffic would have to be stopped, except that of doctors who would have to paint their cars distinctive colours. It had been a warm, dry Spring ; that we welcomed for the joy of it, but we needed rain to help us to break up the big round-ups that dry weather induced. Before I left Liam we agreed to exchange a few young officers who could be attached to our staffs; they would keep our divisions closer in touch and learn of any new developments in our methods cr organization. " I wish you could stay with me," said Liam, " there's plenty of work here for the two of us."

CHAPTER TWENTY-ONE

MAY 1921

★

IN THE CAHIR VALLEY I had difficulty. Military and police were scouring and raiding as I crossed on foot. Lacey's column had fought with and disarmed troops the same day, and had fought their way through an encircling movement. They had captured Potter, a District Inspector of Police. Tincurry had often been raided since I had left for Cork.

" They lie around the house till the dawn," said Mrs. Tobin, " then in they come. You're respectable now, if you please. It's Mr. O'Malley the officers ask for. Oh, he'll be glad enough to meet you, I tell them; but why don't you raid during the night? Are you afraid of one man?"

I wondered where they had found my name, and how they suspected I had been in the valley.

"I'm afraid you can't sleep in your new room yet," she said. "It'd be too dangerous now. I had a dream about you the other night."

My room had been named when part of the house was being rebuilt. It looked out on the yard and had a stairway which would make escape easier. In her dream a house I was in had been surrounded, and it wasn't Tincurry. As I came out to fight in the open, I had been wounded many times, and had managed to get in again. "You were all covered with blood," she said, "so here's a dash of holy water for you and be more careful." But the dream was not to come true for another year and a half.

I climbed the Galtees, sweating under the load of arms, equipment and my haversacks. Near the top I threw myself flat as I heard the whirring of an aeroplane propellor; it passed close to me, probably carrying mail and dispatches to Tipperary barracks. From the crest I could see the Glen of Aherlow beneath, the thin water glint of the Suir, and the woods towards Bansha, from which the peeler once "went on duty and patrollin-o." Away to the north were our friends the mountains of Mid-Tipperary. A black mass with grey splotches, the Rock of Cashel, stood out in the Golden Vale, then the Moat of Kilfeakle; at the side of it Seán was buried. I took a compass-bearing on the Moat of Knockgraffon beyond the Suir, which was to be my landmark on the way to the centre. When I reached the river I shouted and whistled. Soon a boat came over for me. Boats used by us were now hidden away. Raiding troops from Cahir had stove in the bottom of all boats on the river near them to prevent our men from crossing.

At the centre I saw two spies who had been court-martialled. The local men were waiting the G.H.Q. confirmation of their sentence before they shot them. It was awkward to keep spies; they had to be guarded. It was stupid of the enemy to send brave men around trying to link up with our companies or columns. They did not seem to understand the tightness of our organization or the change in the minds of the people. Volunteers who moved away to live in a new county had to have a transfer from their old company, new recruits were known by the men in their area. A stranger had not much chance now in a good area. People would report at once that they had seen a stranger on such a road. Before nightfall he would be rounded up and questioned by us.

I was told that my bag, which I had left in Glenough, had been captured whilst I was in Cork. That explained how the raiding officers knew my name. There was a fair amount of information in my note-books.

Traynor, a Dublin Volunteer, was under sentence of death. District Inspector Potter was offered in exchange. The British refused ; they would allow four named prisoners to escape as if by accident from internment camps if Potter was released. The offer was refused. Traynor was hanged. Potter was shot, and, as a result, seventeen houses in South Tipp. were blown up by military, amongst them Tincurry.

I had chosen Con Maloney as Adjutant for the Division and Dan Breen as Quartermaster. He had a deal of influence with our Q.M.G., and that was often what counted most when arms were distributed. Word came that Con's brother, Paddy, had been killed fighting, with Seán Duffy, Commandant of the Tipperary Battalion, when surrounded by Tans. His father's house and chemist shop in Tipperary had been burnt. My books had been sent from Dublin to his house for safety; I had often gone in to handle them or to take a few away with me to read.

Brigade staffs from the five brigades that constituted the command came to the first council meeting of the Division; but there was a delay. Seán Wall, Brigadier of East Limerick, and Chairman of the Limerick County Council, had been shot dead on his way. The Brigadier of Mid Limerick and the Vice-Commandant of East Limerick had been held up in a running fight with their columns; six of their men had been killed. Two men taken prisoners, after a drumhead court martial, had been shot next day by the British. Our columns had been co-operating with Cork in another arms landing that was to consist of Thomson guns from the United States. The landing had not come off.

South Tipperary, I knew, would have to be the backbone of the Division. It was the strongest brigade and the best organized. Next would come East Limerick. Mid Tipperary, Mid Limerick and Kilkenny were poor. For a month or more Kilkenny was not to be officially attached to the Division. Arrangements were made by the officers present to start small columns in each battalion, and to make brigade columns fight. They were to assist their battalion officers in planning attacks on posts.

Con was to find a suitable headquarters and organize divisional communications whilst I inspected brigades. I visited battalions in the low country around the city of Limerick. They were bad enough. I was told by the brigade commandant that it would be too dangerous for me to go into the city. Soldiers and police were very active; there were many spies, touts and secret service agents. I went to Limerick to see for myself. Military and police patrols moved up and down the streets. They halted and searched people. The police were insolent. I saw men struck with the butt end of rifles for not putting up their hands quickly enough when ordered. They were kicked for no reason that I could see save that the police were drunk. In the night time I heard heavy hammering in the street. I grabbed a gun, pulled on my trousers and rushed to a front door. I thought the noise might mean a raid on the house I was in. The street was blue-white with search lights. Police and military moved outside two houses opposite. They smashed in the doors with sledge hammers and rifle butts. Later three men were bundled into lorries. They were in their shirts and trousers.

In the city the Volunteers had two battalions; but they did not seem to ruffle the surface of enemy occupation. For long there had been internal trouble: a row between our First and Second battalions. It had meant jealousy and bitterness; our effectiveness there suffered. The city was the Headquarters of a British Brigade. I felt that we would have to rely more on the material resources of Limerick than on the driving force of her officers.

I overheard a long conversation between three commercial travellers in the snug of a pub. whilst I was waiting for intelligence reports. They talked of Tipperary town and of the girls whom they looked upon as " good things " there.

Commercials had their own freemasonry, the transient nature of their work made them gallants in the eyes of the stay-at-homes. It evidently helped, as they inferred, to make many who were thought to be staid by the rest of the town, open to reason. The surface life of the small town was changed by many an undercurrent before they had finished their talk.

I toured the seven battalions of East Limerick, a country I had tramped over from the straight slender thrust of the larch plantations on the side of Seefin and the hill-passes leading to County Cork up to mountainous valleys beyond Doon. Here I knew the men. I could appreciate the situation more rapidly. Houses I had once slept in had been blown up by the military as a reprisal for defeats by the boys of the column.

There were many good dug-outs now in the high double banks in the low lands; they were well hidden. Military cycling patrols were active, the net-work of roads helped them. Men on the run were in charge of columns or stocked them; and men from the companies were taking their turns for service. Battalion and some company staffs were now working whole time. Practically every town had an enemy garrison and although most of the people in a town were friendly to us it was difficult to make our men organize and tap the information there. It was harder still for us to obtain information about enemy movement and routine when our reliable I.R.A. men had to leave towns to avoid arrest.

I walked up the sloping rise of the old racecourse where Jerry Kieley, O'Keefe and I had once panted dry-mouthed. I met Owen O'Keefe near Kilteely. He had deep lines on his face. He did not talk much; he was resolute when he did talk. " Welcome back," he said, " some of the boys won't be so glad to know you're round again, but the times have a stir in them now." He told me of what had happened in the past five months. " You remember Martin Conway; he was wounded after a dance, and foolish it was to hold it, for the Tans killed five lads that night and they followed him with bloodhounds, but he killed the first of them before he fell dead."

Martin from the shores of Loch Gur used to drive me in a trap behind a black stallion that spanked away in pride; his fierce dog was a friend of mine. He was wild enough himself. He had spoiled a very good ambush by jumping out on to the road between two lorries to open fire with his long-barrelled Webley-Forbsbury.

"And do you remember Tobin of the Galbally Battalion? Well, he was tracked and died of wounds outside his mother's door, and Martin Scanlan, he escaped from the Tans in Limerick and hid in a hotel cellar. They searched the hotel and the cellar and were going out when a woman said: 'He's there,' and they tried again and murdered him." He had been a school teacher. I had appointed him from the ranks to command a battalion when I was last in Bruree. "I'm the makings of a poor soldier," he had said, "but there's my hand on it that I'll do my best."

Every one of our little fights or attacks was significant, they made panoramic pictures of the struggle in the people's eyes and lived on in their minds. Only in our country could the details of an individual fight expand to the generalisations of a pitched battle. What to me was a defeat, such as the destruction of an occupied post without the capture of its arms, would soon be sung of as a victory. Our own critical judgments which adjudged action and made it grow gigantic through memory and distance, were like to folklore. To an outsider, who saw our strivings and their glorification, this flaring imagination that lit the stars might make him think of the burglar who shouted at the top of his voice to hide the noise of his feet. Actually the people saw the clash between two mentalities, two trends in direction, and two philosophies of life; between exploiters and exploited. Even the living were quickly becoming folklore; I had heard my own name in song at the few dances I had attended.

Many of us could hardly see ourselves for the legends built up around us. The legends helped to give others an undue sense of our ability or experience, but they hid our real selves; when I saw myself as clearly as I could in terms of myself, I resented the legend. It made me other than myself and attuned to act to standards that were not my own. That was different from the other subordination of of oneself to the movement.

"We brought off a good ambush at Dromkeen with the Mid Limericks—a lorry of Tans. Man, we rose them off the road with bullets; we killed eleven of them. I got

this very belt off the D.I. We thought he was dead. He
lay that quiet; after, we heard he was stunned. I got his
gun, too."

I looked at the belt. The ammunition pouch was cut in
a peculiar way. "That's mine," I said.

O'Keefe drew away. "No, it's not."

"It has my monogram on it," I said, "under the flap
and so has the belt. Now, show me the gun, it has four
ridges on the grip."

"That's right," he said. "But it's not your belt."

"Do you remember the night I was surrounded at Bally-
firren House near Oola? I threw my belt at the revolver
flashes. There were two guns in it. That week I had gone
down with you to the cobbler and he fixed the holsters and
pouches to my liking." O'Keefe still looked unbelieving.

"Let's go to the cobbler and ask him if he recognizes
the pouch and holster?"

We walked to the small shop. O'Keefe took the gun in
his hand and handed the belt to the cobbler.

"Did you ever see this before?"

The man blinked his eyes. They were weak. The
light was not good. He handled the leather. "Yes, I
remember now. Last year it was. It's a good job," he said,
patting the leather.

"It's your's all right," said O'Keefe, when he stood on
the road.

"But you own it now. Sometime when the fighting is
over, I'd like to have the belt and the gun back."

"There's my hand on it," he said. We shook hands in troth.

I intended to return the belt. It had been given to me by
a Dublin artist. It had belonged to her brother who had
served in the British Army, and she had taken it from her
house unknown to her people.

* * * *

Con had found a place where he could work in Donohill.
The house was a little off the road; a small bohreen led
to other houses. Close at hand near an old fort were a
series of small hills. The people were good here; they
did not talk. Eight miles away was Tipperary. Oola, Cappaghwhite, Annacarty and Dundrum barracks were less than
six miles from us. Limerick Junction was near; that was
an advantage for dispatches by rail. In a house-to-house

search our position would be dangerous. If we could build a dug-out on the slope of one of the hills with a covered passage for escape we could put up a fight amongst the small hills.

The house consisted of a kitchen and two rooms. "Mrs. Quirke's," it was known. She was a strong character, a tall woman with long bones; untidy hair in wisps stuck out at the back of her neck and on her forehead. She was always at her ease in conversation. I never saw her ruffled. She took satire, banter and discussion at her ease, and she seemed to look on danger as a joke. Her voice was rough, but she was never angry. When we were worried, trying to work out a problem, she poked fun, smiled at us, or later in the evening made us laugh with some trite remark. In her heart I'm sure she thought the boys were only play-acting, God help them, trying to be soldiers. She assumed that I was delicate because I was thin and did not eat much; bottles of an iron tonic which followed me round were a proof that there was something wrong with me. First thing when I got up she had an egg-flip ready for me, and she put whiskey in it. "What good is it without a drop in it, I'd like to know?" Instead of a feather dipped in holy water, the usual good-bye, mine was now an egg-flip and a warning word not to get killed. My welcome whenever she saw me through the half-door or heard my shout in the distance was an egg-flip. Once Con laughed when I had finished my drink: "Do you know why she gives you the egg-flip?"

"No."

"To carry you to the next house the way you won't die here, that's what she said."

If I got up late there was absent the usual moral sense which righteous early risers have and by which they infer the hour one gets up and forget the hour one goes to bed. When I left her word to be called at a certain hour she often would not; then I had to make a hurried scramble in badly-kept-in rage to attend a staff meeting or inspection. If I said anything to her she would say calmly: "Musha, I knew you were tired, God help you, and you wanted the rest." She respected my many papers and maps and did not disturb them, and she had no passion for a meticulously settled organization of articles of furniture. I never knew how unreal our ideas and the—to us—importance of our doings were to her. She was a woman, the house had to be swept, food to be cooked, the small percussions and re-percussions of life to be solved and lived; but she followed with womanly sympathy, helped us with her mothering instinct and her easy, restful strength.

We used a large table in the kitchen. I was working on training notes, intelligence, operations and the quarter-master's department. Dan Breen was away with a column and the paper work of his department fell on me and on Michael Fitzpatrick, the assistant Q.M. He was a well-built boy of middle height with deep red hair and a bad temper. Mick Fitz's temper was more sudden than mine, but it was a sudden flare. He said exactly what he thought, then there was a quiet period until he went up in smoke again. Con was even tempered and easy going. We were tied to our typewriters. Con had learned to type, I was beginning. I hit the keys searching in anguish for a letter, or sat back to curse when I looked at what I thought was a correct sheet.

The administrative work piled up gradually. I found it hard to select officers to fill vacant posts on the staff. It would be better to leave them vacant than to have them filled by men who did not know their work or had not enough energy to begin to learn it. It would be easy enough to work with accepted organization, but here, work, due to uneven standards, reduplicated itself without end. Orders and instructions that were to be passed on by battalions to companies, were often hidden securely and remained there in the dumps specially built for papers, or were burnt at once to avoid risk. Some men gave more time to thinking out excuses for avoiding operations than the actions would themselves need. Outwardly some were efficient whilst procrastination and irresoluteness gnawed at their guts. Tipp. battalion was fairly good, but it had seen little fighting. Troops moved around cautiously and in large numbers. They never raided Donohill.

As I looked at my collection of pens I thought of what Seán Moylan had said the last time I had met him near the Kerry border. He was preparing to blow up a masonry bridge. "We started the war with hurleys and, by God, we'll finish it with fountain pens." Now the pen was almost an indication of our rank. I had four for coloured inks, and two for ordinary use.

After night-fall the neighbours came in one by one for a chat around the fire. The door latch rattled, a voice would say " God save! " and there was an answering chorus of " God save you! " from the fire. They talked of the day's news; most of them now had read the daily paper. They passed comments on the fighting, as reported, and talked of rumours and stray bits of information they had gathered at the creamery or in Tipp. They discussed foreign politics in detail and their judgments were shrewd enough. If they were in a difficulty about geography or history, someone would say " ask himself." That meant me. Change in rank did not mean anything to the people; we were " the boys " to them whether we tried to direct divisions or served as Volunteers on flying columns. Their observations on turnips that needed rain, sheep with the staggers, springing heifers, yaller cows and their calves, " Jaysus " fluid for maggoty sheep, were mingled with the doings of neighbours, the marksmanship of the Tans who shot at their grazing geese, or with a story startling in phrase and in the deft use of words.

I had often thought over our affection for certain figures in Irish history; we spoke of them personally as if they were present or had just left us, and called them by their Christian names or nicknames. This habit was shared both by the book-read and the lip-memoried. Con of the Hundred Battles, Brian of the Tributes, Silken Thomas, Gerald the Earl, The Súgán Earl, Shane the Proud, Red Hugh, Owen Roe, Miles the Slasher, Lord Edward, The Chief. From the fire I would hear the names again. Red Hugh and Lord Edward were the most loved, and yet, Red Hugh had died in Simancas in 1607, but his name flowered like a slow sunset.

I felt I understood the country better now. I had sloughed off some conventional skins, and the layer of the importance of bookish reading which had prevented a closer contact with the life about me. The people had, essentially, warmth, feeling and heart, and they knew of life through living. I had been sponsored by the movement and nurtured by the people. They softened down actuality. A long distance might be " a mile and a bit," or " only a few perches across the fields "; weather about which there could be no doubt as to its rotteness would be: " a soft day, thanks be to God." If I came in feeling like the end of the world from anxiety and hunger, I would be told " Arra but it's yourself is in fine fettle these times." The hovering terror would disappear with " Please God it'll soon be over," though I suspected they thought it might last to the Fair Day of Jerusalem.

I found many changes in home life. The sons of the house might be officers now, away with a column, or on the run. The older people listened to them with diffidence and respect; their opinions were asked for and their remarks were passed on to the neighbours. Houses were neater and the girls tidier; a column might come suddenly to the neighbourhood and men might be scattered in billets, or men on the run from a town might stay with them.

Officers were more serious. They had become graver and more responsible. Administrative work had broadened and danger had hardened and had made them more alert. They spoke in a different and manlier way, their voice had assurance and their thought was clearer and harder. The men had a lithe disarming strength and reserves of staying power. They talked of bloody happenings with zest and laughed about gruesome doings, but they were not callous. In imagination some of them flavoured their interpretation of reality. There was a strange mixture of gentleness and resolute fierceness about some. Many an old score lived in their long land-memory, and was settled, known and unknown to senior officers, with weight of gun.

A bitterness and ferocity came from a present extra- vagant killing or torturing by the British. I cursed blindly for hours when I heard that a man in East Limerick had been tied behind a lorry and dragged until the life burst from him, and when I read a Kilkenny report of a hostage during a fight being made to stand up whilst a Lewis gun resting on his shoulder sprayed a column of our men. Such happenings relit an old race hatred, but it would die down again. I could see it work in the men. They faced their task squarely. They were fighting ruthlessness and they did not want to give mercy.

Our flamboyance had been whittled clean enough, we stood out clearer and bleaker, but we took a lot of time to grow up. Our comradeship in a desperate cause was reducing our disparities and was uniting us in a bond, yet class distinctions would jut out, and our merging in what we were glad to call "the people" was a figment. We could not see any definite social shape or direction to our efforts. We were not critical of our leaders and our work absorbed our judgment in its immediate local use. History might have taught us where in ourselves we would find reaction, but our blind spots were as many as the holes in a strainer.

Going through the country I often felt as would a traveller on a railway journey as he looked at the passing life about him, dissociated from it. The people had to live the round of the soil and solve its problems of economic and of living relationships, which were more of living than my relation to the fighting effort only; beneath the will necessary for the action and decision needed for command was my other less resolute and retiring self. The strain was there always, but work kept it away. Always alert and steeling myself, wondering if peace would ever come, yet pushing on officers and columns to make the fighting more thorough, feeling what the unarmed people were going through, but planning operations that would bring down on them more than equivalent brutality.

I was learning by trial and error. I had been taught the real value of organization by my abuse of it in over-direction ; now I had to unlearn in training, operations and the outward appearance of discipline. I had stumbled from one military book to another in mistake or advance, and from a saturation of their subjects I was revising methods, guided by our changing conditions. Columns were slowly learning what they had ignored at classes. They were familiar with their weapons, the military aspect of the ground they crossed, and protective movement, but they were weak in manoeuvre and musketry tactics. Formerly, brigade officers had directed operations in person, now battalions and column commanders planned their own schemes, but they were slow enough in making fight when it did not fall in their way.

Roads had been more thoroughly destroyed, bridges had

been blown up or torn down by man power. We had very little dynamite or gelignite left; explosives were needed for landmines and barrack attacks. Picks and shovels had to do most of the work and " pickite " became our explosive. British military rounded up the men of a neighbourhood to fill in trenches and remove obstacles, but the roads were pitted corrugations. County Councils that had given allegiance to the Dáil no longer paid men to work on the repair of roads. Lorries of troops carried cranes, cross-cuts and ropes to remove obstacles, and portable steel bridges for crossing gaps made by trenches and broken bridges.

Men in the companies snipped telegraph wires to interrupt enemy messages or cut down poles intermit-tently, scouted for columns, watched out for round-ups, noted movements of troops, guarded prisoners and sniped barracks. They held up trains to search for mails; later they read letters for information, stamped them " Censored by I.R.A.," and left the mail bags where they would be found. They took the goods of boycotted Belfast houses from waggons and burnt them.

A boycott had been enforced by the Dáil on Belfast firms; employees there had been forced to take the oath of allegiance to the King ; those who refused were driven out of work and from the city. There had been heavy bombing, sniping and burning ; the British said they were unable to prevent the armed Ulstermen from operating against civilians who were defended by the ill-armed I.R.A. Curfew had not been imposed nor Martial Law proclaimed, although casualties were twenty times as heavy as they had ever been in the South. In the press the Ulster situation took on a religious aspect.

In some of our areas a brigade levy had been enforced ; people were expected to contribute according to their means, and if they refused their cattle were driven off and sold. We had to pay G.H.Q. for the small driblets of arms that came to us, but our main source of supply was the enemy supplies we captured in action. Our H.Q. did not send us money to buy office supplies or to clothe columns; some of our staffs bought food to reduce the strain on the resources of friendly houses that fed men continually. The people did not complain; even amongst those who had a reputation for being stingy there was an inherent hospitality, or a show of it that could be made more apparent by tact on our part. We could select our own billets now and quarter men on hostile houses. People were jealous if column men were not billeted on them and a column commander had to be diplomatic.

The Tommies looked upon us as 'ill tribes, and that must have connoted something wild and fierce. Official reports from the Castle would always make us appear to act in well armed bands of two hundred men or more. The Tommies were told we would shoot them if they surrendered. All this did not help to resolve their fear of the unknown.

We could not keep prisoners; soldiers and police, when disarmed, were put on the roadside to walk to their posts. Often they identified men who had helped to feed them. The soldiers had become isolated from the people and their leave was cut down; sometimes they would follow the example of their officers who were generally arrogant and brutal in raids and in their treatment of prisoners, but on the whole they kept an essential humanity. To their officers we were " rebels," " Shinners," " cowboys," and " well paid murderers "; their caste system made them see us as the lower orders or " natives."

It would be hard to say which side was under the greatest tension. We had no base and no possibility of reinforcements being rushed when needed. We had to be always on the alert against raiding paries. Our good men were harder to replace, our officers and staff officers bore the brunt of the danger and more of them were killed. Casualties with us were always personal. There was the fear of arrest and of ill treatment or " shot trying to escape " on the road when prisoners, and the diffused sense of terror and helplessness amongst the people.

The enemy could have regular meals, a standard of comfort, the advantage of numbers and training, more than ample supplies of ammunition, and well cared for and efficient weapons, but they were dealing with an unknown element which formerly they had been accustomed to suppress by a display of force. Their imaginative contempt at first and their fears had magnified our strength, and they were operating in a hostile countryside when they left the shelter of their barracks. They were undermined by our intelligence system which created in them distrust of their most tried officials. Their intelligence files even in the Castle were brought out for our intelligence to read and note, and were then quickly brought back. Information came through from the War Office in London and from the Castle sometimes before its contents was issued to the military or R.I.C. to act on. In some of their barracks notices were posted up warning all ranks to guard their tongues. Officers were instructed not to talk between separate blocks of the one barracks about anything that might be construed as information.

Their campaign of terror was defeating itself; it had made conservatives liberals and had treated the luke-warm as extreme; it had affected the discipline of their army and police. Co-operation between their forces was not happy; Auxiliaries and Tans did as they pleased, the older men of the R.I.C. disliked the intruders and their doings. Their civil and political authority resented army interference and control. Unionists stood aloof, they suffered from both sides, but they resented the campaign of Dublin Castle.

In Great Britain Bishops and Ministers of various non-Catholic denominations addressed letters of protest to Lloyd George; professors and lecturers in the University of Wales united to dissociate themselves from his policy in a long letter. Leaders of the Intellectual Life of Great Britain published a manifesto in which they protested against their Government's campaign of terrorism.

Taxes continued to be forwarded by County Councils to the British Local Government Board in Dublin, but now some councils refused to forward the monies. The Dáil was slowly gaining control and in increasing that control was our main effort. The British could defeat some of our columns and round-up our men, but they could not maintain civil administration when they had lost the support of the people.

The Dáil endeavoured to isolate customs offices; but in the burning of the Dublin Custom House, one of the finest buildings in the city, all its records were destroyed and British administration was disorganized. Auxiliaries and military rushed to the burning buildings; seven of the I.R.A. were killed, eleven wounded, and 101 arrests were made. My brother, Cecil, a medical student, had been amongst those arrested. I found later he had to jump from a top window with a companion who was shot dead as he jumped. A passer-by cross-eyed with excitement brought home word that my brother had been killed and that the dead boy was a prisoner.

* * * *

Liam Lynch and I had arranged that our two divisions would co-operate in a series of attacks on a certain day. Few of our battalions had carried out operation surveys according to my instructions; some sketches and plans of the vicinity of posts and barracks had come in to me. On the evening of the day arranged for the operations our divisional staff, which had carried out the only attack on police in our area, met with Dinny Lacey's column. He had about thirty-five men, but had done nothing that day.

Lacey had brought his column many times through South Tipperary, but it had seen very little fighting; that was due partly to bad luck, the uncertainty of enemy movement, and our faulty intelligence system. He was very religious; he fingered his beads often as his well-spread-out column crossed country. He was strict and had his men well in hand; he did not talk much, and then decisively. He was very stubborn. In anger a white temper paled his face and his voice stuttered or came in a swifter rush. Strong and well-built with regular un-emphasized features, he was very much admired by his men who called him " Captain Dinny," though he was brigade vice-commandant.

Some of the column wore green-grey uniform, but most of the uniforms in the area had been captured by enemy raiding parties during the past five years. Some wore their caps back to front; a few had uniform caps, one boy had a triangular forage cap, and there were hats with pinned-up sides and turned-down brims. All wore riding breeches and leggings. His men had rifles, khaki slings of ammunition or leather bandoliers; some had grenades slung dangerously by their levers in their belts. There was a Hotchkiss gun section. There were a few ex-soldiers who had served in the world war, but as they had been trained only in trench warfare they lacked individuality and initiative and looked too much to their N.C.O.'s for guidance; they were little adaptable to our conditions.

The men had an air of assurance, constant exercise had hardened and burnt them; they were looked up to as old soldiers by the men in the areas through which they passed. The men were young, cheery and fond of " caffling." The column had its own slang; when the men were in a house where long flitches of bacon hung from the ceiling they were content; " the sky looks good," they'd say to each other, as they looked up at the rafters.

I said what I thought to Lacey. The main intention of the combined operations was to relieve the pressure on the First Southern, and here he was with thirty-five men yet had made no attempt to fight; as brigade vice-com. he could have arranged for fights in at least three battalions. " We can't meet the beggars," he said, " they go too cautiously now."

" Why don't you go into the towns? if the British won't come out we'll have to go in." I sent the Tipperary battalion commandant to get information about the strength of the military evening patrol and of movements of Tans in Tipperary; next evening at dusk half the column, reinforced by local men and scouts, would move into the town to attack and bomb the patrol and Tans.

We were not going to give any quarter to the Tans that night or worry about the mixed company in the hotel bars and pubs that we would bomb and shoot up. The Tans in Tipp. had never spared either the countryside or their prisoners. The battalion commandant and I had worked out a defence of the town against reprisal parties, and we felt easier in mind about the night's work.

Next day we worked around until we were close to the town. I intended to leave the machine gun section in a position to cover the retirement of our men from the town. Towards dusk we moved through a grove of trees north of Tipperary and close to it; our advance guard made prisoners of disconcerted courting couples whom they sent back to our reserve to hold until shooting began. I was with the advanced guard. Close to a road the Tipperary Commandant shouted " Halt!" to a man who began to run; a thick hedge held us up. When we got through the man was on the road. " He's a tout," the commandant said, " he's always with police and he'll surely report us." The man had seen a number of our main body in front of a grove

of trees. Police and military would be on their guard
now, or might be rushed out to where we had last been
seen. The column marched away into the night towards
Donohill.

CHAPTER TWENTY-TWO

MAY—JULY, 1921

★

EAMONN PRICE, Assistant D.O. came down from Dublin to
a council meeting of the Second Southern Division. At
its first meeting brigade officers had objected to the intimation from G.H.Q. that two of the divisional staff
would receive £5 a week each as salary. None of the other
whole-time officers in the brigades were paid. After a
debate it was decided that salaries would not be accepted
until officers engaged solely on army work and the men in
columns, were paid; that would be Tibbs' Eve, we knew.
Price told us the C.S. insisted that myself and the adjutant
must accept money as a " disciplinary measure," and he
would enforce his command. We took the money, but
transferred it to the divisional arms account with the Q.M.G.
Séamus said, " It looks as if they want to have men in
charge of divisions they can call H.Q. men." It was
strange we thought, that the C.S. should treat our refusal
as indiscipline.

Price wore city clothes; he did not carry a gun, but he
borrowed a Webley which made him rise in our esteem. I
brought him through the central plain of Mid Tipperary.
We had to cross bridges and water ditches; we threw
ourselves flat when we heard the noise of lorry engines. We
crawled close to enemy posts to show him their defences and
squelched at night through water-logged bottoms. At the
end of the third day his trousers were in flitters. Jim
Leahy, the brigadier, was with us; usually we were our
own scouts, moving in the various thinnesses or breadths
of a triangle, in line or in file. I could not rely much on
scouts supplied by the companies. They were never alert
save when an objective danger was pressing. Small streams,
stone walls, barbed wire and long wet grass were natural

enough to us in a tramp, but they were strange to him, and we did not select the easiest way. As he was the first member of the Head Quarter's Staff to inspect the Martial Law area I wanted to show him conditions and expose him to the same risks as our senior officers.

One evening above Dovea, we were making for Borriso-leigh. In the distance was the gap in the Devil's Bit flat against a pale lemon sky. The light was failing as we crossed a marshy field rising up to a road, judging by the telegraph poles. We could hear voices in the stillness, and the wind rustled in the purple-topped reeds. We saw six figures behind a stone wall on the road; they halted to watch us as we stood. They had rifles on their shoulders. Price was the rear point of our triangle. " Police," shouted Leahy, " and there's no cover." The field was bare. " Let's rush them," I said. We ran up hill, Leahy and I shouting. We might as well be shot going forward. The group near the wall scattered, but no shots came. When we reached the road we saw two men with spades on their shoulders; the others had run away. " You're both mad," said Price.

Near Thurles next night Leahy whispered to me as I worked at a table with Price, " Come outside a minute." The sentry from the local company had refused to stay on sentry duty. " He told me to go to hell," Leahy said. " You'd best settle him." I talked to the sentry. Why was he picked? he wanted to know; he had been working all day. He was tired; we were tired, too, I said. The briga-dier had told me the man had not been on sentry duty for the past three months, and he would be relieved inside of three hours. He was a fat faced man with a dribbling moustache and scowling eyes. I was tired and there was a long walk before us next morning. " You can be court-martialled for disobeying an order on active service, and you know what the result might be," I said.

" I'm not going to do sentry work," he said slowly. I took off my Sam Brown belt; two guns were slung in the open holsters. " Take one," I said, " we'll fight it out beyond that clump of trees over there. I'm fed up driving men to do their duty."

He looked at my belt. " I'll do my share of sentry work," he said. We shook hands.

Near Emly in East Limerick a scout rushed into the house where Price and I were in bed. " Soldiers searching the next house. Hurry out! Quick!" In trousers and long boots with my shirt in my teeth I got through a back window; we dressed behind a hedge. The soldiers passed the house we had been in and searched the next house on the roadside. Two lorries of soldiers dusted a road as we crossed a bog; we lay flat, but they had not seen us. Later in the day we nearly ran into a cycling patrol from Kilmallock; trying to avoid them we found ourselves close to sentries who were guarding a long convoy that had halted on the Kilfinnan road. I counted twenty lorries through my glasses; officers and men, white with dust, were standing on the road. We watched the convoy move off as we sat on the slopes of Slievereagh. " I've seen as much as I want to of East Limerick," Price said with emphasis. Next day I would be able to pass him on to the Corkmen and be free from anxiety.

Tomás Malone had part of the East Limerick column near a pass that led into County Cork. This was a country of steep hills and narrow defiles between the Galtees and the Ballyhoura range. The people were very staunch; our columns rested up here and troops found the hill country difficult. We had good protection now. In the early morning someone grabbed my shoulder hard. " Get up quick, the soldiers are making up the bohereen." I spread the column men behind a hedge and waited. Later a scout came; a British cycling patrol had searched a house at the end of the small road leading up to our position and had then gone back to the main road. " It's the Galbally patrol under Shaky," he said. An officer from the Galbally post had been nicknamed Shaky, because he suffered from a mixture of shell shock and drink. He was an eager collector of candlesticks; when he raided a house he placed the candlesticks on a table, compared them and took away any he fancied for his collection. Such was Shaky in folk-lore. Price and I went back to bed. " They won't come back by the same road," I said. An hour later I heard a shout outside. " They're coming!"

" Where are they? " I asked, as I buckled my belt.

" Searching the second house on the bohereen." Ours was the fourth. I told Tomás to cover the approaches to the house and to guard his flanks well. Then I went back to bed.

An aeroplane made a forced landing fourteen miles from Limerick city; a battalion column rushed to the landing place to find pilot and observer attempting to burn their papers. The column men set fire to the plane. That was the second plane the East Limerick men had burnt. In their dispatches was an order from Dublin to the Limerick military to raid at once for Michael Brennan and his column which were in Roxborough, close to the city. There was a list of houses to be blown up and information true and imaginative about us. "Columns are being broken up," one report stated; "this may be the last kick, but remember the last kick is always the hardest." Word was sent at once to Michael Brennan, Brigadier of East Clare.

We were becoming almost popular. Respectable people were beginning to crawl in to us, neutrals and those who thought they had best come over were changing from indifference or hostility to a painful acceptance, with the knowledge that some kind of a peace settlement would be made.

Soon we would have to destroy railways, the main supply artery of garrisons. That would mean a food survey and arrangements for exchange of surplus food between areas and a closer contact between our divisional staffs and county, city and borough councils and Dáil members. The Dáil, unable to meet as a body, carried on its work in committees. It was not safe for it to meet as a Parliament. As we destroyed communications Dublin would be cut off from the country; we would have to build up civil control by areas, and the First and Second Southern would act together. Liam Lynch and I had exchanged our ideas on, and our plans for the future. We saw what hardening was to come. The people of this country would have to give allegiance to it or if they wanted to support the Empire they would have to clear out and support the Empire elsewhere. Race did not matter; it was a question of allegiance to Ireland that separated Celt, Viking, Norman, English, and their intermixture there.

On inspection I brought a list which Con called "The Hundred Awkward Questions." At councils and staff meetings I questioned officers in turn. I checked their information at the next visitation, often there were wide discrepancies. I could evaluate brigade information when I attended battalion staff meetings or councils, and both brigade and battalion statistics when I inspected companies. Facts and figures, I might find, had been given out of pure airiness of mind or from desire to make a good show. Supervision was irksome, but I needed to know the individual officers personally down to company captains, and to understand as far as I could the actual difficulties of each area to form judgment on development, possibilities or lack of activity.

I found in many companies that only a few of the men had seen grenades or rifles and that training schemes had never been enforced or orders carried out. Some companies neglected to block roads when ordered. That meant our small columns were open to sudden raids or round-ups, and due to this negligence men were killed or captured. Information captured or sent through our intelligence was often not forwarded quickly enough by dispatch riders, and again men were killed as a result.

I had thirty-two battalion areas to cover, and close on 7,000 men to be responsible for. To sit down and attempt to direct might have been possible if battalions had any uniformity in armament, ability, experience or desire for action, or if there was any possibility of information being forwarded quickly so that I could keep in touch with the situation in battalion areas. Staff work dealt too much with the building up of administration, but soon it would have to tackle operations seriously.

* * * *

I slept out with men from Rosegreen company at the Centre under a tent which had once been a hay rick cover; some had hammocks which they slung in the hedge from tree branches. I was working in 47 when a scout came to see me. Three men had been captured on the hillside; they were British officers, and the Rosegreen men had them in a dug-out lower down. I met the two boys who had captured them. One had a rifle and two rounds of ammunition, the other an empty bandolier, when they saw the three men coming across the fields. The boy with the rifle halted them; the men began to run. He fired. One of the men was wounded slightly; the others came back and all three surrendered. Each had an automatic in his pocket and an identification card. Two were gunner officers from Fethard Artillery Barracks, five miles across the hill. I sent two boys up the hill to find out where the officers had stopped and what they had been doing. Later one came back. The officers had been searching hedges; at a house on the slope, they had asked about dug-outs. They had questioned the young man of the house.

I brought them up one by one. They gave me their names, ranks, the name of their commanding officer. They had been out for a walk, they said.

" Any officers we capture in this area are to be shot until such time as you cease shooting your prisoners."

" We have nothing to do with the shooting of prisoners," one said.

" This is not a personal question. Our men whom your men may capture and later shoot will have nothing to do with your being shot. My mind is made up about it. You will be shot at dawn to-morrow."

" Can't you consider the matter? " one asked.

" You will have to consult your officers," another said, " you can't do it without authority."

" I happen to be in command of this area. This is my authority. It would be better to prepare your minds. I will get food ready for you." I gave them cigarettes. A boy with a rifle lay near the entrance to the dug-out.

A scout rushed down to where I sat. Beside me were six riflemen who had been mobilized in the meantime.

" Soldiers with a machine gun. They've just come over the brow of the hill and they're searching."

" Easy," I said, " the officers will hear you." The scouring soldiers came from Fethard. Other sections of troops would possibly be making their way in our direction.

I blindfolded the officers so that they could not see where they were going. The covering on their eyes made them helpless; their hands were free, but tying a man's hands was not a job we liked. Men held them by the sleeves so that they could walk more easily. One of them limped. He had a slight flesh wound. I put him on a cart.

" If we are surrounded," I said to the one whose face I liked best, " I'll let you go. I'm not going to shoot you like dogs." The guard of riflemen grumbled.

" But you'll shoot them to-morrow anyhow," said the Brigade Q.M. " Where's the difference? ."

The Q.M. was right, but it was tough to have to turn on them suddenly when we were hard put in a fight to shoot them like injured beasts.

One of the officers said, " We can do first-aid for your wounded if there's a fight."

A sloe-skin dusk came slowly down on the steep western slopes of Slievenamon and across the woods there. It blurred the valley of the Suir below the Comeraghs; hedges of tangled hawthorn with fresh leaves, in amongst the neat stems of spruce, stood out against the rise of hills. There was a strong, spicy smell carried across from the bright pink blossoms of a corner hedge of wild crab.

We halted at a gateway. A horse and trap came up. The officers got up into the seats. A young girl came out from a house. She peered at the men in the half light. " Who are they? " she asked.

" English officers," said a guard.

" Shooting's too good for them," she said, bitterly, as she looked up at them. They looked down at her with set faces.

" Oh, leave them alone," I said.

" God help the poor boys," said a woman beside her, " perhaps they'd like a sup of milk." She came back with a large jug and three delph mugs. The officers drank. They thanked her.

We walked into the closing-in darkness, riflemen in front and behind the trap, until we were a distance from where the officers had been captured. I expected a big round-up in which the countryside would be combed by troops from Cahir and Clonmel—both strong military posts. They would probably converge in the triangular area of which Fethard was the apex. We came to a farm-house up in the fields some way off the main Clonmel road. Sentries were posted. The girls and women of the house got ready supper; they did not ask any questions. A fire was lighted in the room where the officers were. After supper I went into the room. The blinds were drawn so that they could not look out. It was a large room. They were seated at a table. One had his head in his hands.

"Would you like to see a clergyman of your own religion?"

"No," said one. The others shook their heads.

"Would you like a civilian, an Imperialist, to stay with you?"

"No." They did not need any one.

"Here's writing paper and envelopes. You can write to anyone you wish. If you give me your words of honour that you won't mention anything of military importance, you can seal the envelopes yourselves."

Each gave me his word. There were beds for them to sleep on.

I sat in the kitchen by the fire. The women of the house had gone to bed quietly. None of us spoke for a long time. I was putting myself in the place of the men inside. My turn might come, too, and soon. It seemed easier to face one's own execution than to have to shoot others. "It's very dark outside," said the Quartermaster. "I hope the boys are keeping a good look out." He strode into the darkness.

He was an elderly man. Freckles showed through a wind-red face. There were thin folds in his neck. He had a long skillet of a jaw, he showed the wide gaps between his teeth when he smiled. His step was as deliberate as a gander's. He would have his say no matter what happened; he was accustomed to jump objections—for that was a quartermaster's offensive. He could advise about a round of ammunition as seriously as we would discuss or draw up a plan of operations. He was the oldest of us, about thirty-five years. He spoke slowly and carefully, toothing his words in a dry humour.

None of us was twenty-four; the youngest officer inside was about that age. One was tall and dark with brown eyes. He had illtreated prisoners in Tipperary, one of the Rosegreen men said. He had been insulting when on raids. One was stout with a thick neck, his hair was a little thin. He had been more anxious to talk and to remonstrate than the others. The third was quiet and reserved. He had a sensitive face and he did not talk. I liked him best. I was worried about him because he was wounded. It was an accepted convention that a wounded man should not be shot until he was able to walk. I did not bother about the convention, only the presence of the wounded man made its own conditions.   I did not see any sense in keeping him for a few days longer.   It would be harder on him if his companions went first.

" I wish it were over," I said to the Q.M.   There were two other men seated on chairs making a round of the fire.

" It'll be over soon enough," he said.   He was calm enough about it.   I knew that I would continue to shoot their officers.   Of that, there would be no doubt, but this kind of work was hard enough.   If we shot enough of them it would make the others think a little.   I don't know what we talked about.   Odds and rags of conversation about men in other battalions, the relative merits of different kinds of explosives, the making of improvised Stokes guns and the history of this part of Desmond.   Two men went out to relieve their comrades.   I walked outside in the darkness. The night was misty, the moon shone softly through cloud veils.   Sounds carried well, away through the distance came the lonely bray of an ass ; it was answered in sardonic harshness near by.   Sheep coughed drily in the shelter of a hedge and a cow chewed loudly.

" It'll soon be dawn," said the Q.M.   I knocked at the door.   They were seated around the table.   Their faces looked worn and drawn.   None of them had slept.

" Have you written your letters? "

" Yes," said the thin swarthy one, " here they are."

" If you would like to send your money or valuables to your friends or relatives I will forward them for you."

" We would like to send them with a note to our C.O., Major King, in Fethard," the quiet one said.

I found an empty Fry's chocolate box on a side table. They put their watches, money and rings inside.

" Would you like some tea ?   It'll soon be dawn and we'll have to be on our way."

" No thanks, we don't want anything."

We walked down the sloping fields towards the roadway. The sky was clouded with heavy grey.   The light was dim, a cold dawn wind blew across the thick hedges.   It ruffled the grass which was shiny with dew drops.   Men with rifles formed an extended five-pointed figure.   An officer walked on each side of the Q.M.   I was behind with the

third. " It's a mistake," he said. " It won't do any good.
We could be good to prisoners."

" None of us want to do it," I said, " but I must think of
our men." I could not see the ultimate implications of our
proposed action. The sky lighted silvery grey, the wind
dropped. We caught up with the three in front. " Stiff
banks those for hunting," said the tall, swarthy officer.
They smiled as if they had thought of horses and the sight
of a red-brown fox. " There's not much hunting now," I
said. We had stopped hunting through the Martial Law area.

We reached the roadway. There was a wall in front of
a church. The three officers were placed on the green grass
edge of the dusty road.

" Do you mind?" I said, as I placed their handkerchiefs
around their eyes. One handkerchief was of silk and
claret coloured.

" No."

" This is good-bye," I said.

They shook hands with the Q.M. and myself. Their
hands were cold and limp. They shook hands with each
other.

The six men of the firing squad stood near the other side
of the road. One of the men fumbled for a while with his
magazine. He could not click it into place. An officer
pulled down his handkerchief and looked at us, then he put
it back over his eyes. Perhaps he thought we were trying
to frighten and test them and that we did not intend to shoot.
" Ram in the magazine," I whispered to the Q.M.

" Are you ready? " asked the Q.M.

One of the officers nodded. They joined hands, " Good-
bye, old boy," they said, inclining their heads.

" Squad." . . . " Ready " . . . " Fire."

The volley crashed sharply. The three fell to the
ground; their arms twitched. The Q.M. put his revolver
to each of their foreheads in turn and fired. The bodies lay
still on the green grass. We stood to attention. Then slowly
we went up the hill across country making for the Centre.
None of us spoke till we had crossed a good many fields
where wind had snaked the rye grass.

*   *   *

Enemy columns wearing civilian clothes and equipped
somewhat like our columns, or in full war kit with helios

for signalling and blood hounds for tracking, had been moving through parts of Tipperary and Kilkenny. They slept during the day, usually, and tramped into the night. Another column might try to pass itself off as one of our own from an outside area. A man with an Irish accent would act the prisoner; with hands tied behind his back he would be kicked down from a lorry and left in a kitchen to talk to the women about the local lads and ask that word be sent to them for a rescue. His supposed captors would leave rifles lying about and act in a seemingly careless way in hope that an attempt would be made to free the prisoner.

I inspected Kilkenny Brigade. The brigade staff had seldom sent our orders to battalions; they had never been on inspection. On the western border of the county enemy patrols were numerous. I had a running fight with one at night. Further south towards Mullinavat I was surprised by a sudden round-up. In the darkness we moved through their cordons and lay out for the dawn. Early in the morning with two officers I took cover suddenly as we were about to cross a road.

Two lorries passed quickly. I saw a man upright in the first lorry. He was tied with ropes by outstretched arms to the tailboard. There was blood on his face and clothes. Later in the day I was told he was a dispatch rider who had been captured the previous evening with a dispatch of mine on him. He had not talked.

The weather continued dry, the grass was burned with heat; fine weather helped sweeping operations and round-ups. The division, which in men, arms and extent was the second most important of our units was not fighting enough, and was not helping to draw off troops from the First Southern. Kilkenny and Limerick, two cities at the extreme limits of our area, were not being made use of to radiate strength and to supply good officers and material to their surroundings.

Divisional spirit was hard to build; I was handicapped by having no brigade of my own to back me. Liam Lynch had North Cork in which he had lived continually. It would have been better, I now thought, to have placed Séamus Robinson in charge; he could fall back on the resources of Tipp. 3. That brigade, our best, lived too much on its reputation. Tracey, Robinson and Breen had created a tradition and had done most of its fighting; battalion officers, however, were now inclined to fight it it out when surrounded. Staffs in three battalions recently had fought it out to their end, but columns in East Limerick had seen more fighting. It was a continual worry to me that I was not improving the division more quickly, some one else in my place would do better work I felt.

I was not getting enough support I knew, and I found it hard to define the cause whether it lay in myself or came from the brigade officers. Micky Fitz, Con and I discussed the situation frequently with our Divisional Engineer, Bob de Courcey of Limerick, and our Intelligence Officer. The division partook of our general decentralization; the Martial Law area was solving its own problems by itself. G.H.Q. issued general instructions, but our operations were our own. We had not yet reached the stage when we could carry out operations on an extensive scale to a H.Q. plan or even to a divisional plan.

I decided to organize a divisional column of one hundred men. We would move in three parallel columns and begin in county Kilkenny, the area which had done least. As time went on, I knew we would have to strengthen some of our columns to close with the British columns which were beginning to move round in our area. We needed careful training in manoeuvre, and we would have to go into the towns to look for fight. I intended that we would sleep out; that meant hay-rick covers, ground sheets and blankets. I sent word to brigades to select men for the new column. Our men in small columns could, I felt, meet the same number of men or more in the open, but as our numbers increased our officers would be more liable to be out manoeuvred by the British officers. I hoped that as a result of our new action I could select some officers whom I would send to sleepy areas for organization, training and operations. I knew that action and comradeship would knit more closely the officers and men of a column, and that any later orders to them would be more promptly obeyed.

I began the organization of a divisional company. Its sections would act as a permanent guard to our headquarters and could be used for dispatches. Our Q.M. would equip the men with grenades and through our Q.M.G. we might be able to arm them with Mauser automatics. I intended to train the company as N.C.O.'s and give them a thorough grounding in scouting and in protective work.

There was no munitions factory in our area. Grenade tops, now of aluminium, since the capture of a Headquarters' factory in Dublin, were sent through our Quartermaster-General. Steel piping for bodies were made in Limerick or supplied from Dublin, but in action the new grenades burst in one direction or might fail to detonate. " Cheddar " for grenades and "war flour" for land mines for attacking armoured cars and steel-plated lorries, were made in Limerick, but in small quantities.

There had been rumours of peace. Lord Derby, a Catholic, to please the Vatican after Archbishop Clune's repulse, and Lord Haldane and others had come over to size up our leaders so that the English Cabinet could resolve the strong and weak points of their opponents. Cope, the Assistant Irish Under-Secretary, was busiest of all in Dublin. Michael Collins began to appear in print; he was called the Irish de Wet. Brugha, Dev., or Mulcahy were never mentioned. Sir James Craig, the Northern leader, had met de Valera, and General Smuts had talked with him. Rumours came about the removal of prisoners from the internment camps at the Curragh, Ballykinlar, Beare Island and Spike to a far-away British possession. The battalions on guard duty were badly needed for service. Nineteen fresh battalions of infantry and marines came over.

There were rumours about a withdrawal of all British troops to the coast and the use of a blockade; the internment of all Unionists so that the remainder of the population outside the new camps could be treated as active enemies. The British intended to man railways, post offices, telegraphs and telephones, with troops, issue passports; but that would mean a special enlistment in England of 50,000 men for service in Ireland. The Chief Secretary, Hamar Greenwood, had a plan for Martial Law in three provinces if the Southern Members did not attend the Southern Parliament on the 14th of July. Executions of our men had stopped; official military blowing up of houses had ceased, perhaps they realized that a castle of their friends counted more than a cottage of ours. Destruction of town halls and the burning of creameries and farm supplies had slowed down.

In December of 1920, a Government of Ireland Bill had provided for a Southern Parliament of twenty-six counties and a Northern of six. At the elections in the South, 124 Republicans had been returned and four Unionists representing Trinity College. King George opened the Northern Parliament in June; the Southern Parliament was not a success. Only the four members from Trinity came to the opening. The other members had given their allegiance to Dáil Éireann, the Government of the Republic, and they would not sanction the partition of their country made by the British Parliament.

On the 9th of July, a Dublin boy came to Mrs. Quirke's whilst I was away. A dispatch rider was sent for me. The boy would not tell his business to any other member of the staff. He handed me a typed order.

In view of the conversations now being entered into by our Government with the Government of Great Britain, and in pursuance of mutual conversations, active operations by our troops will be suspended as from noon, Monday, 11th July.

RISTEARD UA MAOLCHATHA,
Chief of Staff.

Two days from now on the 11th of June at noon we were to see that all officers and men in the Division observed the terms of the Truce which had been agreed to by the British. There was no intimation as to how long the Truce would last.

Con typed my orders to the five brigades. We sat down to talk about the news in wonder. What did it mean? and why had senior officers no other information than a bald message? Would the Truce last a week, or perhaps two weeks? We were willing to keep up the pressure which had been increasing steadily; soon, in a month or more, the division would begin operations in the towns and use columns by sections. Bewildered, we waited for Micky Fitz, the Quartermaster, to discuss the speeding up of " cheddar " and " war flour." And so ended for us what we called the scrap, the people later on, the trouble; and others fond of labels, the Revolution.

*   *   *   *

Put on the kettle now and make the tay, and if they weren't happy, that you may.

Some excerpts from reviews of Ernie O'Malley's *The Singing Flame* (Anvil Books 1978).

'... destined to become the classic of the great tragedy that was the civil war...'

'What makes this sequel of greater significance than the other book (*On Another Man's Wound*), fine as it was, is its probings into the sources of nationalism... His legend has waxed and waned during the twenty years since his death. Will this book recommend it to a new generation? I hope so...'

—*Francis Stuart, The Sunday Press*

'... as exciting and gripping as his first book... the first major work from the point of view of a person who was so highly placed on the Republican side.' —*Nollaig O Gadhra, Mayo News*

'... a remarkable man... fascinating reading... a literary masterpiece... and a work of great historical importance.

—*David Neligan, The Irish Independent*

'*The Singing Flame*, his plain but moving account of the Civil War, is a soldier's book... It is certain to hold a permanent and important position in the literature of Irish resistance... will go a long way towards explaining genuine Republicanism to a new generation.'

—*Prionsias MacAonghusa, Hibernia*

'... not alone valuable but invaluable... an extraordinary man... he had a tremendous gift of language...

—*Tim Pat Coogan on RTE's Folio*

'... an absorbing, personal account of one man's very active involvement in the Civil War at a very high level... an outstanding national record... It will be read and it will keep the flame alive.' —*Kevin Boland, The Irish Press*

'Many have been awaiting this book... It is his own history, fascinating and revealing of himself and his comrades and their motivation... O'Malley was a writer of quite exceptional capacity... This is compulsive reading.'

—*Michael McInerney, The Irish Times*

'He had an unerring eye and ear... his evaluation of comrades and opponents must contribute to the total history of this period... there can be few Irish history books better than it.' —*John Flatley, The Connacht Tribune*